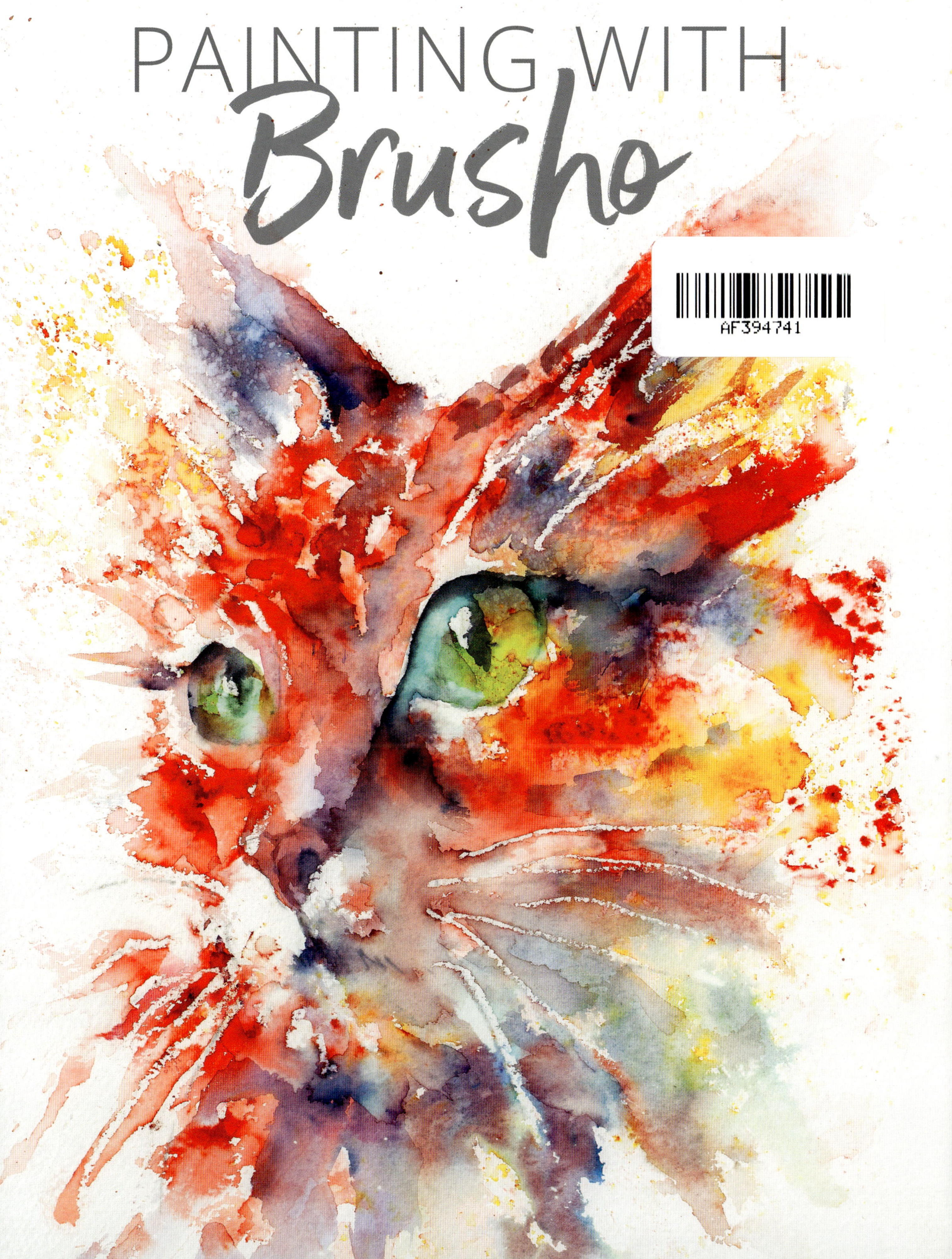
PAINTING WITH
Brusho
AF394741

Dedication

I dedicate this book to my husband Geoff.
I know without a shadow of doubt that without his support and
encouragement this book would never have been written.
Geoff has never painted a picture in his life, but it is fair to say he now
knows more about painting with Brusho than most.

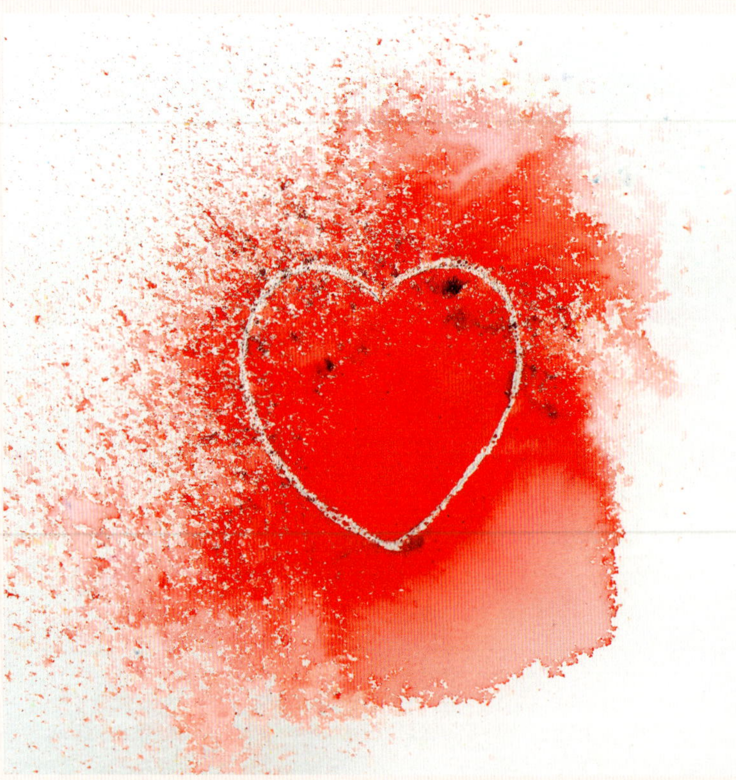

Acknowledgements

Colourcraft (C&A) Ltd for producing such an exciting medium to work
with, painting with Brusho always brightens my day.

Search Press for having the faith in me to produce this book.

Lyndsey Dodd, my encouraging, supportive editor, for working
alongside me with a medium she was unfamiliar with... I think I may
have converted her!

My good friend, Jane Lawton, who gave me my first box of Brusho
many moons ago.

To my family, you should know that your love, support and
encouragement is worth more than I can express.

A special thank you to my dear friend Catherine Aston for her
neverending friendship and her unwavering faith in me even when
I had none! I am truly grateful.

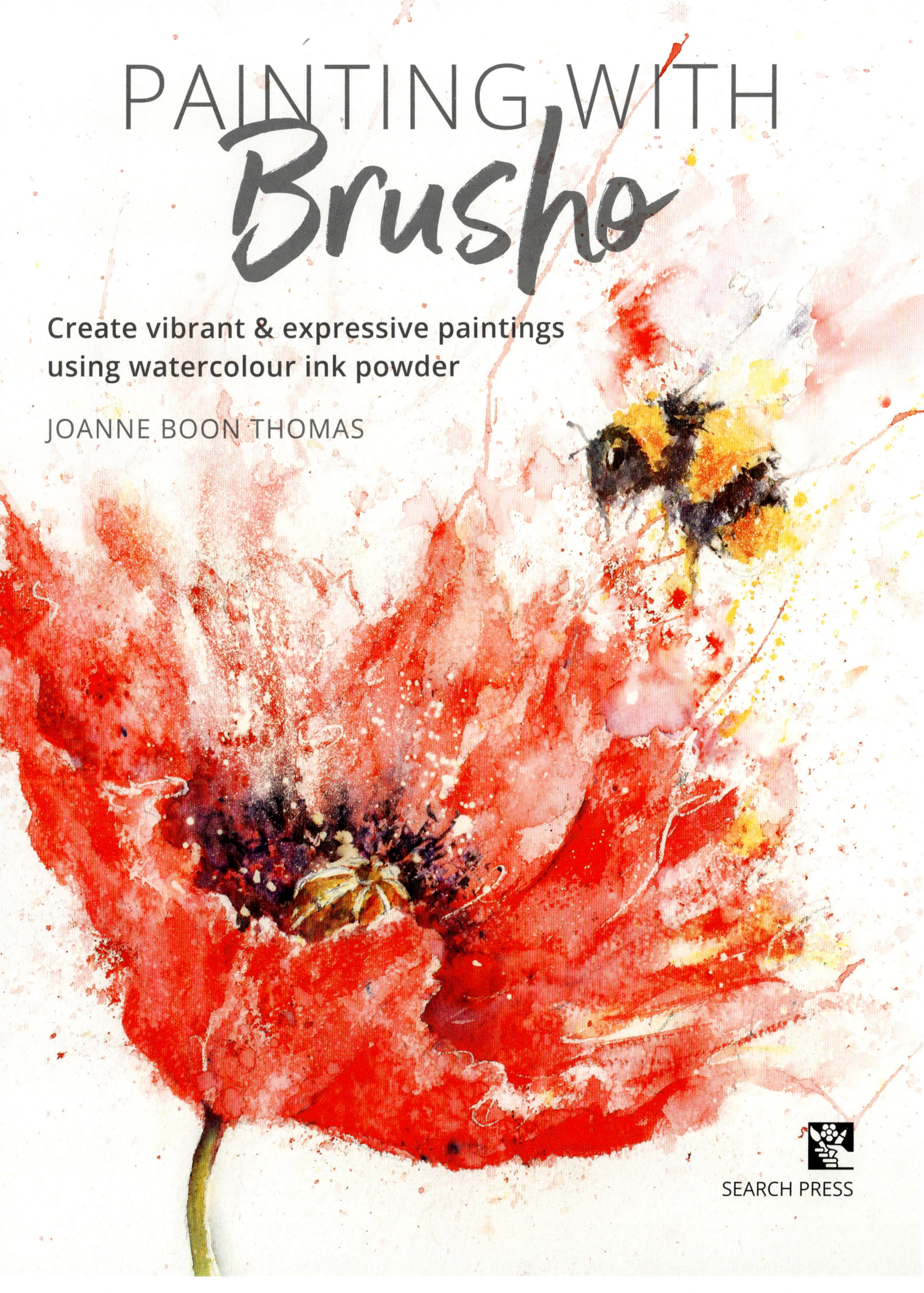

PAINTING WITH
Brusho
Create vibrant & expressive paintings
using watercolour ink powder
JOANNE BOON THOMAS
SEARCH PRESS

First published in 2023

Search Press Limited
Wellwood, North Farm Road,
Tunbridge Wells, Kent TN2 3DR

Reprinted 2024

Text copyright © Joanne Boon Thomas, 2023

Photographs by Mark Davison at Search Press Studios

Photographs and design copyright
© Search Press Ltd. 2023

ISBN: 978-1-78221-962-0
ebook ISBN: 978-1-78126-956-5

Suppliers
If you have difficulty in obtaining any of the materials and equipment mentioned in this book, then please visit the Search Press website for details of suppliers: www.searchpress.com

Colourcraft
Colourcraft (C&A) Ltd is the manufacturer and supplier of Brusho®.

Outlines
Extra copies of the outlines are also available to download free from the Bookmarked Hub: www.bookmarkedhub.com. Search for this book by title or ISBN: the files can be found under 'Book Extras'. Membership of the Bookmarked online community is free.

You are invited to visit the author's:
Website: artbyboon.co.uk
Instagram: @artbyboon
YouTube: https://youtube.com/@JBOONTOM
Patreon: www.patreon.com/joanneboonthomas

Publishers' note
All the step-by-step photographs in this book feature the author, Joanne Boon Thomas, demonstrating how to paint with Brusho. No models have been used.

Cover image: Summer Joy
Page 1: Feline Friend
Page 3: Perfect Pollinator
Below: Jumbo

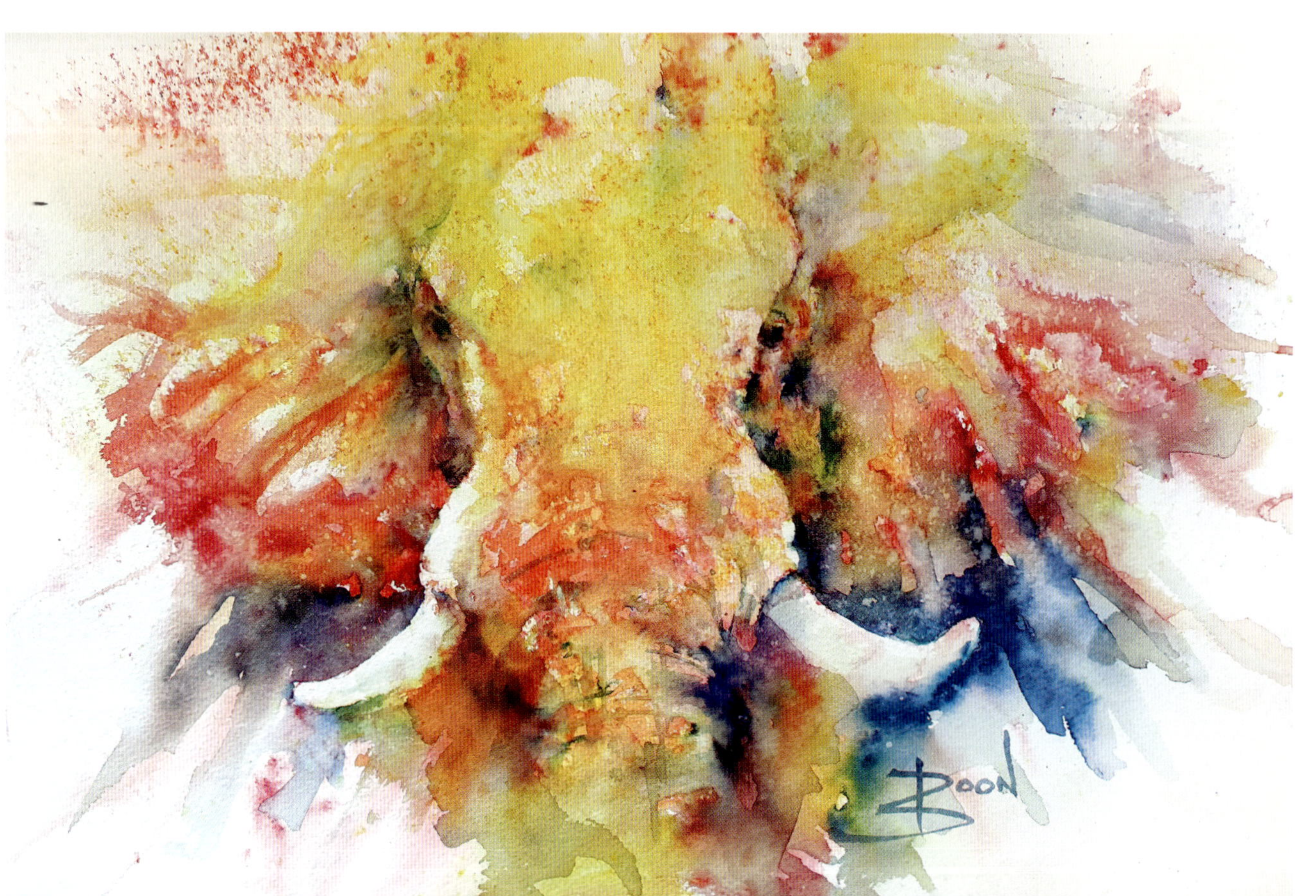

Contents

Introduction

I have been creative from a young age and initially focused on watercolour as this medium suited what I was trying to achieve, both in looseness and expression. I also enjoyed experimenting to create different effects using watercolour and mixed media and loved the results.

I was introduced to Brusho over ten years ago by a friend who teaches in a primary school. Initially, the box of paint sat on my studio shelf for months before I even opened it. I was utterly perplexed by this powder paint used in schools – I just didn't know what it could offer me, or even where to start!

I slowly began to play around with this new medium, at first using it like watercolour, mixing the Brusho powder with water to create colourful washes. Although the washes were bright and vibrant, I wanted to explore the possibilities of Brusho via experimentation. I set aside any preconceived rules and began to test the boundaries of the medium.

After weeks of practice I found that Brusho had so much to offer. I sprinkled small amounts of powder onto watercolour paper and spritzed it with water to watch the delicious pigment explode into colour. This fascinating process still excites me every time! I started to exploit the characteristics of Brusho to produce dynamic and totally individual artwork, finding that I could paint the same picture several times and each one would be slightly different.

I went on to experiment with bleach and discovered that I could lift colour away using different ratios of bleach to water. I also tried different watercolour papers to see how they reacted to the bleach. As I have always enjoyed using the wax resist method with my watercolours I started to incorporate this technique with Brusho. I was pleasantly surprised that this technique was just as effective with Brusho, allowing me to create subtle light highlights within the colour washes. The potential of working with Brusho is endless, and I am continually experimenting and finding new and exciting ways to create unique Brusho art.

Painting with Brusho is achievable for those who are just starting their painting journey as well as the more experienced artist. The best advice I could give to a Brusho beginner is to play and experiment without trying to create a masterpiece! Familiarize yourself with the medium and its properties. I'm not going to say it is easy, but if you follow the simple steps outlined, by the end of this book you should be well on the way to creating your own distinctive artwork. I like to sketch a rough outline in pencil before laying down any paint. Once the paint has dried, I erase the pencil lines. If you would like to use my outlines for your own work, they are at the back of the book.

It is wonderful that Brusho has become a popular medium here in the UK and now all over the world. I am thrilled to have played a part in spreading the Brusho love.

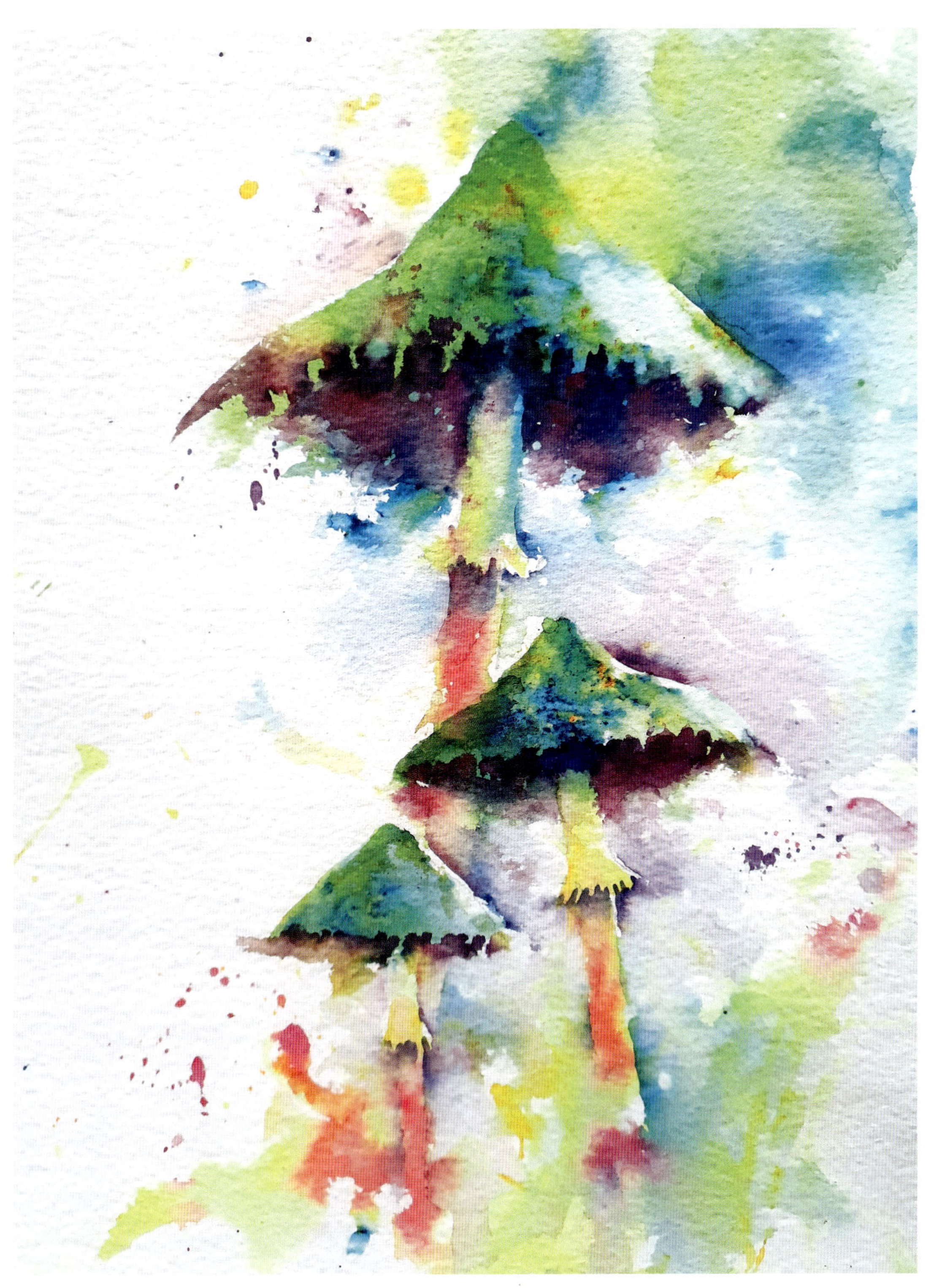

" I genuinely believe that anyone can learn how
to paint; it just takes the desire, good tuition,
plenty of persistence and the knowledge that art
is so very good for the soul. "

About Brusho

What is Brusho?

This is the question I am asked most often, either when people see my Brusho artwork or in my workshops.

Brusho is a highly pigmented water-based paint powder manufacturered and supplied in the UK by Colourcraft (C&A) Ltd. By activating it – that is, adding water to it – you can dissolve the powder to make paint. It can be used to create beautiful smooth washes as well as gorgeous texture, making it a great option for loose and impressionistic work.

The spontaneity of the medium and the way the water carries the powder across the page means that no two Brusho paintings will be exactly the same. If you add water to Brusho and give it a good mix you'll get one even colour (see page 16), but if you look at the individual crystals of powder, you'll see that each colour is made up of different coloured pigments. The black Brusho is a great example of this (see page 46).

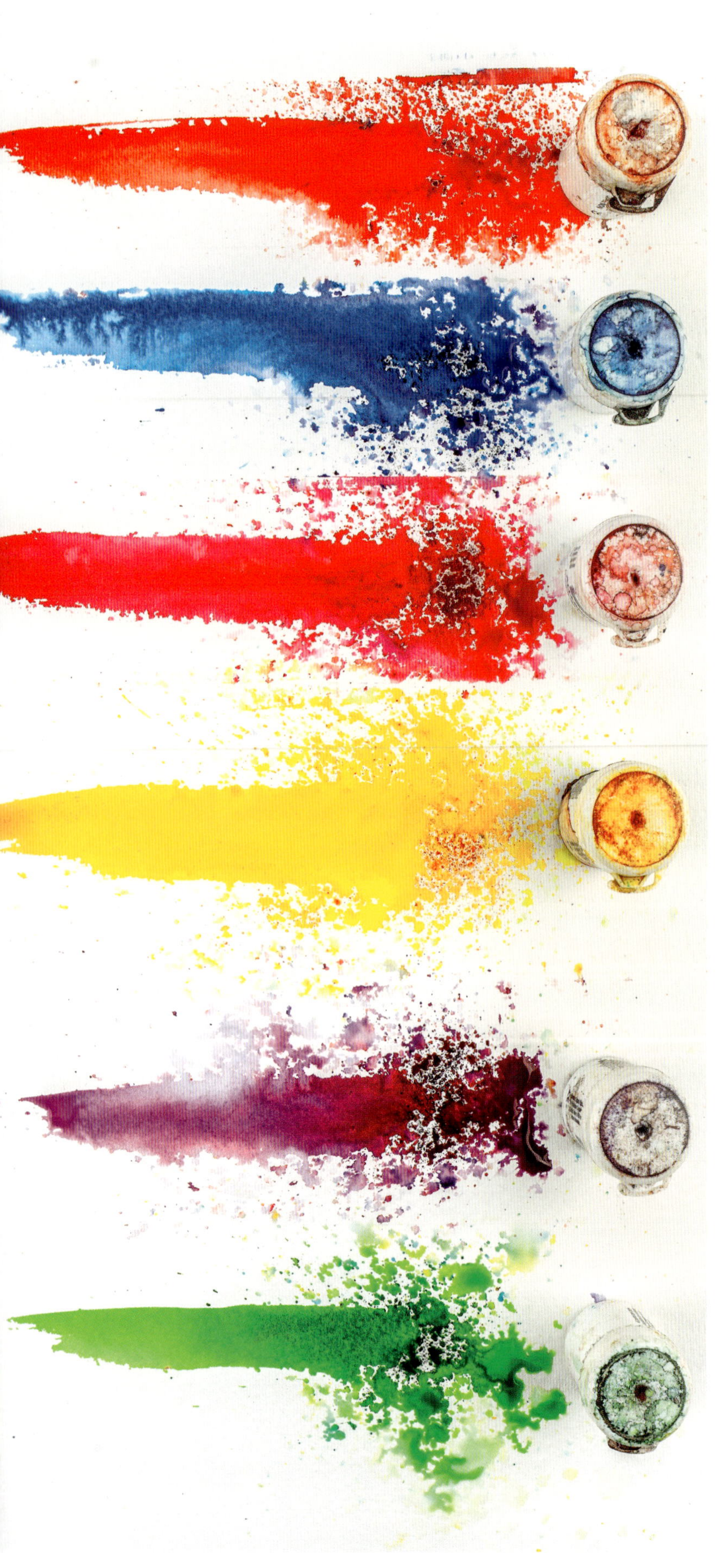

Here you can see the plastic tubs of Brusho, the corresponding powder sprinkled onto dry paper then sprayed with water, and the paint smoothed out with a brush.

Is it lightfast?

Brusho is as lightfast as any other similar type of watercolour. I have Brusho paintings on my wall that are over ten years old, framed in the traditional way with no varnish and they are as fresh as the day I painted them.

Check the manufacturer's information about lightfastness so that you are aware of the longevity of the paint, and always consider where to display your paintings to avoid hanging them in direct sunlight.

Throughout this book I will show you how to exploit the unique characteristics of Brusho. Even if you've never painted with Brusho before, you will learn how to create a beautiful wash or an intricate area of texture with almost no effort at all! I am confident that once you try it you'll be captivated...

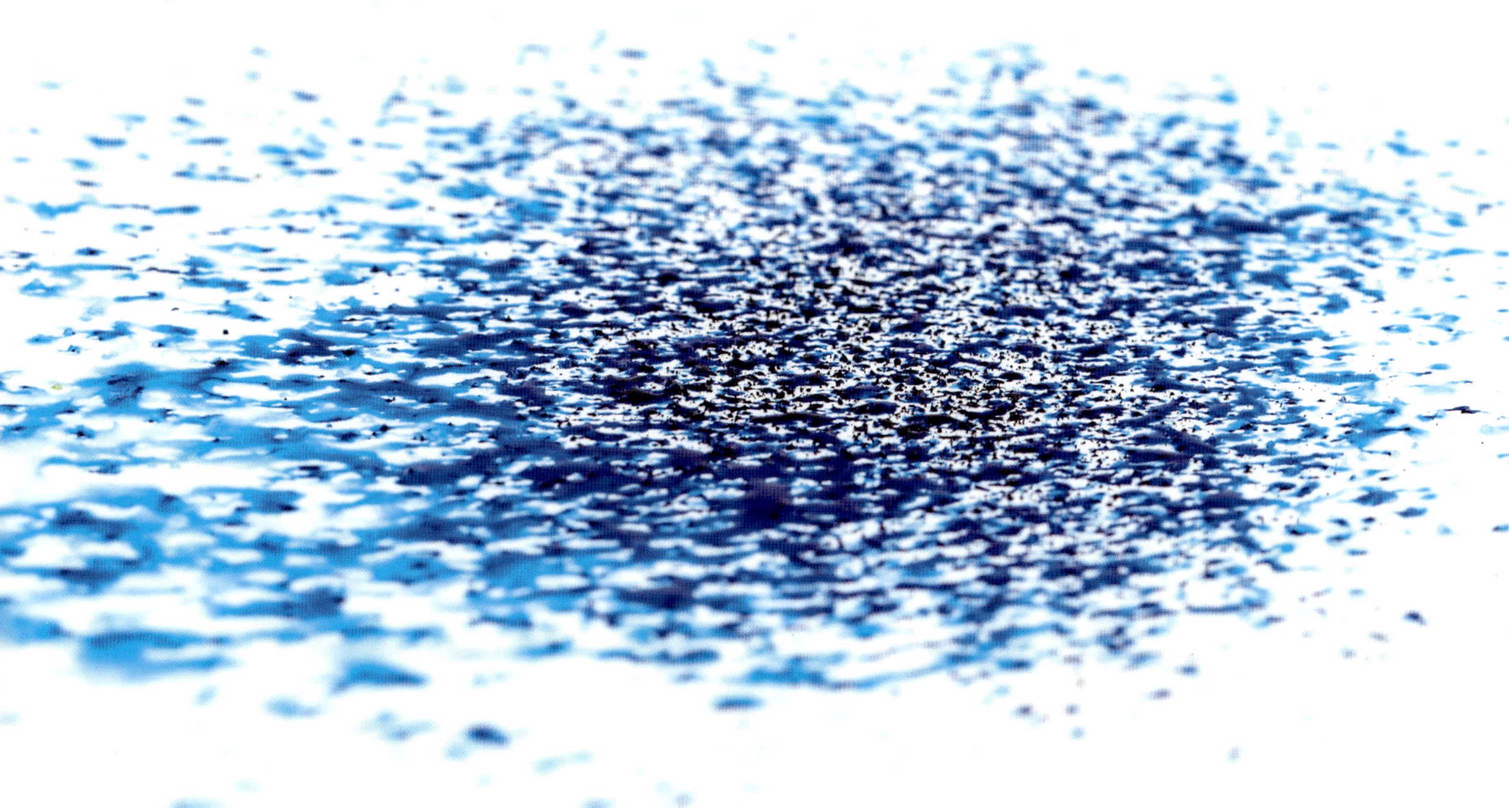

You will need

1 Brusho colours Brusho powder is available in an extensive range of exciting colours, sold as individual plastic pots or assorted packs. The colours I use in this book are:

scarlet	brilliant red	crimson
alizarin crimson	violet	purple
sunburst lemon	gamboge	orange
turquoise	ultramarine blue	cobalt blue
leaf green	sea green	black

However, I rarely use more than three different colours in any one project. At first you may be tempted to use all your colours at once, but my advice is that a limited palette of two or three colours is enough. You will be amazed at the variation of colour you can achieve using just the three primary colours: red, yellow and blue.

2 Watercolour paper I like to work on a Bockingford 300gsm (140lb) Not surface. Unless stated, all of the projects and demonstrations in this book are painted on Bockingford watercolour paper. There is no right or wrong paper to use, but please be aware that different papers will react in slightly different ways, so it's a great idea to experiment until you find your favourite!

3 Watercolour brushes I find a size 8 and 10 round brush suitable. I sometimes like to use my sword brush or rigger.

4 Old watercolour brush To use with bleach. Make sure you clean it thoroughly after using the bleach.

5 Toothbrush Use with bleach to create a spattering effect.

6 Pencil I usually apply a very light pencil drawing as a guide. Once the Brusho has been applied it can cover my drawing, making it difficult to see the pencil lines, so I wait for the wash to dry and reapply the pencil drawing on top of the dry wash. Another option is to create a wash of Brusho colour onto my watercolour paper and then apply my pencil drawing on top of this dry wash. I usually use a soft lead such as a 3B or 4B because a hard pencil line can be difficult to erase and can permanently mark the paper.

7 Eraser For removing pencil outlines from a painting.

8 Black waterproof pen I use this for line drawing before applying Brusho. I always use a waterproof pen as I don't want the line to bleed or run. I have used a size 0.8 black waterproof ink pen with a medium nib in the projects.

9 Spray bottle/atomizer One with water and a second in the ratio of 1:1 bleach and water.

10 Scraps of paper I like to use scraps of the same paper that I will use for my finished painting because it gives me an idea of how my chosen colours will react. I use the scraps as a palette for testing out colours, for spraying my bleach solution onto, or for tipping my Brusho powder from.

11 Palette I alternate between using a palette or scraps of watercolour paper to test out my colours. I like to use a ceramic palette because all types of paint will eventually stain a plastic palette.

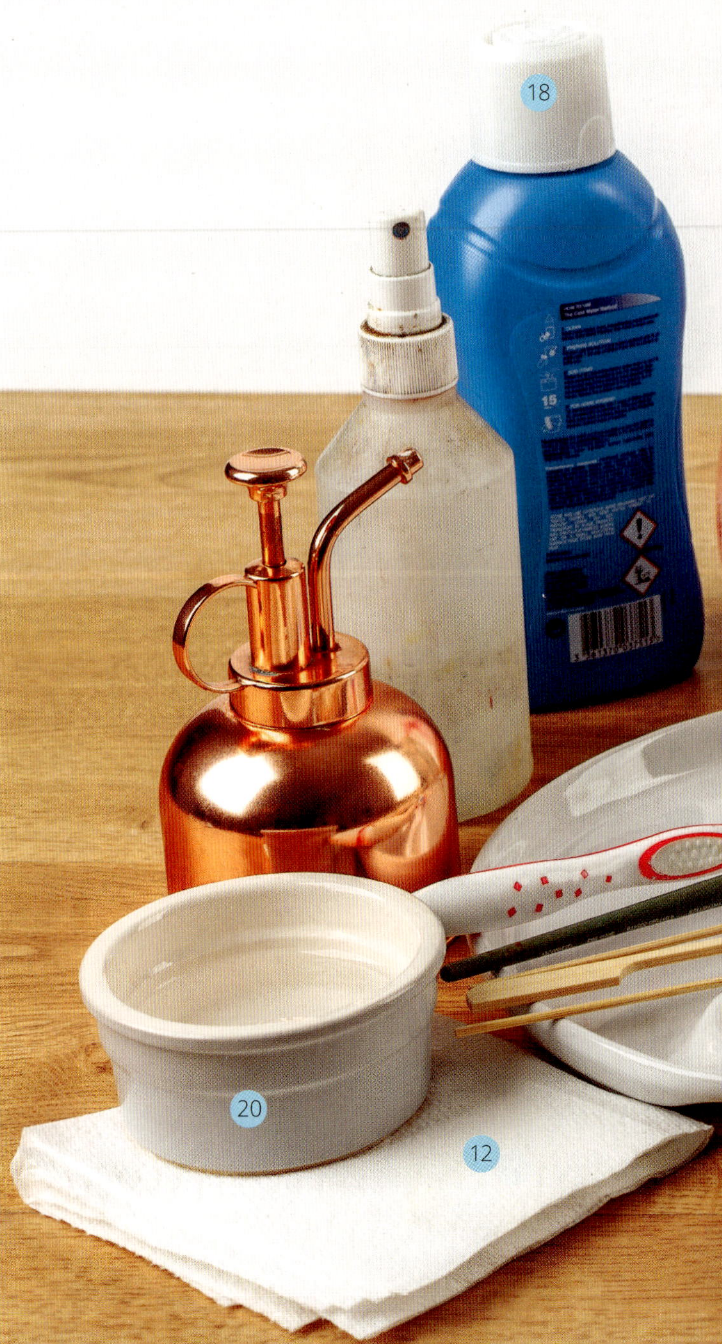

12 Kitchen paper I am a messy painter! I get so engrossed with my painting that keeping my workspace tidy is the last thing on my mind. Therefore I always have a big roll of kitchen paper or an old clean tea towel to mop up any mess. It is also useful for lifting out excess colour.

13 Drawing board I use mine on an incline to encourage the paint to flow.

14 Skewer or small knitting needle To prick a small hole in the lid of the Brusho pot. You can cover the small hole with a piece of masking tape or a pin.

15 Masking tape Use this to secure your paper to your drawing board. You can also use it to cover the hole in the lid of the Brusho tub when you have finished using it.

16 Drawing pins I use these to block up the hole in the lid of the tub of Brusho.

17 Wax A clear or white wax crayon, or a chunk of candle wax will work well for resist effects.

18 Bleach Choose between the kind you use for cleaning the bathroom or Milton fluid which is less toxic and is used for sterilizing babies' bottles.

19 Jug of clean water For cleaning your paintbrush between washes.

20 Ramekin For cleaning your bleach brush or holding a small amount of bleach solution.

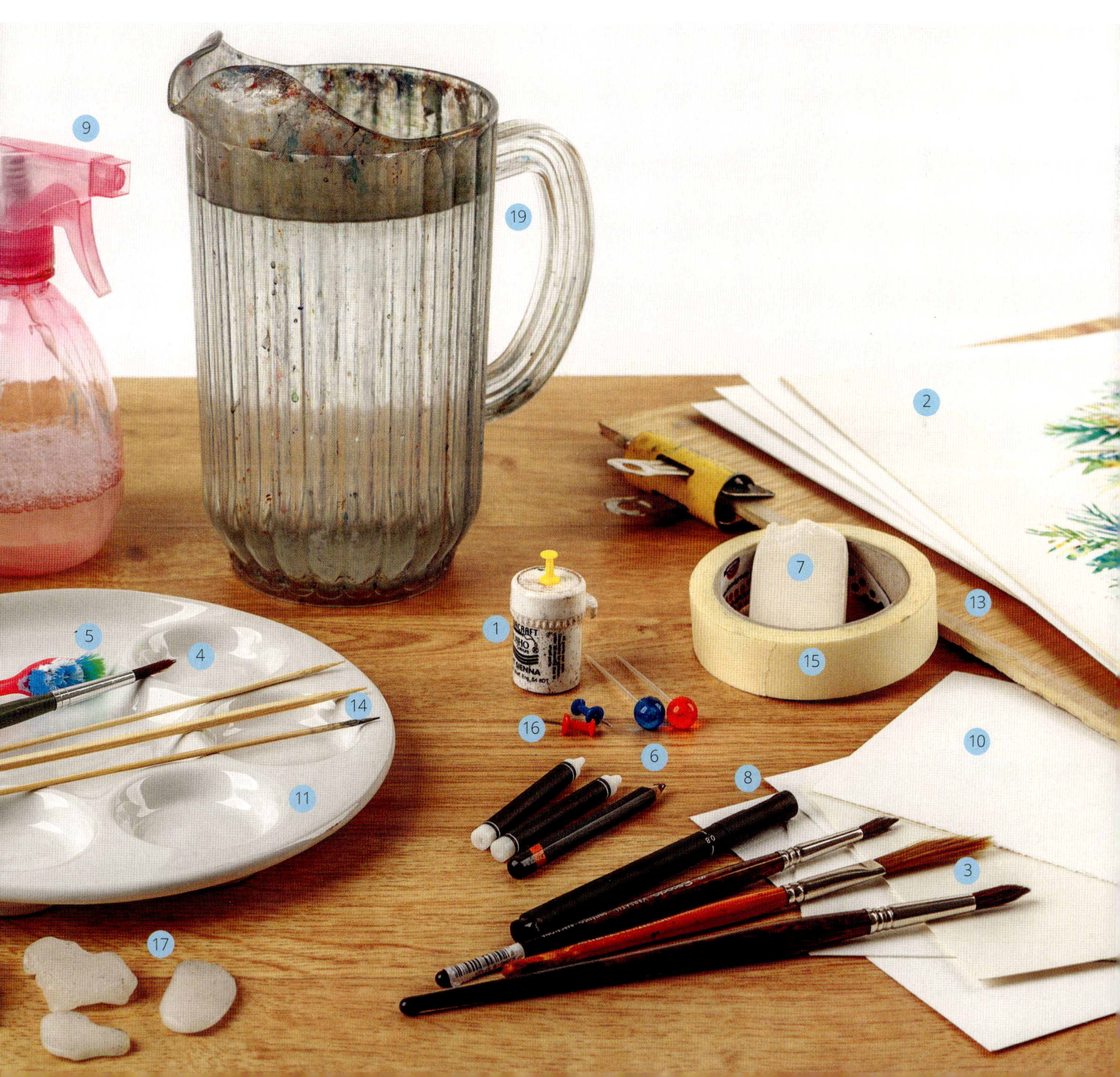

Let's get started

Look at these wonderful Brusho feathers. They demonstrate a range of techniques to show you how versatile Brusho is and how many unusual effects can be created, even with the same subject matter. I have used different techniques for each feather. These techniques will pop up throughout the book, so once you have read through the techniques section that follows and familiarized yourself with the demos, why don't you have a play and create your own unique feathers? This will help you to get to know Brusho before diving into the projects.

The techniques I choose to use will depend on the subject matter, for example most of my Brusho floral artwork uses the sprinkle and spray method (see pages 15–16). At other times I like to use Brusho as I would with my watercolours and start with washes of flat colour.

One colour

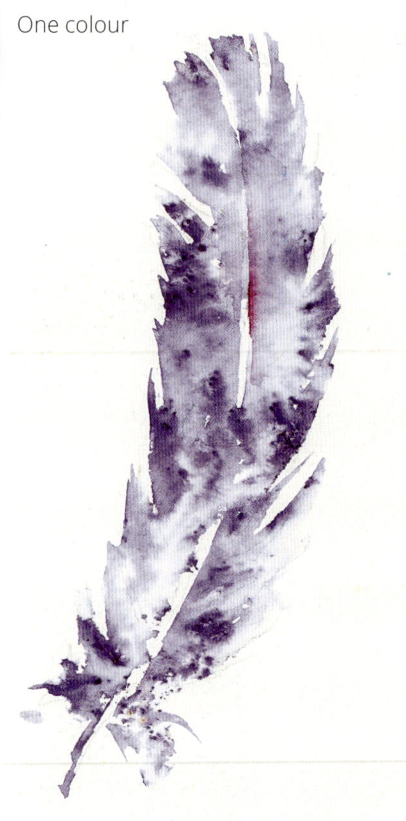

Wax resist

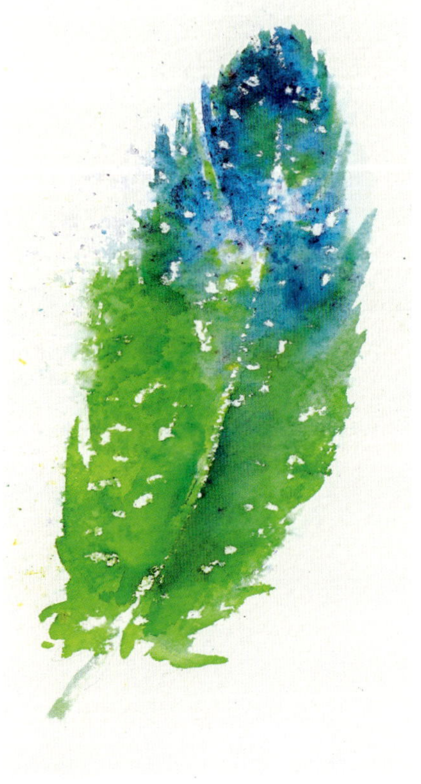

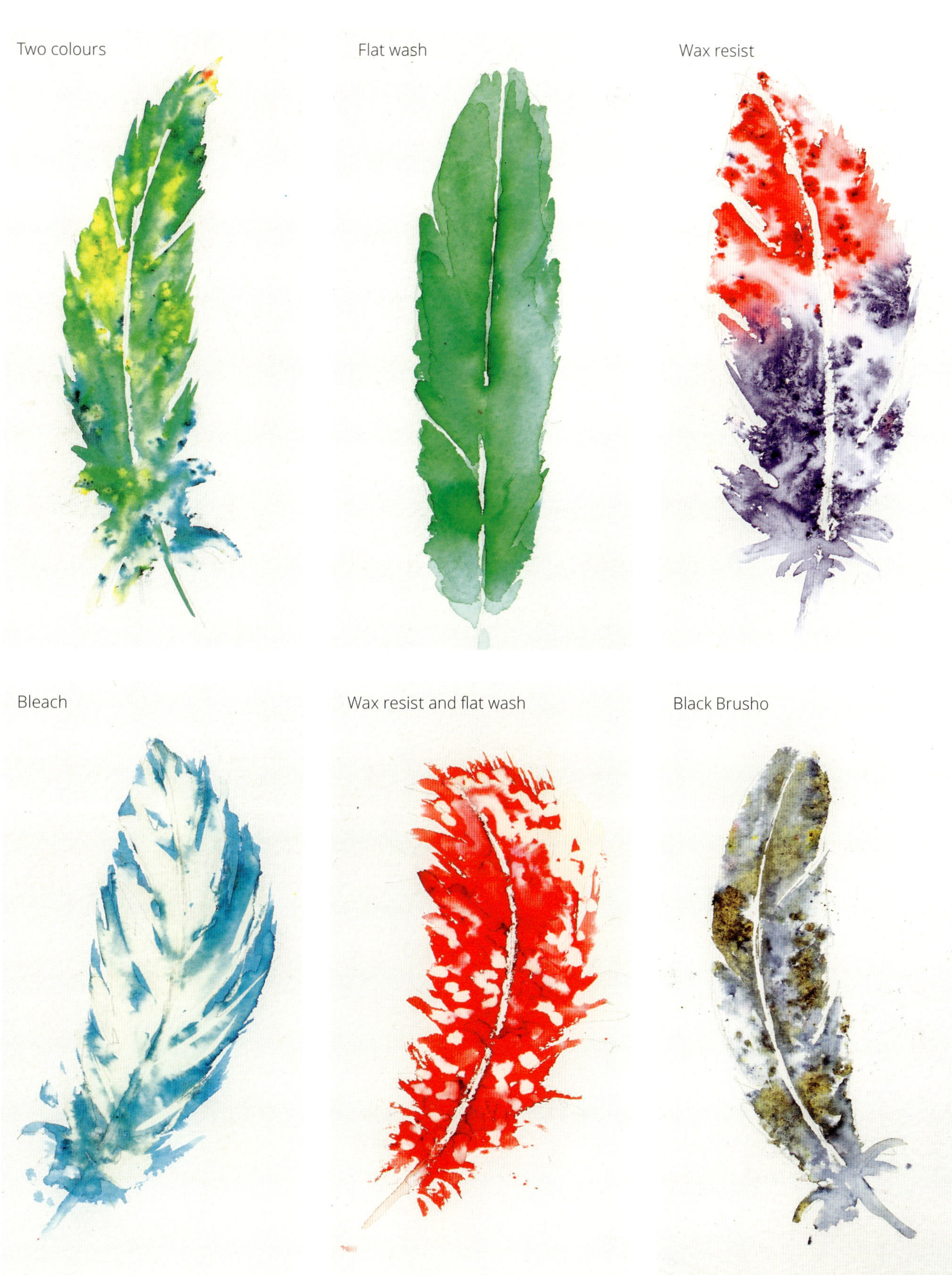

Two colours
Flat wash
Wax resist
Bleach
Wax resist and flat wash
Black Brusho

GETTING BRUSHO OUT OF THE POT

I recommend leaving the lids *on* your Brusho pots! It's all too easy to mix your vibrant colours together and contaminate them, not to mention making a colourful mess in your working area!

You only need a miniscule amount of Brusho powder, but it is difficult to restrict how much comes out the tub at once. I puzzled for a while how to overcome this, but the solution is easy and gave me much more control over the powder: I make a small hole in the lid of each pot with a cocktail stick or skewer. I then sprinkle the powder onto the paper using the same motion as tipping salt or pepper onto food (see picture opposite). This allows you to control the dispersal of Brusho.

If I want to be extra careful about restricting the pigment I tip out, I sprinkle a little Brusho onto a small scrap of paper and tap it from there onto my watercolour paper, giving me even more control.

I like to cover the small hole with a drawing pin or a piece of masking tape when not in use to avoid any powder escaping.

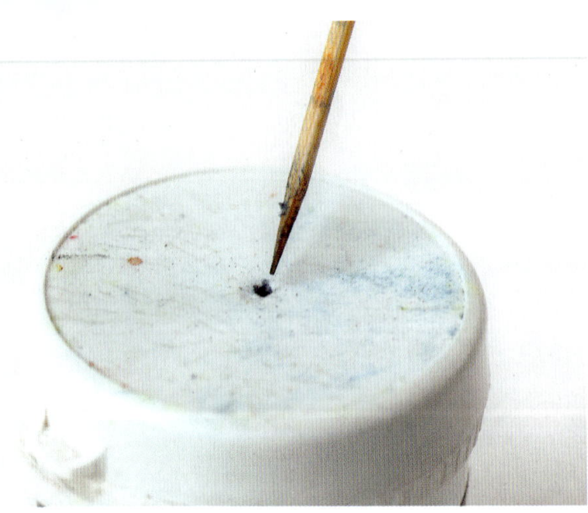

Use a cocktail stick to pierce a small hole in the plastic lid. (Mind your fingers when you do this.)

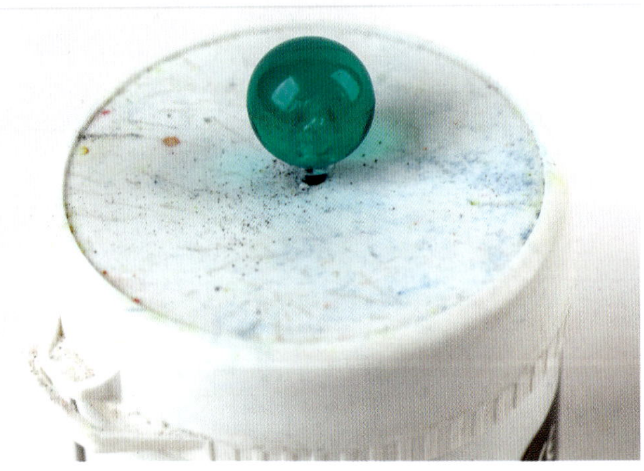

Use a drawing pin to block up the hole to avoid any spillages. The small amount that inevitably ends up on the lid becomes a visual reminder of the colour inside.

SPRINKLE AND SPRAY

I use this technique for many of my Brusho paintings. I sprinkle Brusho onto dry watercolour paper and then spritz with my water bottle. It's as easy as that!

Sprinkling

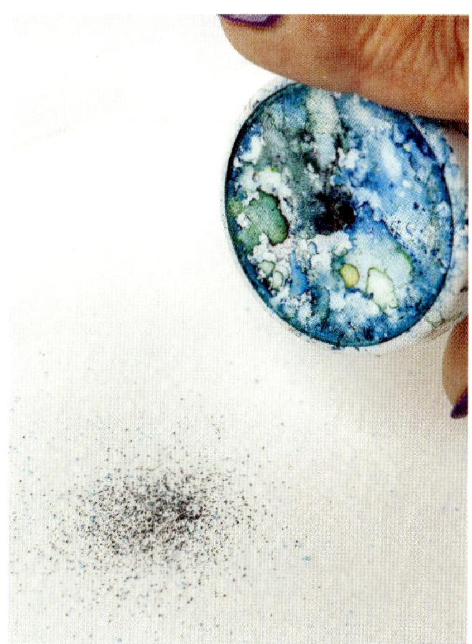

Very gently tap the top of the tub with your forefinger. Imagine you are adding a light seasoning of salt or pepper to your dinner. This will allow you to control how much powder ends up on your paper.

Brusho goes a long way so only sprinkle out a small amount – you will be amazed that so little powder can create so much colour when water is added! I have found that being too generous with the pigment can result in overly powerful dull washes, so less is best.

> **Tip**
>
> Brusho colours can look the same as each other on the paper when dry. Don't worry if your brilliant red Brusho powder doesn't look brilliant red at this stage!

Spraying

A gentle spritz of water is all that is needed to create a beautiful Brusho texture. Set your spray bottle to a fine mist. I recommend that you hold your spray bottle at a distance when spraying onto your watercolour paper. This will ensure you create a light spray rather than flooding your paper and the Brusho wash. Spray from directly above and start with one or two pumps of water. The direction of spray will affect the direction that the paint travels in.

> **Tip**
>
> Wait a few seconds for the paint to activate before adding more spray.

LIFTING USING KITCHEN PAPER

Kitchen paper is an essential part of my Brusho painting kit, especially when I am using the sprinkle and spray method (see page 15) which uses water sprayed directly onto the paper. I place a few pieces of kitchen paper or an old tea towel on top of this wet wash to soak up some of the water and Brusho colour while also retaining the texture. Sometimes I scrunch up a piece of kitchen paper to dab the wet wash if I want to lift certain areas rather than the whole painting.

   When sprinkling Brusho out of the tub it is easy to get carried away and tip out more powder than intended, resulting in too much colour flooding the paper. Using kitchen paper to lift areas of paint away helps to soften down the colour and prevents your page looking garish.

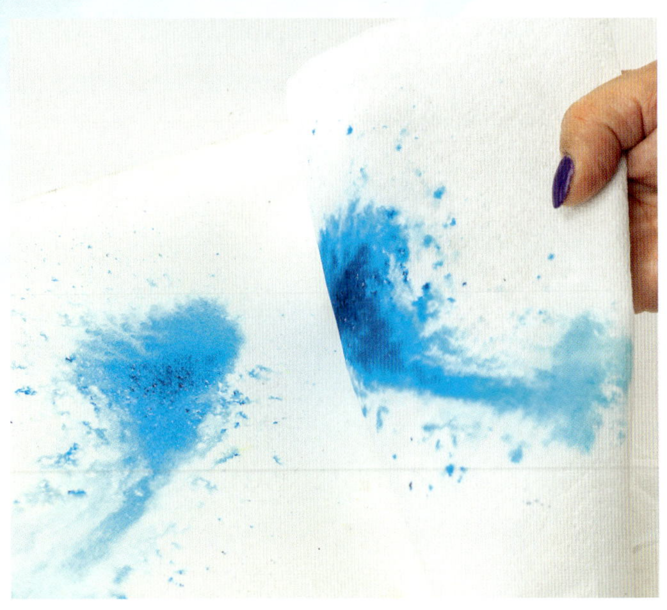

MAKING A SMOOTH WASH

Start with the sprinkle and spray method. Dip your brush in a jug of clean water. Smooth the brush in horizontal strokes over the top of your paint, ironing out the texture you previously created. Make sure you do this while it's still wet.

   This technique allows you to retain the texture created by the spray in some parts of the painting, while adding a smooth wash to other parts. It looks very effective.

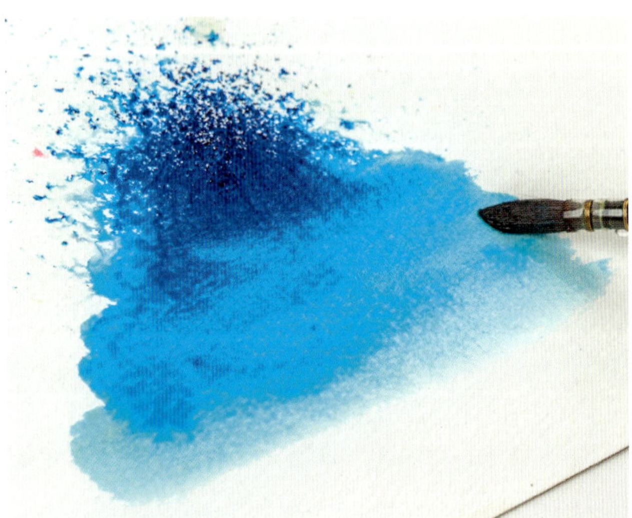

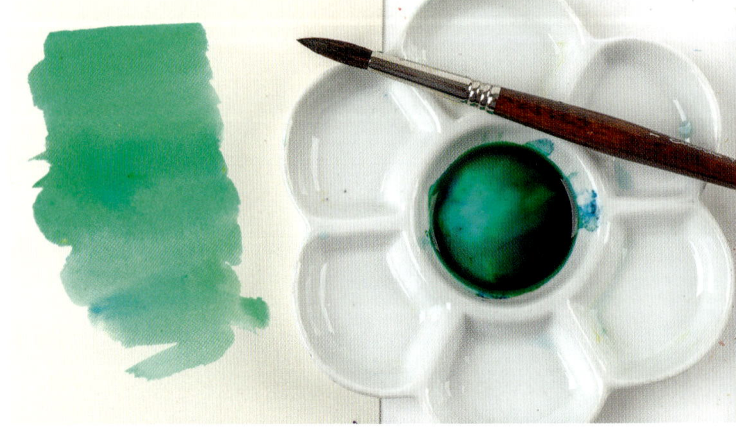

If I require a pure wash of Brusho I will sprinkle the Brusho powder into a palette and mix with water so I have nice clean washes of colour. I can then paint with the Brusho as I would with watercolour.

SPRINKLE AND SPRAY USING TWO COLOURS

You can use the same sprinkle and spray technique shown on pages 15–16, but this time using two different colours. I like to use two primary colours to create a secondary colour. Sprinkle both colours onto the dry page first and then spray the water.

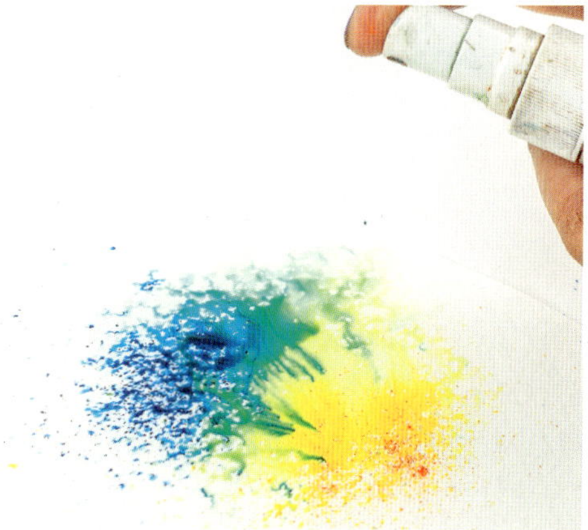

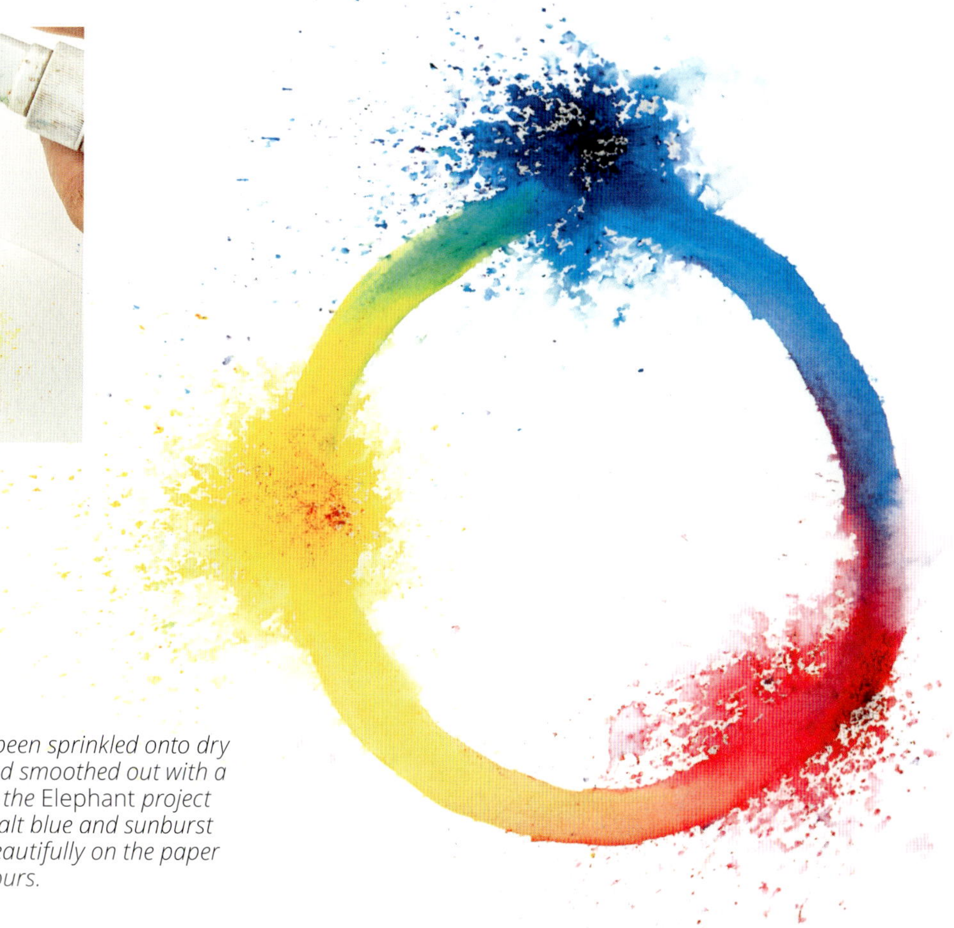

Using three colours

Look at these three colours that have been sprinkled onto dry paper and then sprayed with water and smoothed out with a brush. These are the colours I used for the Elephant *project on pages 88–99: alizarin crimson, cobalt blue and sunburst lemon. See how they blend together beautifully on the paper and create magnificent secondary colours.*

SPRAY *THEN* SPRINKLE

Now you are familiar with the sprinkle and spray method, it can be fun to reverse the order by spraying your paper with clean water first and then sprinkling on the Brusho powder. If you prefer, you can wet your page with a brush rather than spraying it.

This technique is great for floral paintings as the paint disperses from the middle, which gives the impression of the flower's centre and then the petals.

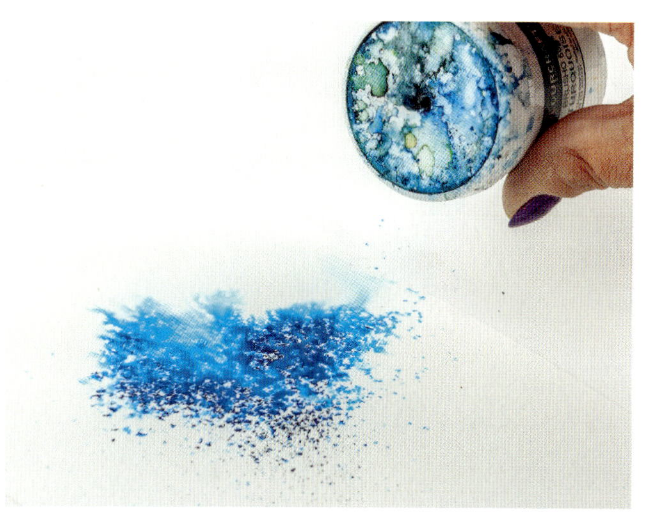

Demo one

Sprinkle and spray using one colour

This simple demonstration is a great example of how Brusho reacts when sprinkled and sprayed with water. We will be using just one colour to create a simple blue floral painting of a small section of a hydrangea. You can use any colour you choose for this exercise, but I find that darker colours work best.

I use my pencil outline to suggest just three small flower shapes emerging from the textured wash. I use a soft pencil for this initial outline because it won't indent the paper if I need to rub it out and redraw it.

You could explore this technique further by painting a full hydrangea floral that is made up of lots of tiny flowerheads (see page 123).

YOU WILL NEED

- Bockingford watercolour paper 300gsm (140lb) Not surface, quarter imperial (28 x 38cm/11 x 15in)
- 3B pencil
- Eraser
- Brusho paint: turquoise
- Size 8 brush
- Spray bottle with water
- Scrap of paper
- Kitchen paper

Steps

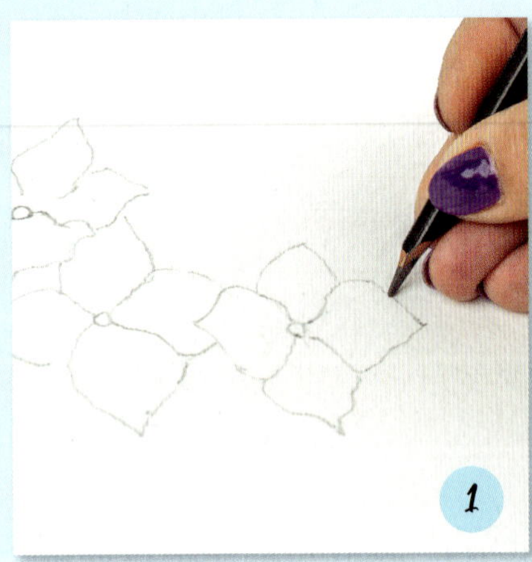 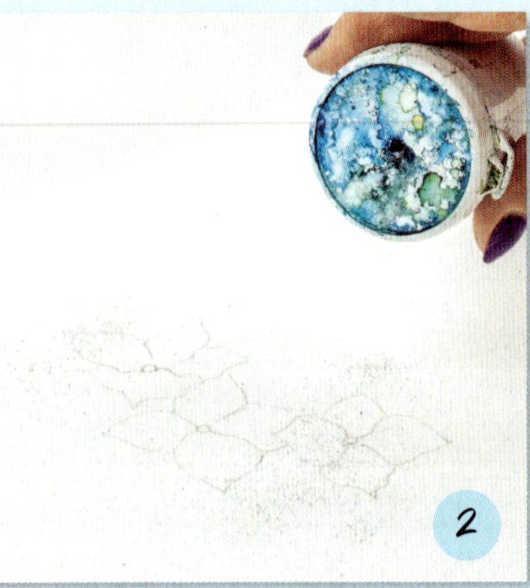 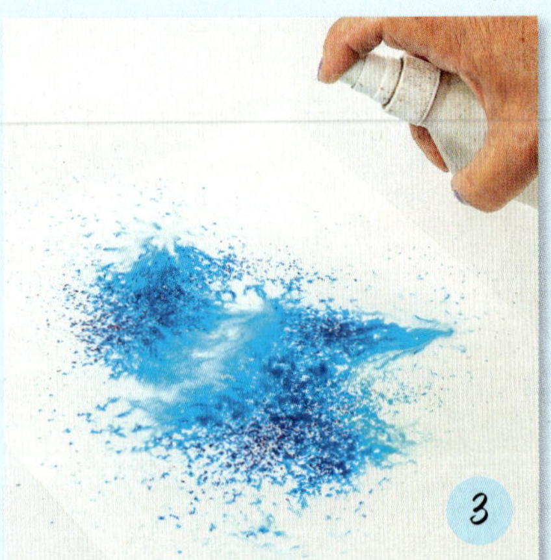

1 Use a soft pencil to outline three small flower shapes as a guide for you to work around.

2 Sprinkle the turquoise Brusho powder onto dry paper. Don't keep your Brusho within the lines.

3 Set your spray bottle to a fine mist and spritz the turquoise Brusho on the paper with water. Immediately you will see the beautiful texture that can be achieved by simply spraying your powder with water to reveal your line drawing underneath.

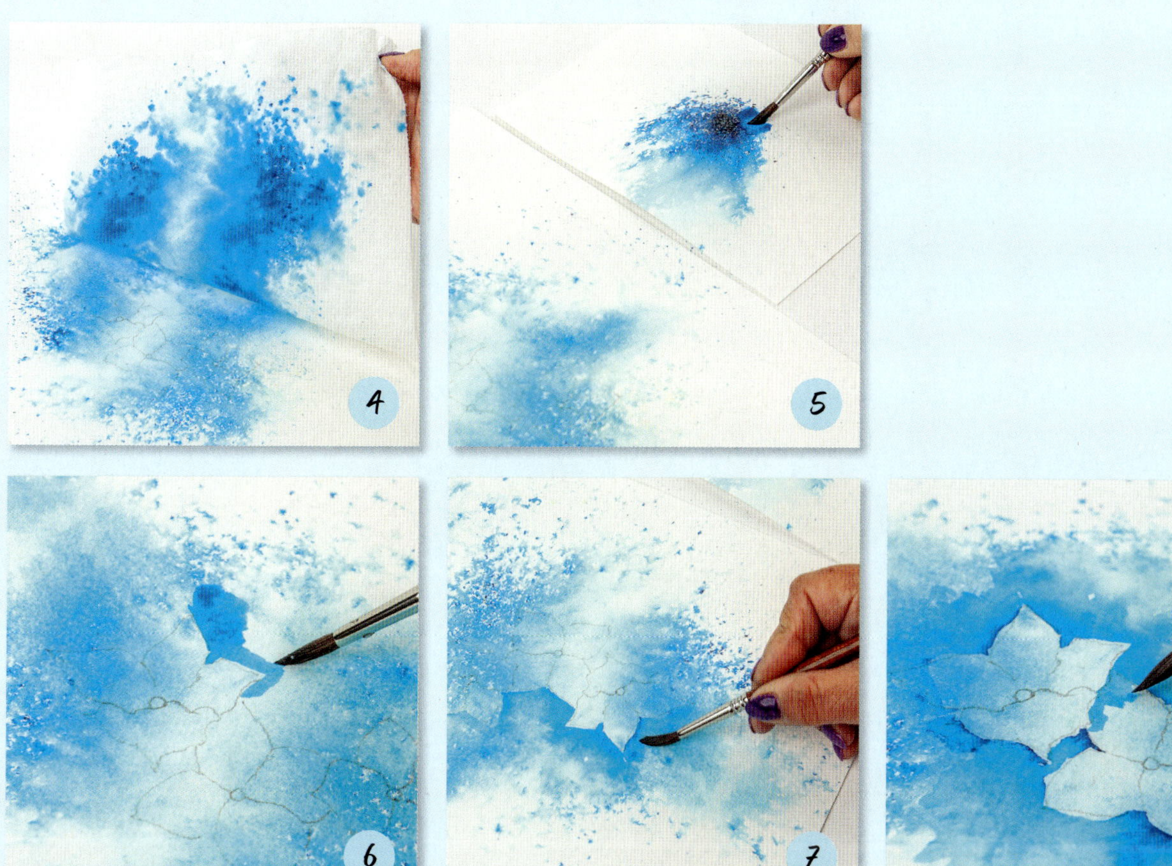

4 Lay a piece of kitchen paper over the top to remove excess water, then allow the page to dry.

5 Using a wet brush, mix a darker wash of the turquoise onto scrap paper, using it like a palette.

6 Using your wash, start to add a few darker areas around your small flower shapes to define them.

7 Rinse the brush before softening the edge of the wash. Rotate your paper if you find that easier.

8 Paint another layer underneath the top flower to knock it back. Repeat with a darker wash against the bottom flower.

9 Add details to the flowers, adding a dark wash around the centre shapes.

10 Soften these washes away from the centre.

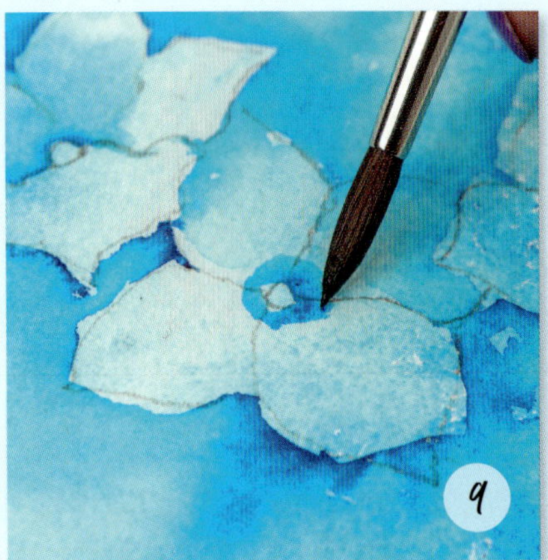

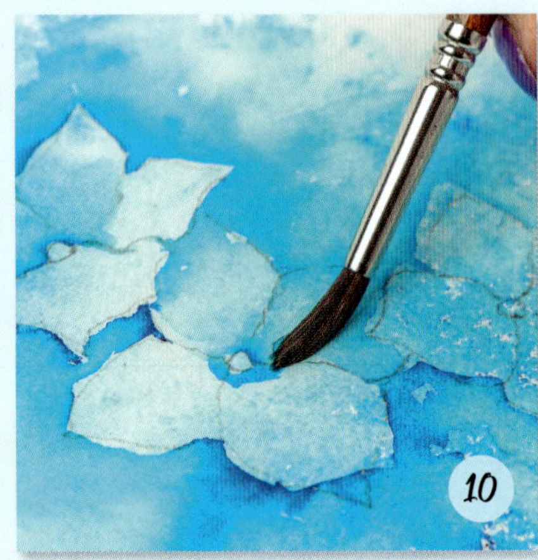

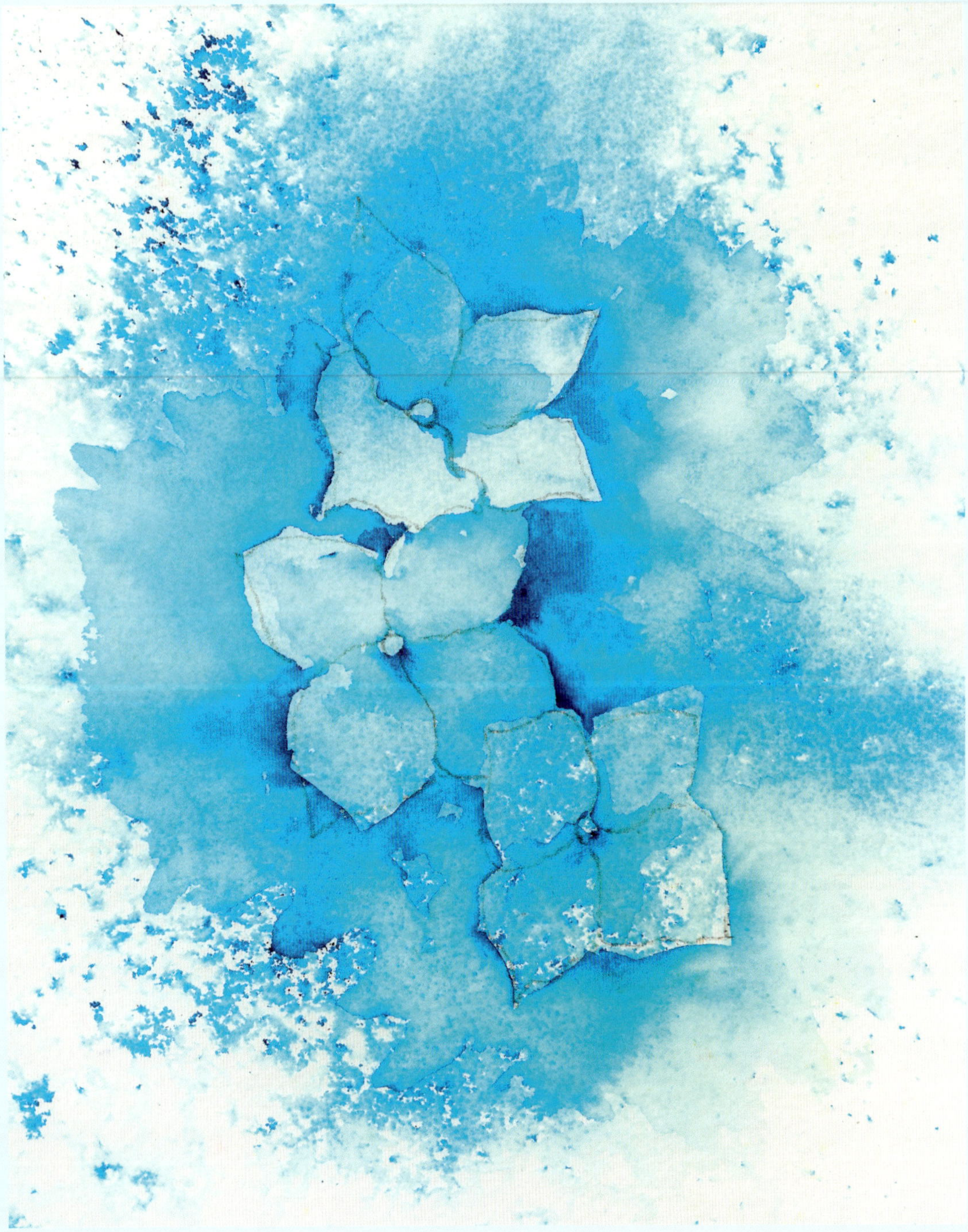

Amazing results using one colour only

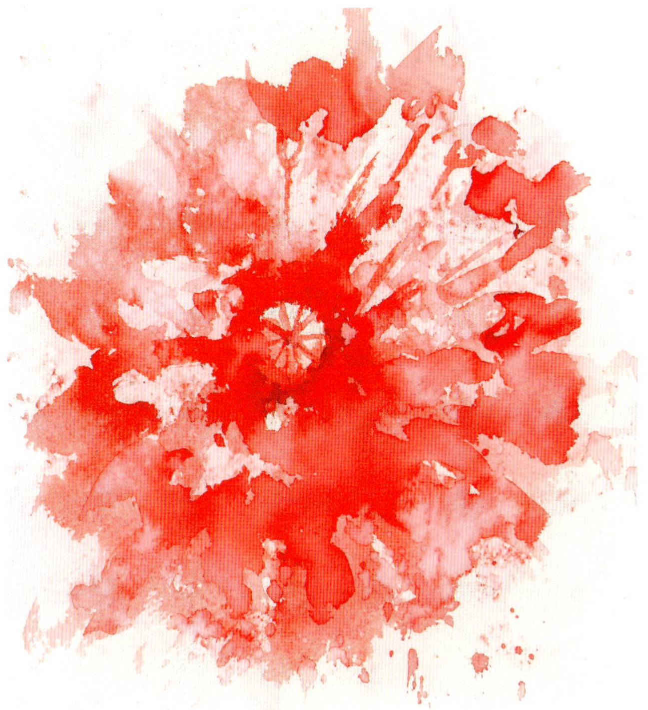

Poppy

I used just one Brusho colour, rose red, to create this vibrant poppy. The poppy started life using the sprinkle and spray technique.

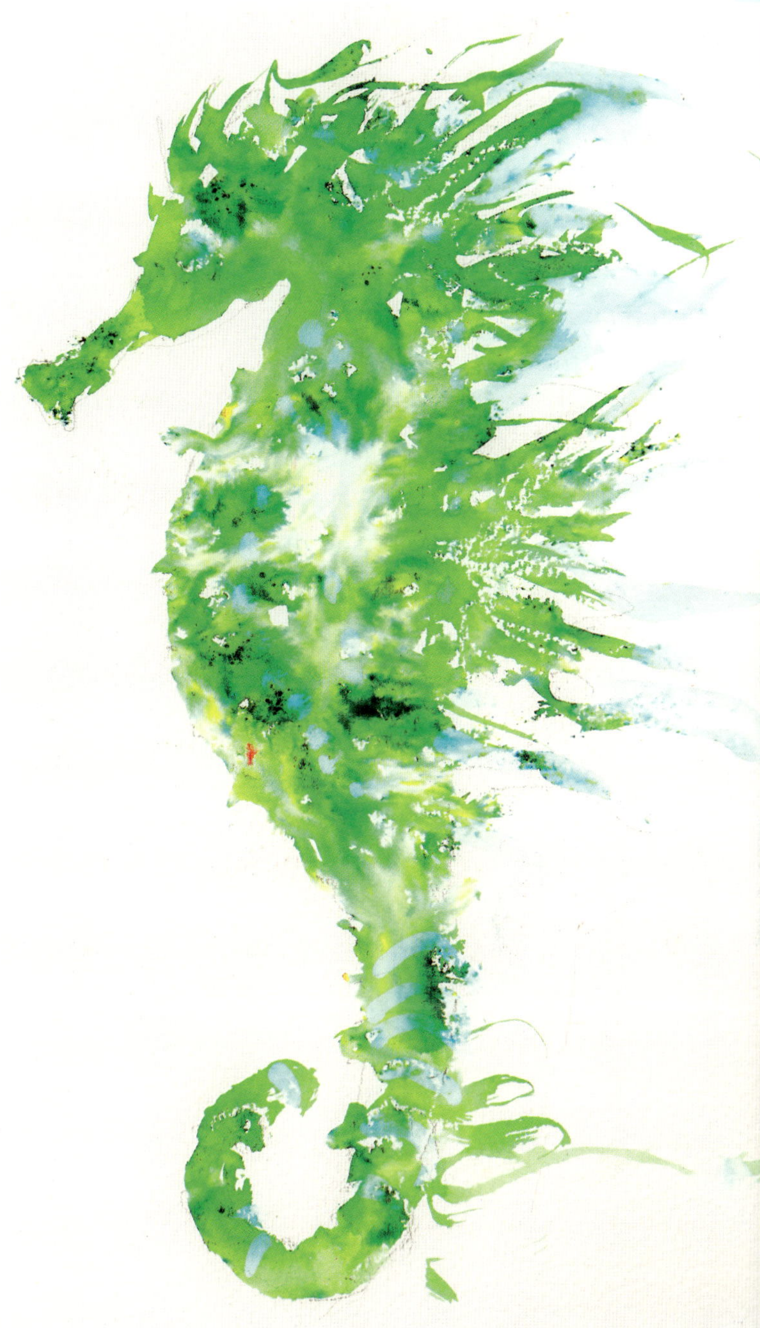

Seahorse

A simple yet effective seahorse is brought to life by wetting the seahorse shape and sprinkling the sea green Brusho onto the wet paper. I added a few linear brushstrokes to give the seahorse more shape and movement.

Demo two

Using two colours

Let's explore Brusho further and create a wash of two Brusho colours that blend together on the paper rather than in a palette. I hope you will be excited by what can be achieved using just two Brusho colours.

This beautifully delicate butterfly is a perfect exercise for you to practise mixing two Brusho colours together. Have fun creating a unique butterfly of your own. Play around with different colour combinations to see what works together and is pleasing to the eye.

YOU WILL NEED

- Bockingford watercolour paper 300gsm (140lb) Not surface, quarter imperial (28 x 38cm/11 x 15in)
- Brusho paint: crimson, violet
- Size 8 brush
- 3B pencil

Steps

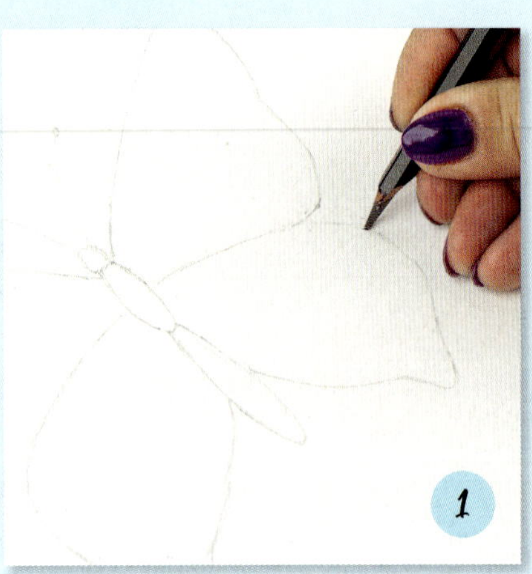

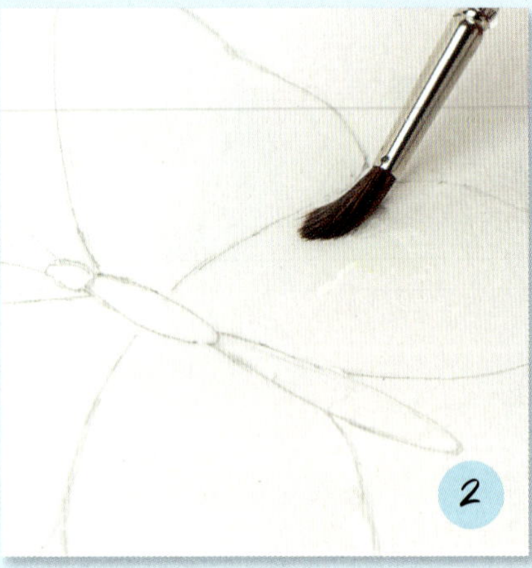

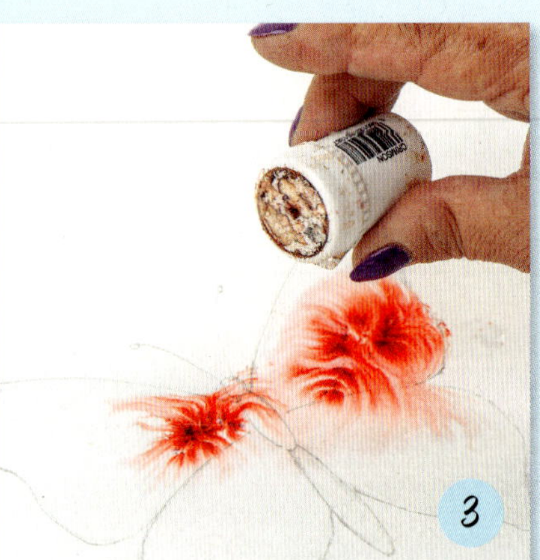

1 Draw a simple butterfly outline in pencil. There is no need for details as we are going to let the Brusho do all the work for us!

2 Wet the whole butterfly shape with your brush and clean water.

3 Sprinkle crimson into the wet area. You will see the paint swirls forming which give the butterfly its markings.

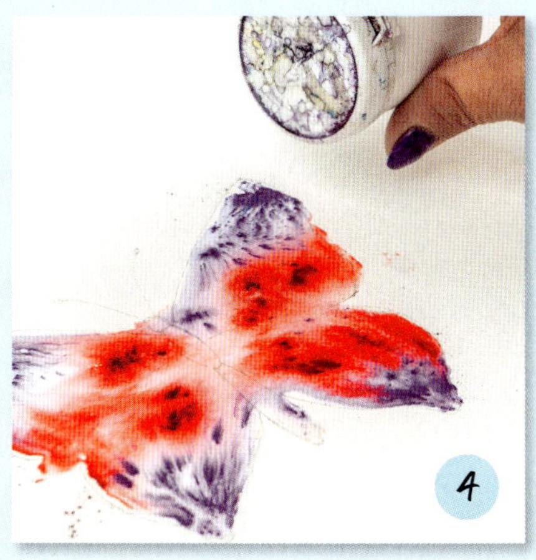

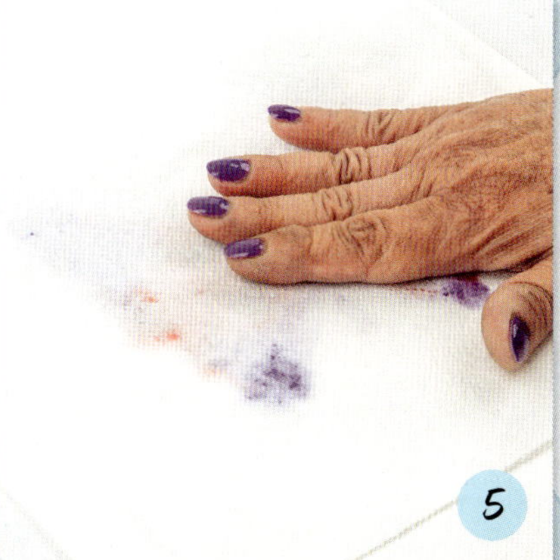

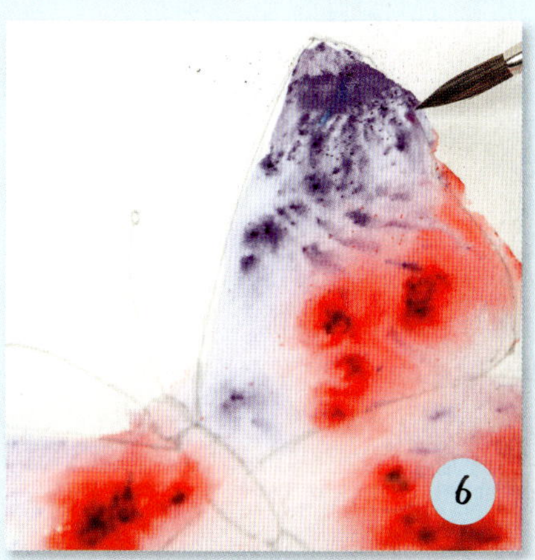

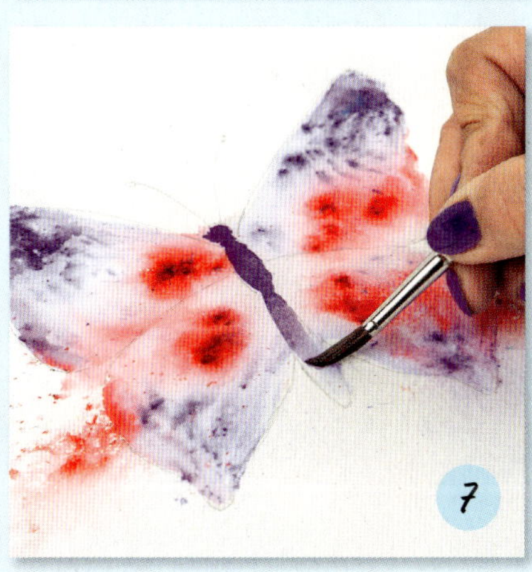

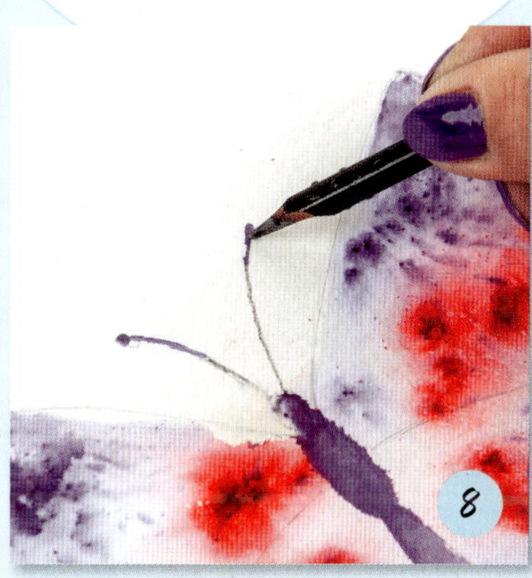

4 Sprinkle violet into the wet area. Allow the colours to blend beautifully on the paper by themselves.

5 Place a piece of kitchen paper over the wet area and press down to seal the textured colour combinations. This aids the drying process.

6 Using clean water on your brush, retouch any areas that the Brusho may have missed. Try not to overwork at this stage as you don't want to lose all that lovely texture.

7 Mix a darker wash of the violet on a scrap of paper and apply to the body using your brush.

8 Using the same wash, dip your pencil in the paint and lightly draw in the antennae. This allows you greater accuracy than using a brush.

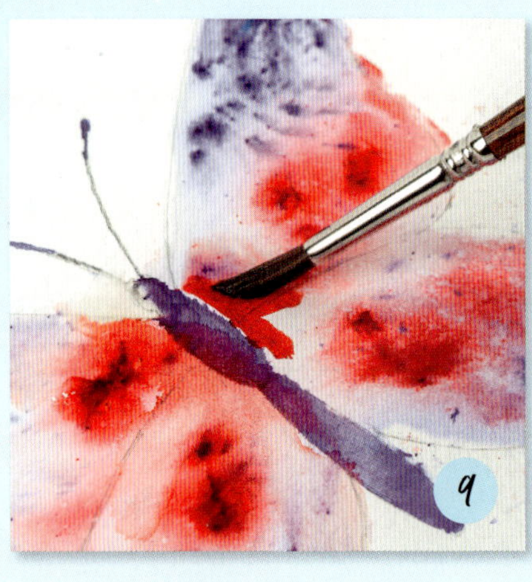

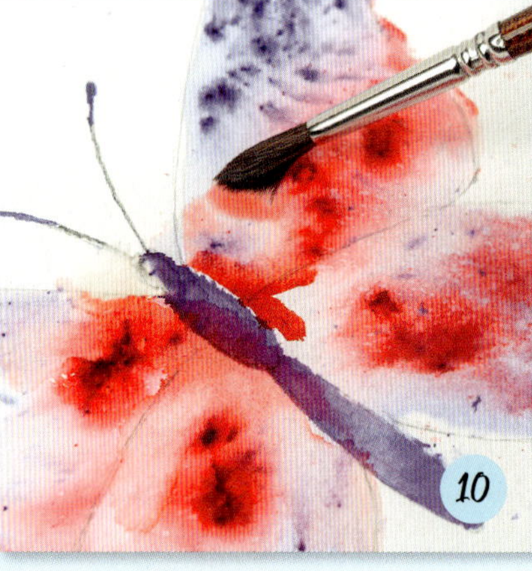

9 Mix a wash of crimson on your scrap paper and apply with your brush either side of the body.

10 Use your brush to smooth out the paint.

Each butterfly will look different to the next. If your butterfly isn't symmetrical, you can sprinkle on more Brusho powder to balance the colour. Then activate the new powder with a spray of water.

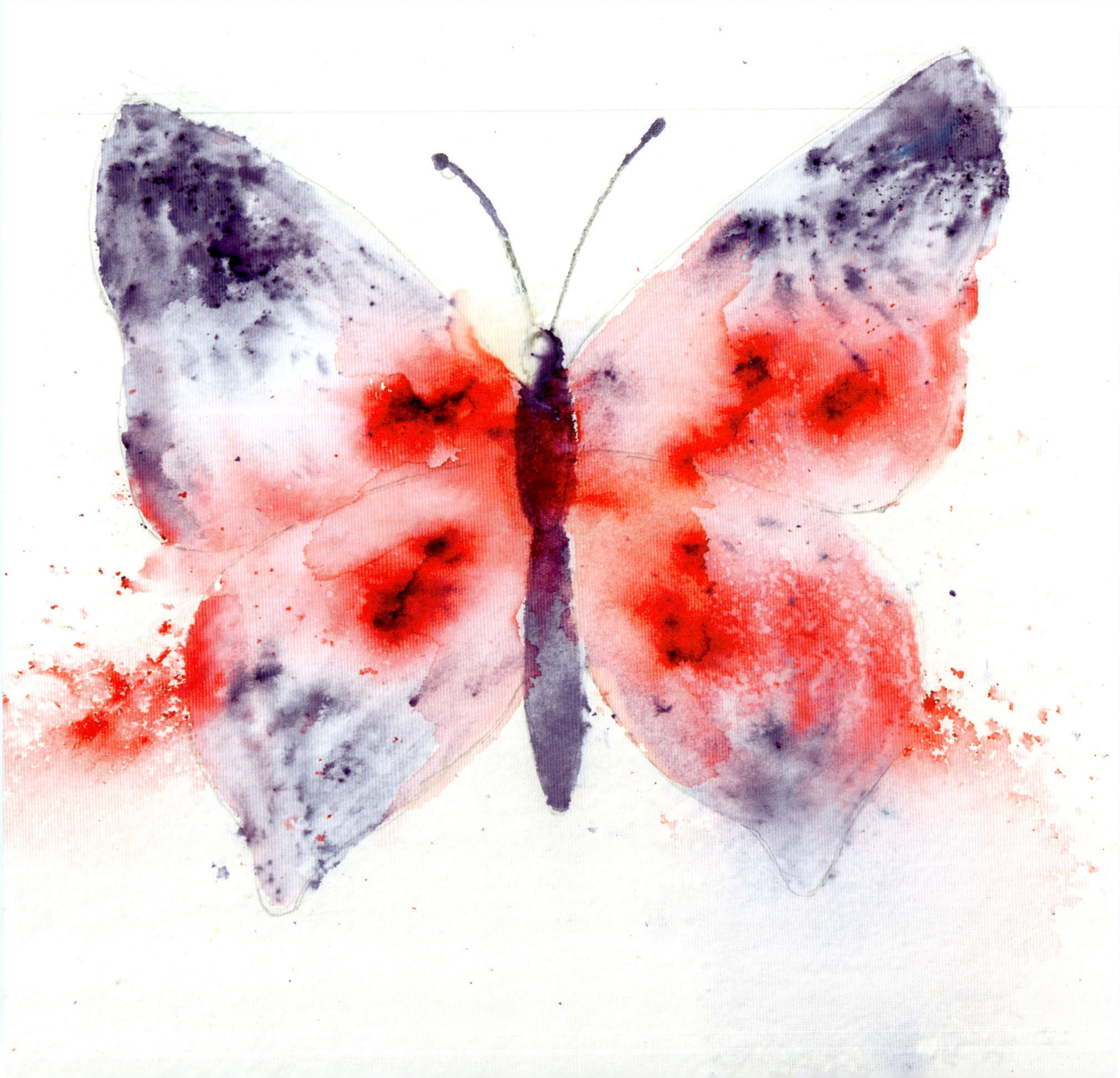

Demo two

Get creative using two colours

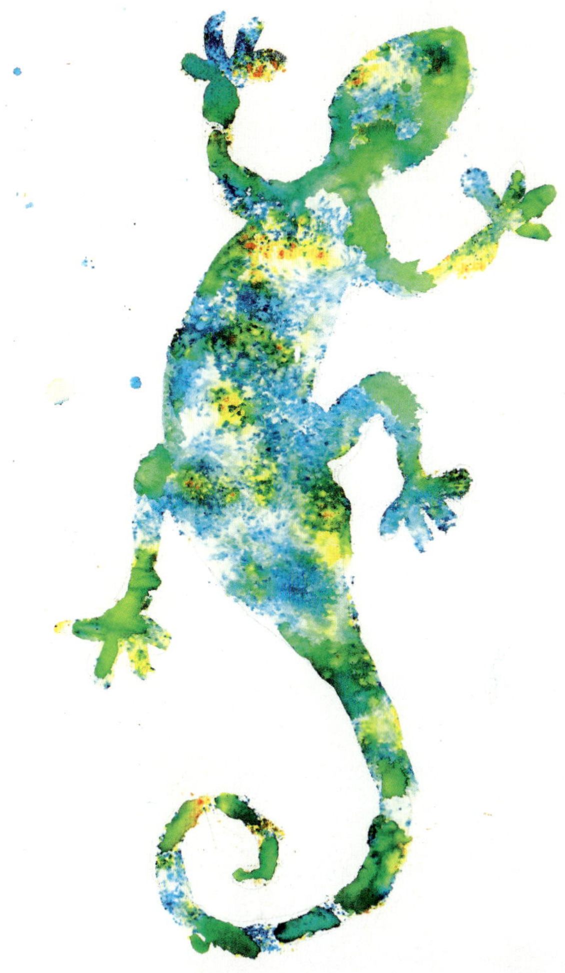

Gecko

I used just two Brusho colours to create this colourful gecko: turquoise and lemon yellow. Using a pencil, I created the outline of the gecko. With a clean brush and a jug of water I wetted inside this pencil area before sprinkling two colours into the wet area. I allowed them to blend on the page to create a textured wash.

Colourful Trees

Here I am using two different colours to paint these atmospheric trees: rose red and black. This painting didn't require a drawn outline as I sprinkled the two colours onto the dry paper and then spritzed with my water bottle to create the Brusho foliage. Using my brush, I pulled the colour down to create the tree trunks and a little foreground.

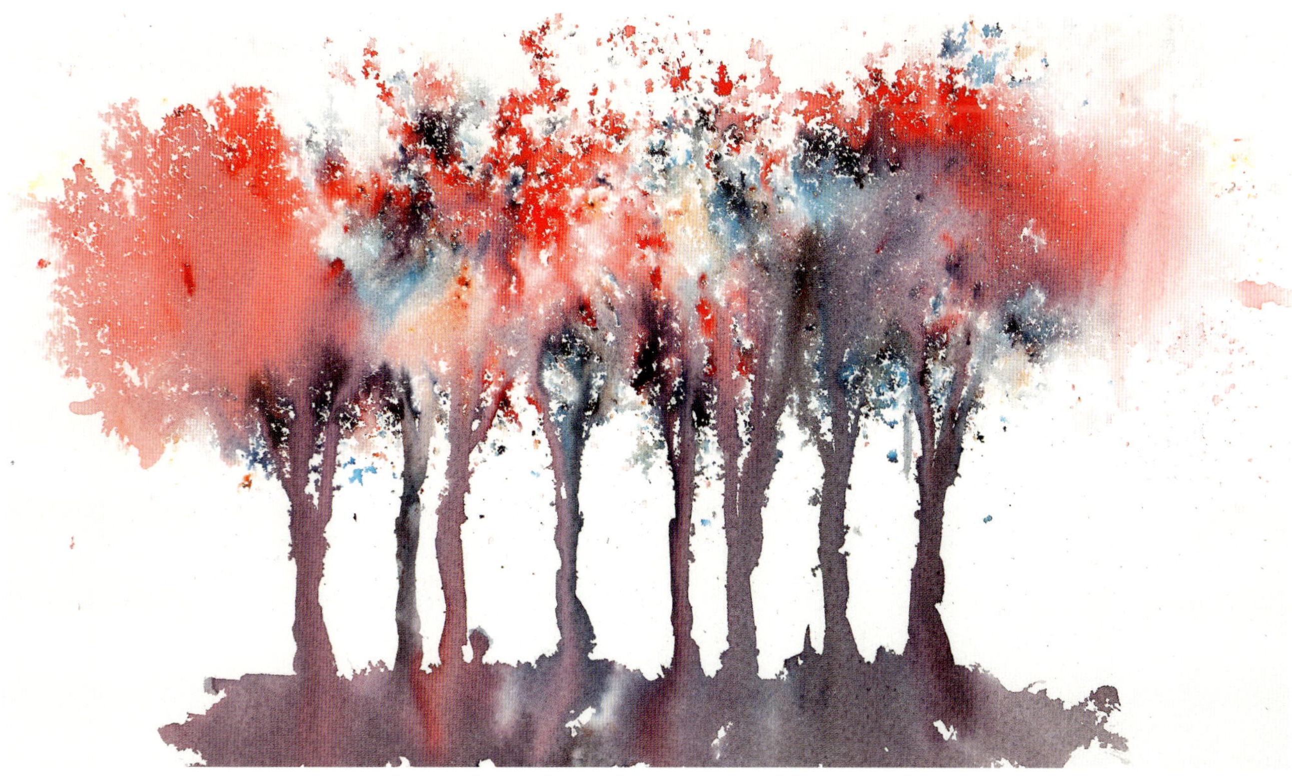

USING WAX RESIST

One of my favourite ways to preserve the white of the paper when working with Brusho is to use the wax resist technique. The wax acts as a barrier and prevents the paper from absorbing the paint. If you want an area of your painting to appear white or would like a sparkly white texture then wax is a very effective tool. It is important to note that once the wax has been applied to your paper you cannot remove it, so it is best used sparingly.

I like to use broken pieces of candle wax with sharp edges to create linear marks, or larger pieces to drag along the paper to create areas of sparkle. You can also use a white wax crayon or purchase wax resist sticks from your local art supplies shop.

One drawback of using the wax resist technique is that it can become gimmicky if used too often or you are heavy-handed with your application, so try reserving it for areas you really want to sing with light. Most of my paintings incorporate a little wax resist, but I try to integrate it rather than make it stand out too much.

Think about the different ways you can use wax to create interest in your paintings, for example you can block in a whole area, create linear marks or letters, or make subtle little dots of wax to produce a sparkle effect in a Brusho wash.

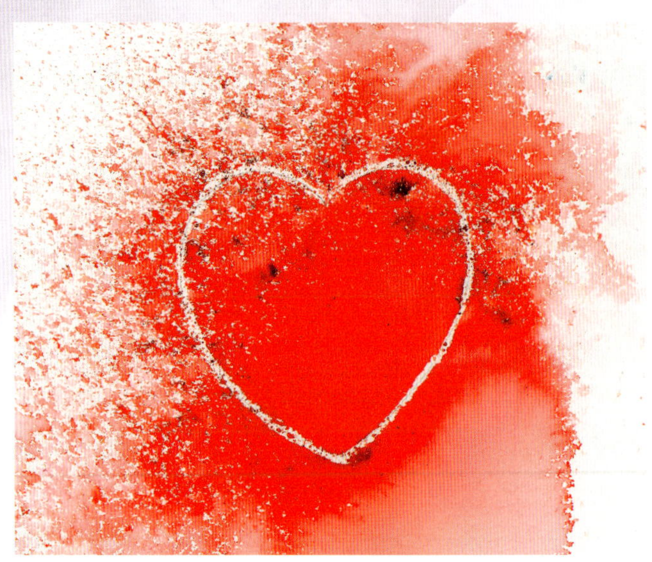

This would make a lovely St Valentine's Day card.

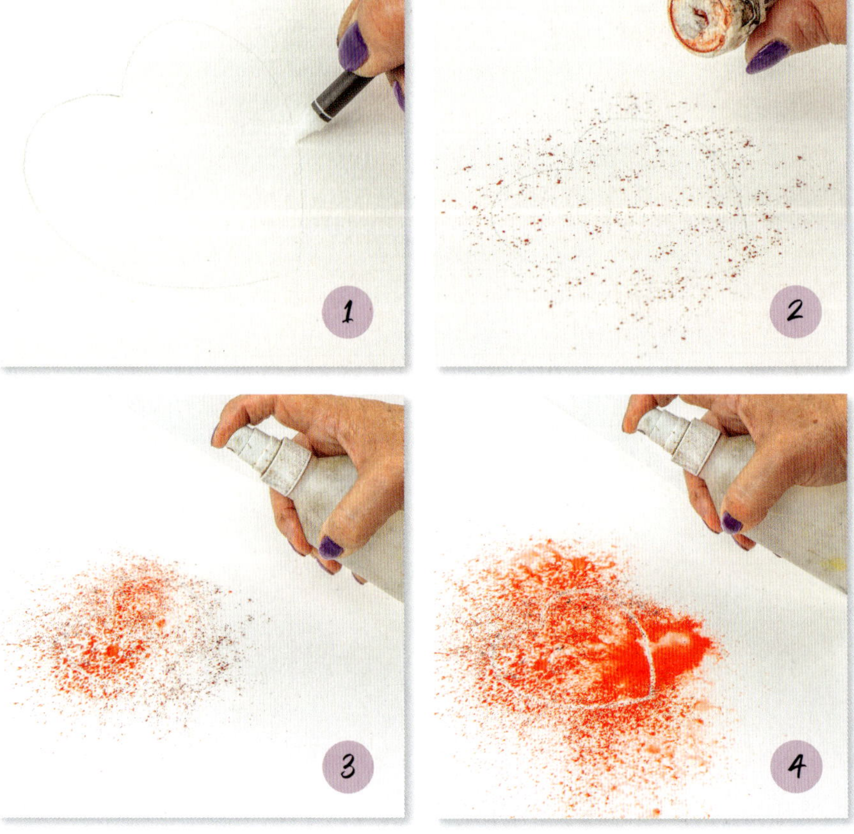

1 Press firmly over your pencil outline with a wax crayon or shard of wax candle.

2 Lightly sprinkle brilliant red Brusho all over the pencil outline and over the wax. Don't worry if you can no longer see your outline.

3 Spray the paint powder with water, starting with the top half.

4 Spray the bottom half and you will see the wax showing through.

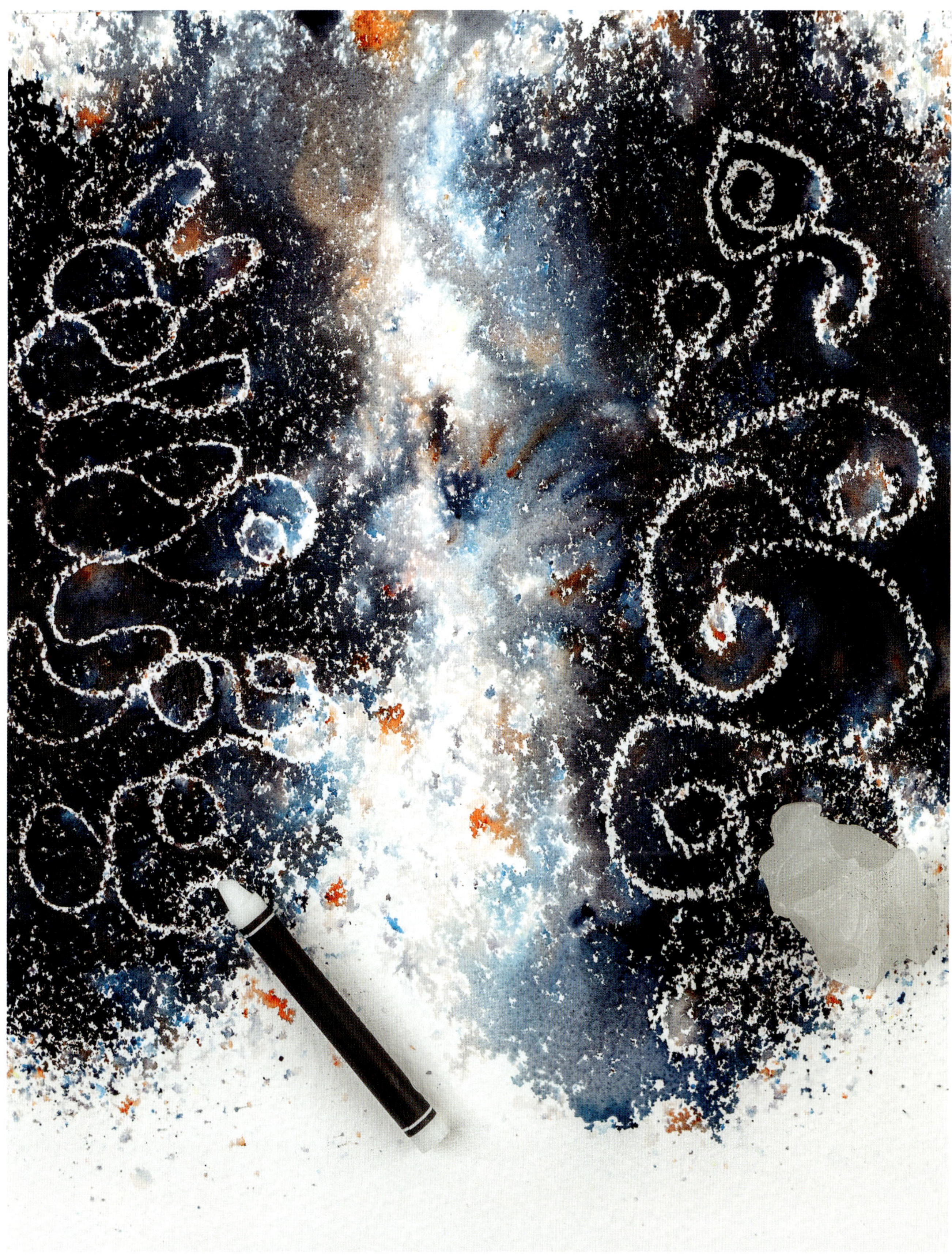

Here you can see the marks made by a white wax crayon (left) and a piece of candle wax (right).

Demo three

Using wax resist

This Brusho spider's web painting uses the wax resist technique. It looks really dynamic yet is so easy to create as well as a lot of fun to paint with a limited palette of just two colours and the sprinkle and spray method.

There is no complicated drawing, just the web and you can of course include the little spider that hangs from his web.

Look at all the juicy texture that the sprinkle and spray method has created and how the dark textured washes resist the wax areas which help to highlight the waxy web.

YOU WILL NEED

- Bockingford watercolour paper, Not surface 300gsm (140lb) half imperial (38 x 56cm/15 x 22in)
- 4B pencil
- Eraser
- Brusho paint: black, purple
- Size 8 brush
- Spray bottle with water
- Wax crayon or candle wax
- Old towel
- Kitchen paper

Steps

1 Using a pencil, sketch the spider's web. Use your piece of wax to draw over the pencil lines of the web. You won't be able to see your wax resist lines untill you start to add your Brusho.

2 Sprinkle black Brusho generously over three-quarters of the web area.

3 Sprinkle purple in the bottom quarter of the web.

4 Spray the dry Brusho powder with water. Now the waxy marks you applied earlier will start to show through the paint.

5 Once you have sprayed over the web, tilt your paper towards you and add more spray under the web, allowing the paint to drip down into the bottom half of your paper.

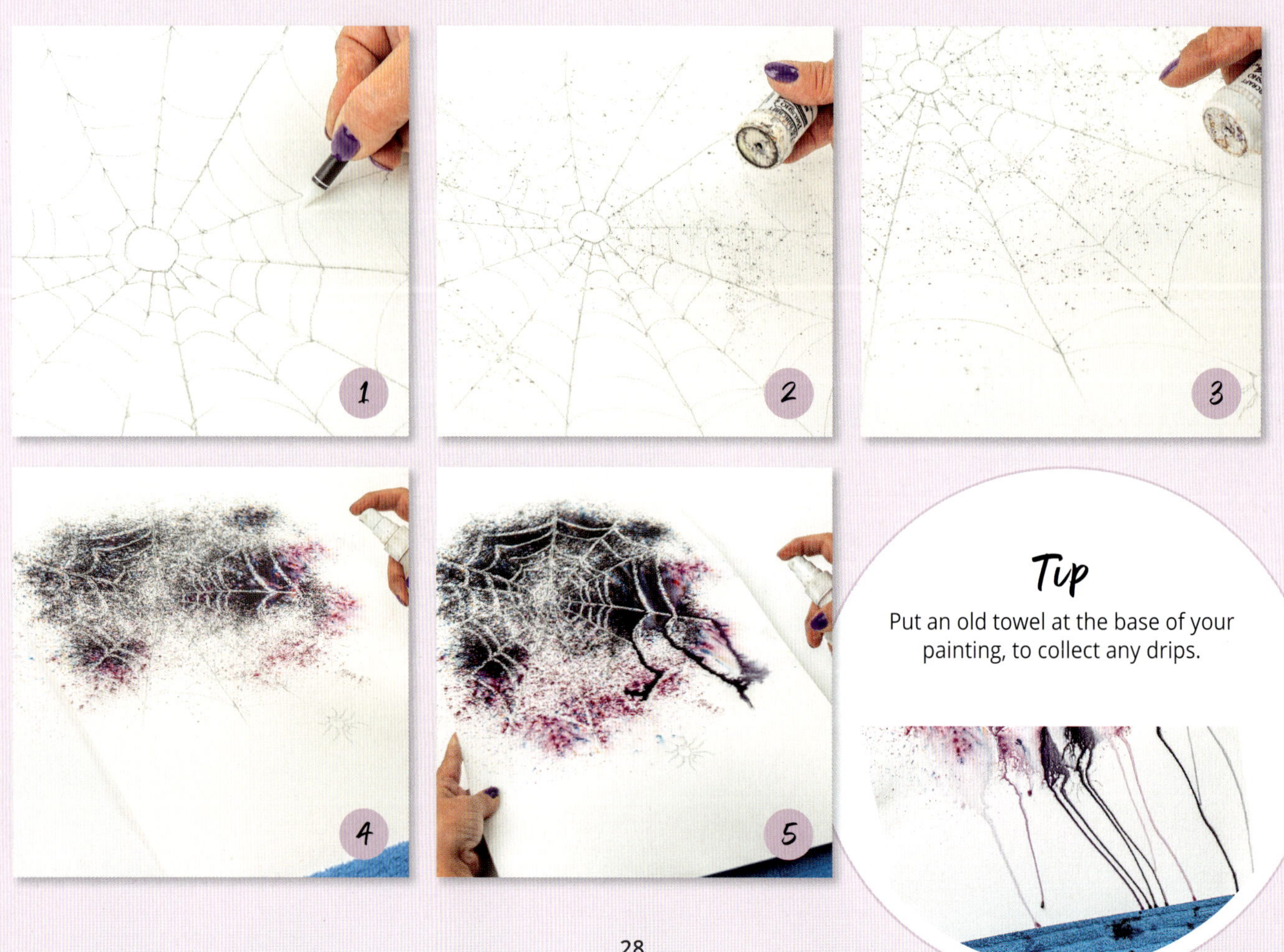

Tip

Put an old towel at the base of your painting, to collect any drips.

6 If needed, dab with a piece of kitchen paper to mop up any excess paint. This also helps to fix the paint to the paper.

7 Once your web is dry you can paint in a little black spider hanging from a thread of his web. You will notice that the spider has moved – that's what spiders do! The original pencil outline was hidden when the paint ran. I removed any remaining pencil outlines with an eraser, then redrew the spider in pencil. I added a dot of wax to his body to create a highlight, before filling it in with black Brusho.

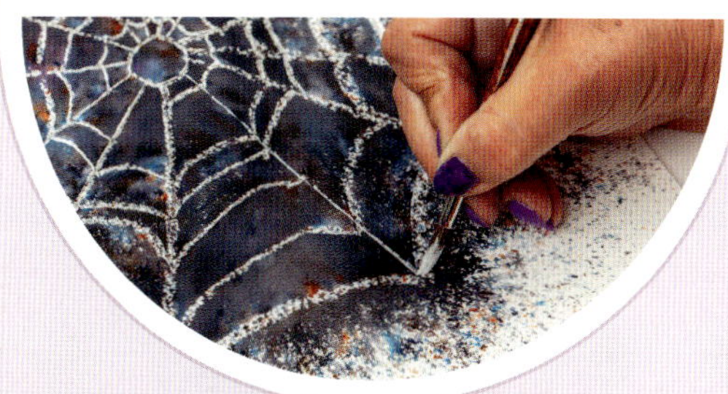

Tip

If you accidentally miss a strand of the web with the wax, you can add it in afterwards with white acrylic.

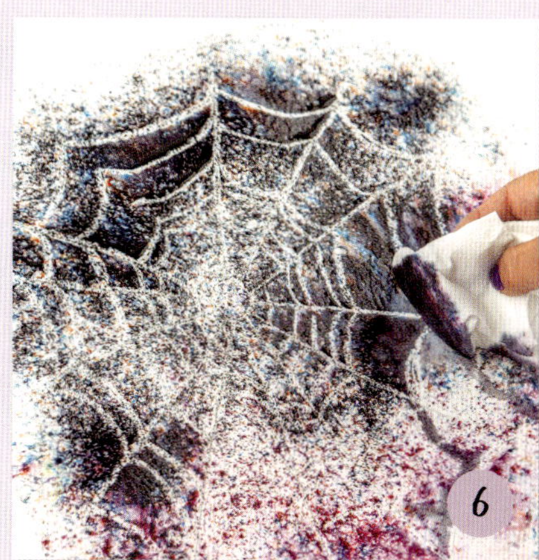

6

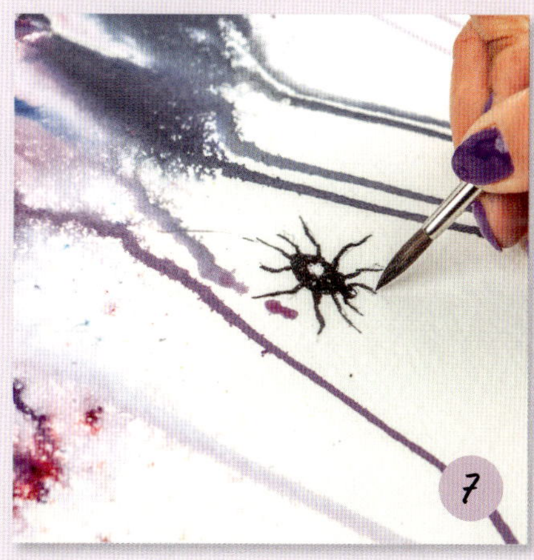

7

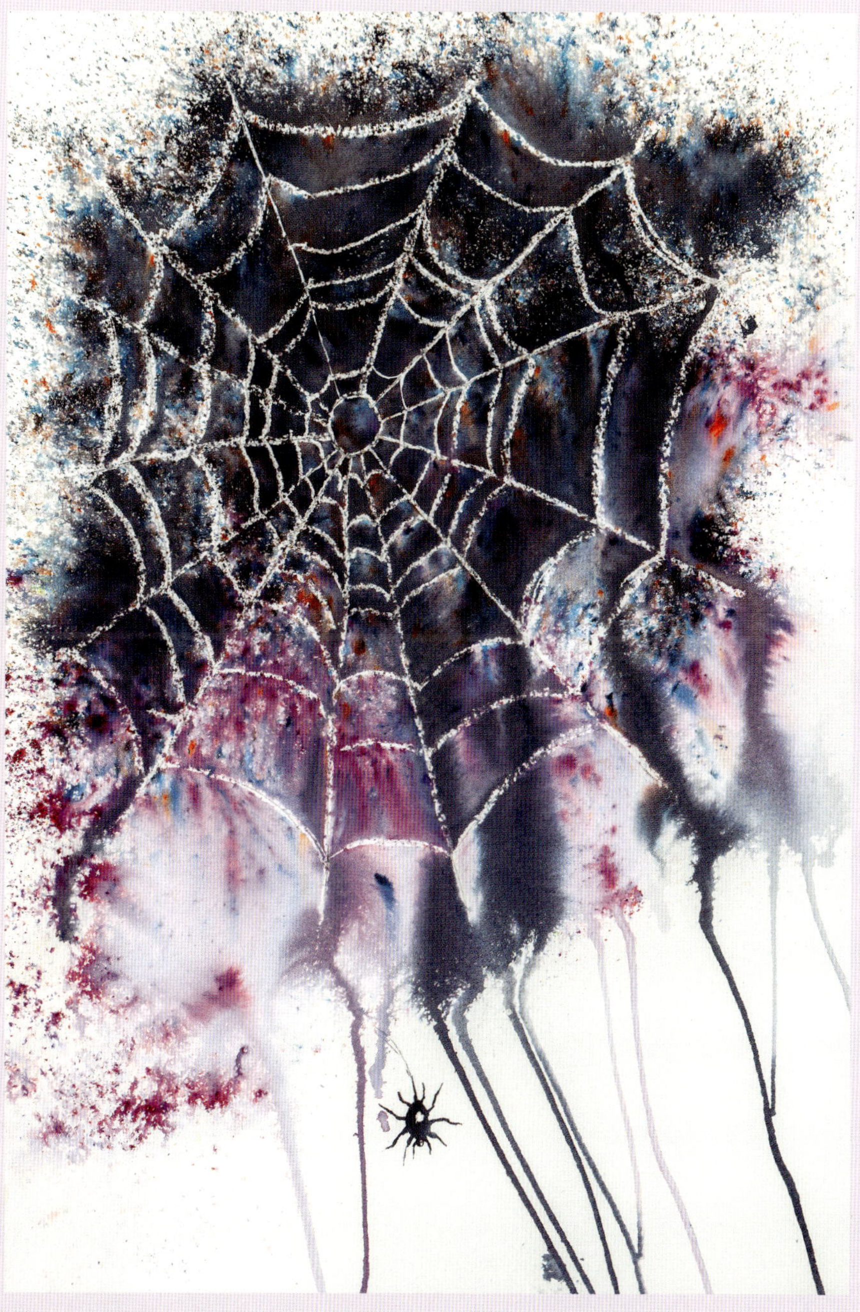

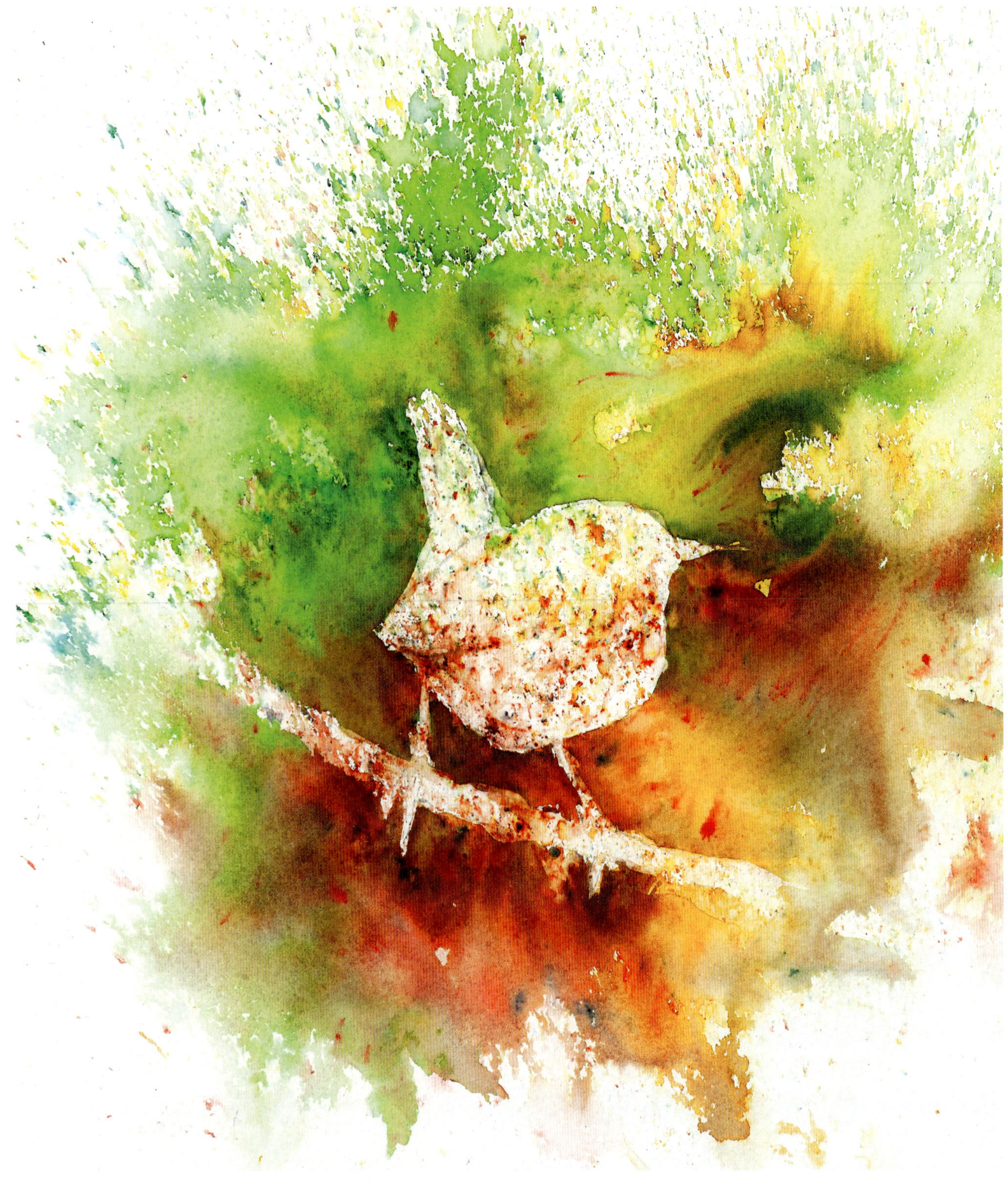

Little Wren

This simple little wren was created using the wax resist technique. Using a pencil I sketched in the shape of the bird and then applied candle wax to the dry paper all over the bird shape and the branch it is perching on. I then applied a wash of Brusho. I like how the Brusho crystals have sneaked into the wax area, creating a subtle texture rather than the pure white of the paper.

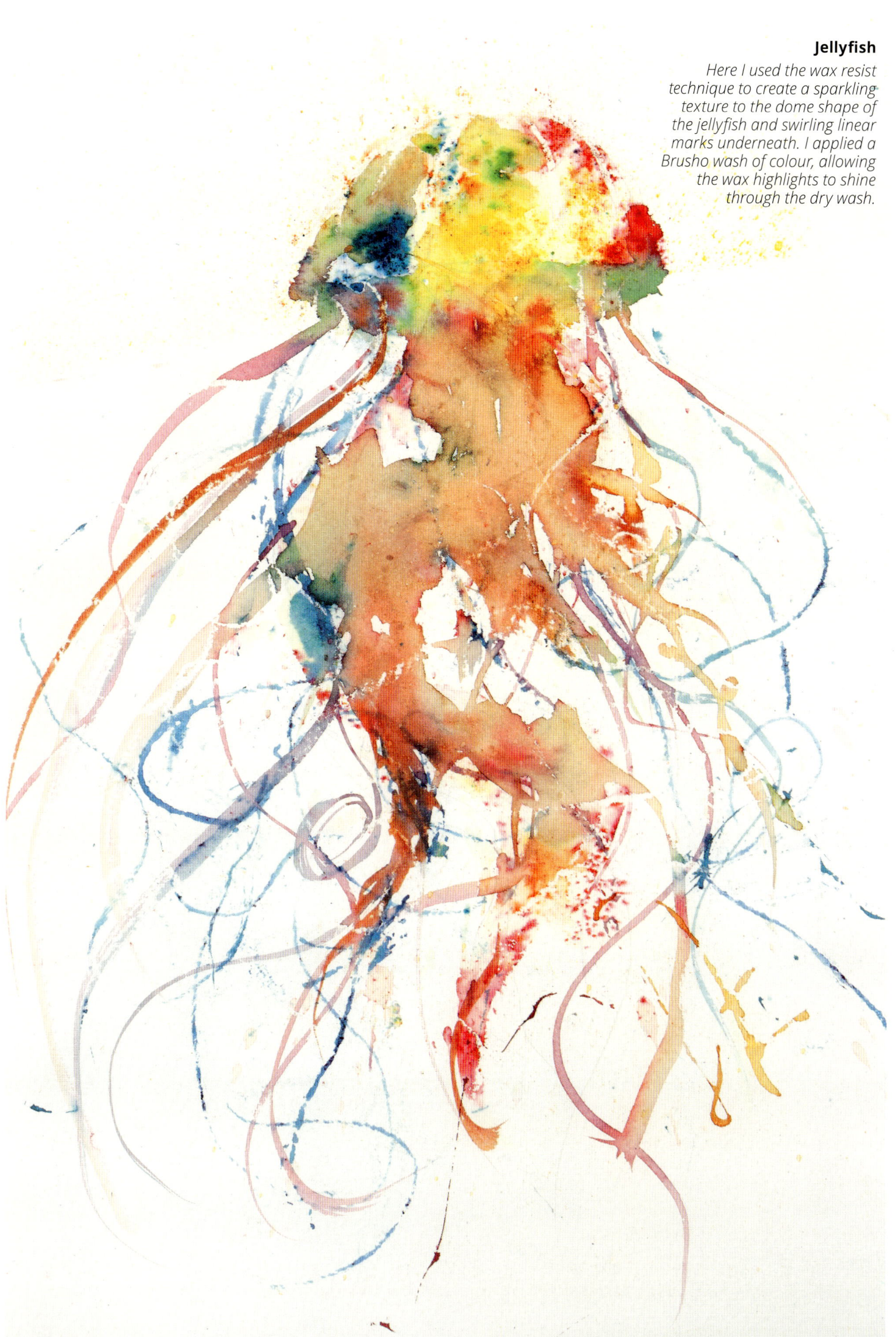

Jellyfish
Here I used the wax resist technique to create a sparkling texture to the dome shape of the jellyfish and swirling linear marks underneath. I applied a Brusho wash of colour, allowing the wax highlights to shine through the dry wash.

USING BLEACH

You can create wonderful results and a range of amazing effects when using bleach to lift off Brusho. Ordinary household bleach can be used to achieve stunning effects, and of course bleach is something we tend to have in our store cupboards. I like to dilute my bleach 50 per cent bleach to 50 per cent water and keep it in a spray bottle clearly marked 'Bleach'. I also have a set of old brushes that I use when working with bleach – you do not want to ruin your good brushes! Don't worry about the effect of bleach on the watercolour paper; it is strong enough to cope with it. However, each type of watercolour paper will react differently to a bleach solution, so experimenting with different papers and noting the results is a good idea.

  If you feel uncertain about using bleach, Milton solution is a good alternative. It is a used for sterilizing babies' bottles and is just as effective at lifting Brusho paint from your paper. Tip a small amount into the lid or a palette and apply with an old brush. Always work in a well ventilated room and wear protective gloves if you prefer.

Bleach chart

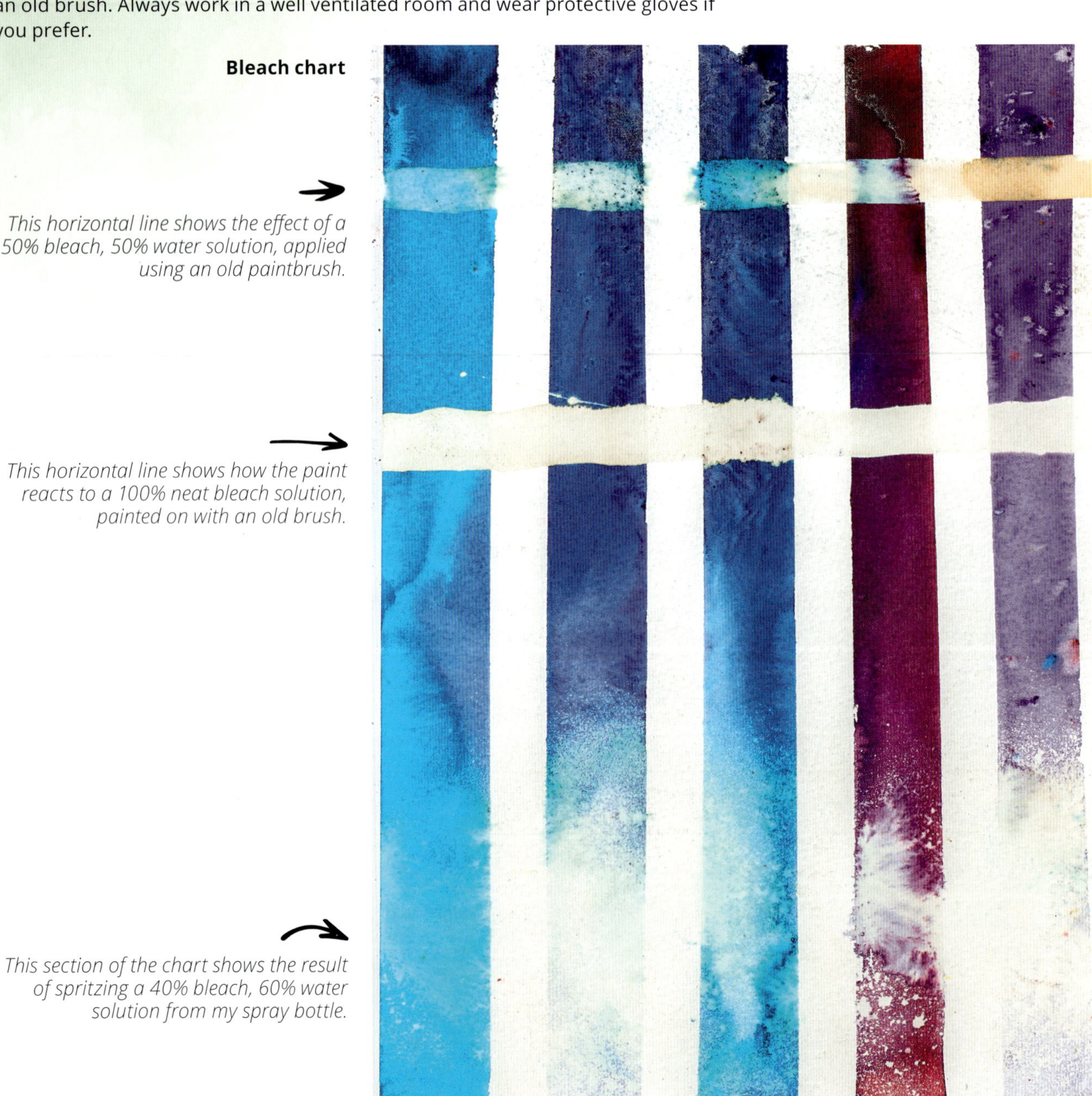

This horizontal line shows the effect of a 50% bleach, 50% water solution, applied using an old paintbrush.

This horizontal line shows how the paint reacts to a 100% neat bleach solution, painted on with an old brush.

This section of the chart shows the result of spritzing a 40% bleach, 60% water solution from my spray bottle.

I made the Brusho and bleach chart (shown below) to see how different Brusho colours react with varying strengths of bleach solution. It is interesting to see how the bleach reacts with the Brusho colours and how some colours lift better than others. I recommend creating a similar chart to give you an indication of the results you can achieve using different amounts of bleach.

I have used Bockingford watercolour paper, but it is worth experimenting with different papers as the results will differ.

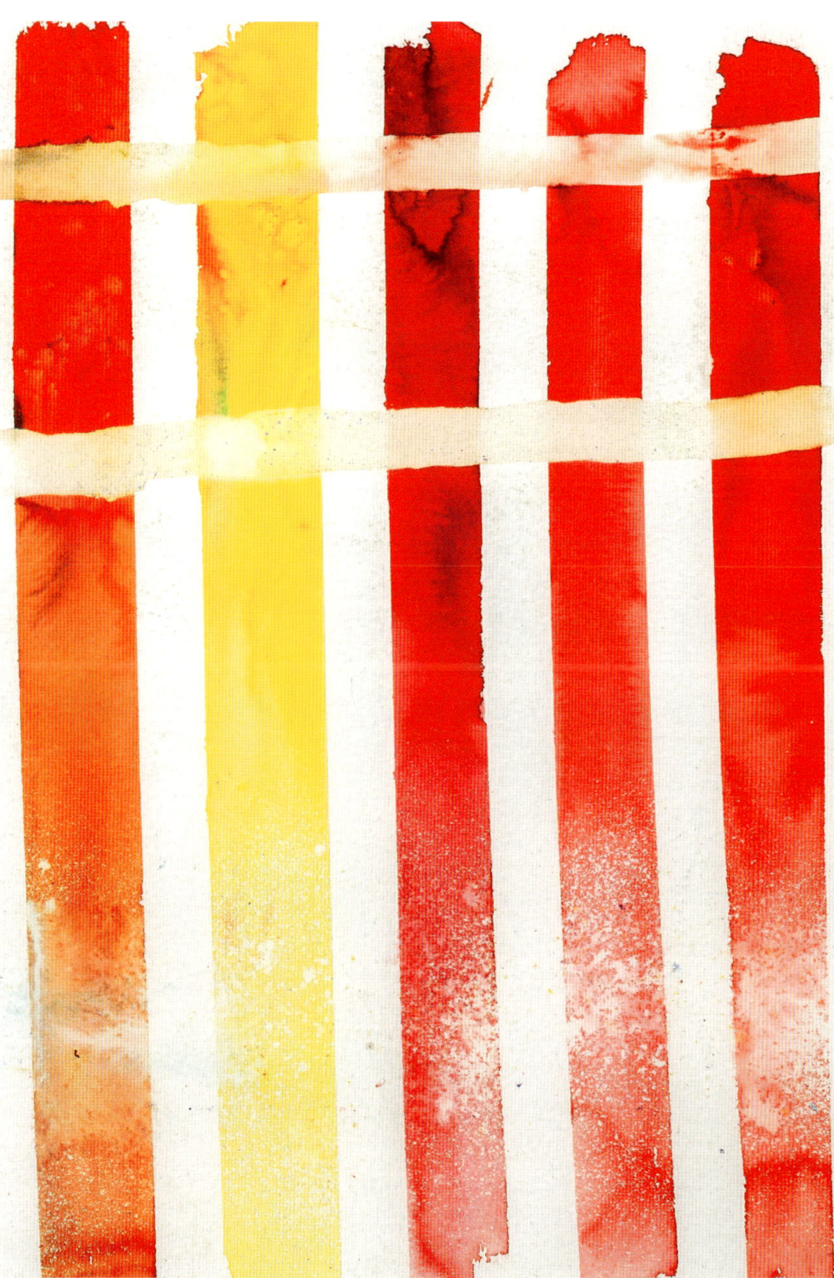

| Orange | Sunburst lemon | Crimson | Brilliant red | Scarlet |

Using bleach

This splendid daisy will give you an opportunity to put into practice some of the techniques we have previously covered such as using a sprinkle of Brusho colour to create texture in the centre of the daisy, large areas of colourful washes and a little bleach to lift away some of the colour to indicate the white petals.

It's hard to believe, but most of the white petals have been achieved by lifting off the Brusho colour with a solution of diluted bleach. You can choose whichever colours you prefer for your daisy.

YOU WILL NEED

- Bockingford watercolour paper, Not surface 300gsm (140lb) half imperial (38 x 56cm/15 x 22in)
- 3B pencil
- Eraser
- Brusho paint: sunburst lemon, orange, crimson, turquoise
- Size 8 or 10 brush
- Old brush for bleach
- Spray bottle with 50% bleach, 50% water solution
- Jug of clean water
- Ramekin with clean water for bleach
- Palette
- Kitchen paper

Steps

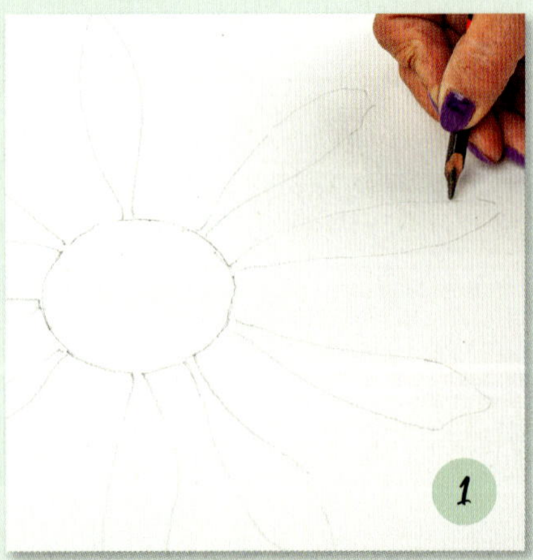 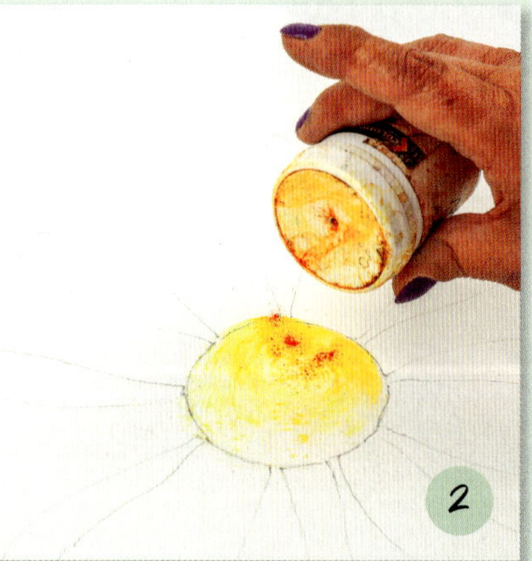 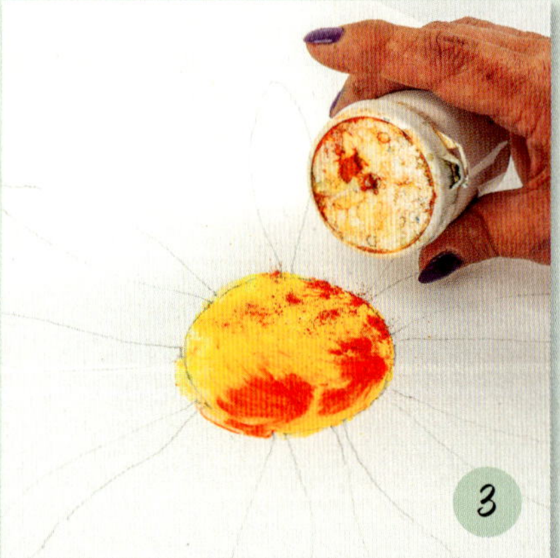

1 Using a soft pencil, sketch the daisy shape on your paper, keeping it simple with very loose detail. You don't need to outline every petal. We will add more later with the bleach.

2 Wet the centre of the daisy with clean water and a brush. Don't worry about keeping the water within the lines – we will allow the paint to run. Sprinkle sunburst lemon.

3 Sprinkle orange Brusho over the top of the sunburst lemon.

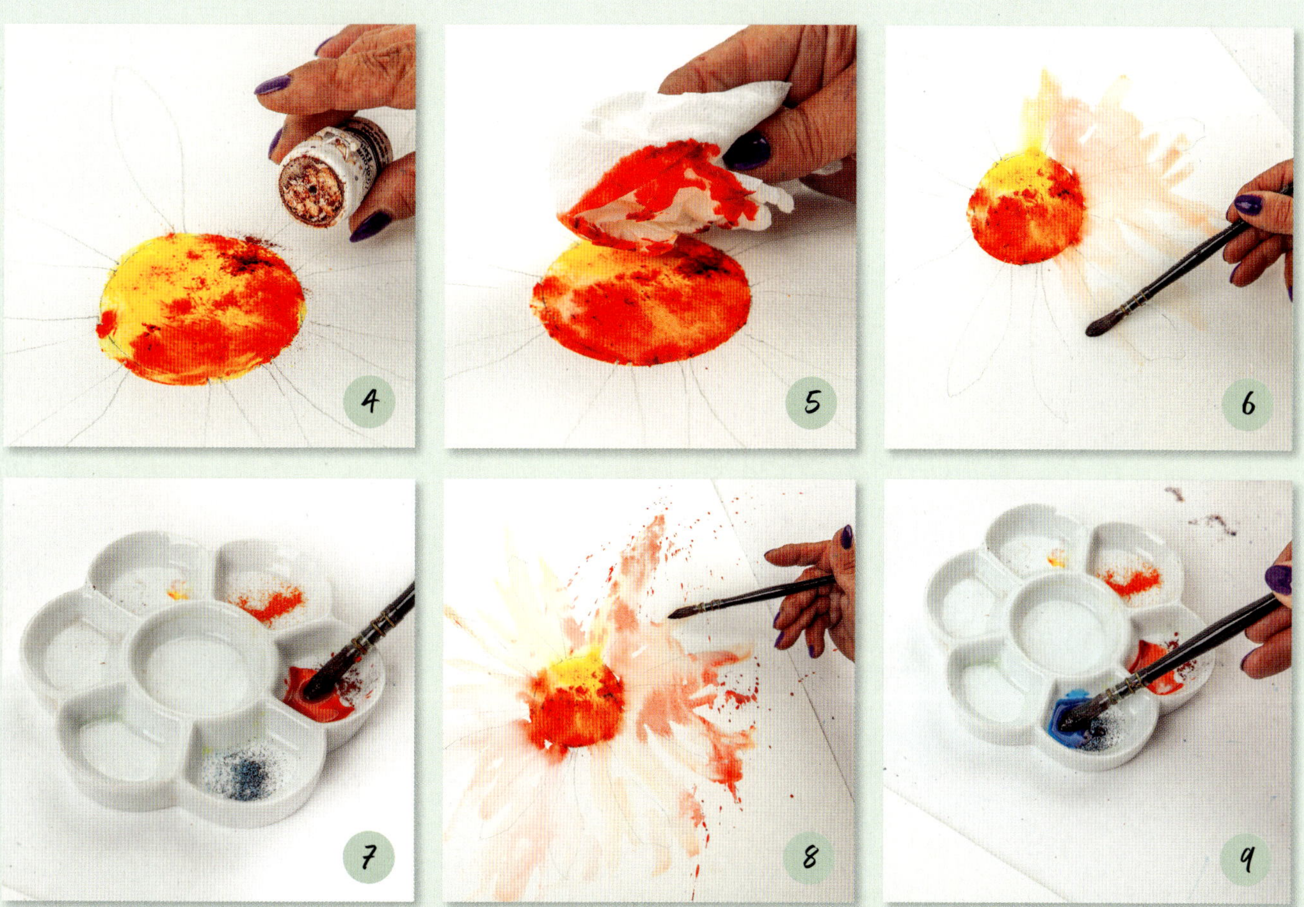

4 Sprinkle a small amount of crimson.

5 You can dab this area with kitchen paper if needed to remove excess wet paint.

6 Use clean water and a brush to reactivate the orange paint. Draw the paint from the edge of the flower's centre and work your way round the flower pulling the paint out so that the pale orange radiates from the middle into each of the petals.

7 Mix a wash of crimson in the palette.

8 Add the crimson mix to your painting by lightly tapping the end of the brush to give a spattering effect.

9 Mix a wash of turquoise and sunburst lemon to make a green in the palette. Alternatively, you could use any green Brusho.

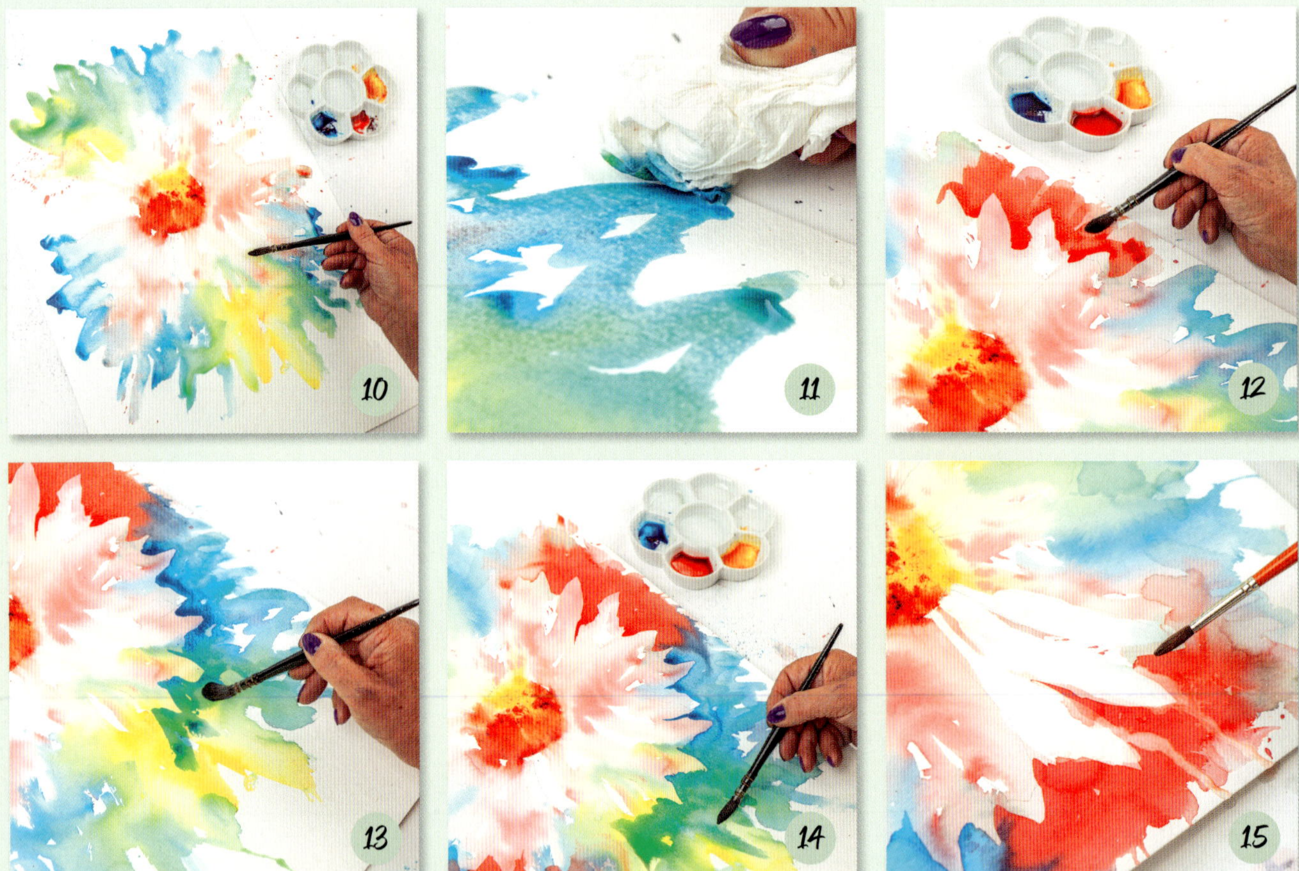

10 Use these two washes to paint around the petal shapes. Don't worry about being too accurate at this stage as we will use bleach to lift away unwanted paint later on.

11 Scrunch up kitchen paper and dab the excess wet areas around the edges.

12 You can now add a crimson wash and allow it to mix with the turquoise and yellow colours while negatively painting around the petal shapes to make them stand out.

13 Repeat with the turquoise wash. Soften the edges, using the belly of the brush to pull out the petal shapes. You can rotate your paper if you find it easier.

14 Again, the turquoise and sunburst lemon combine to make a zingy green. Allow to dry.

15 Spray bleach into the corner of the page at the bottom. Use the point of an old brush to lift out the petal shapes, working from the centre of the flower outwards.

Tip

Negative painting is defining a shape by painting around it with a darker colour.

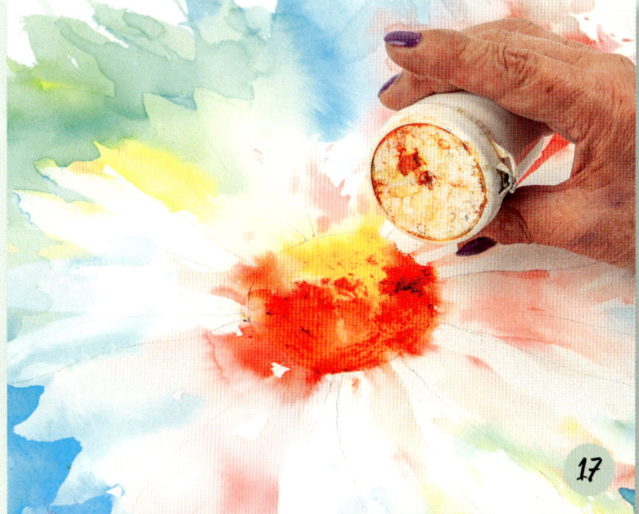

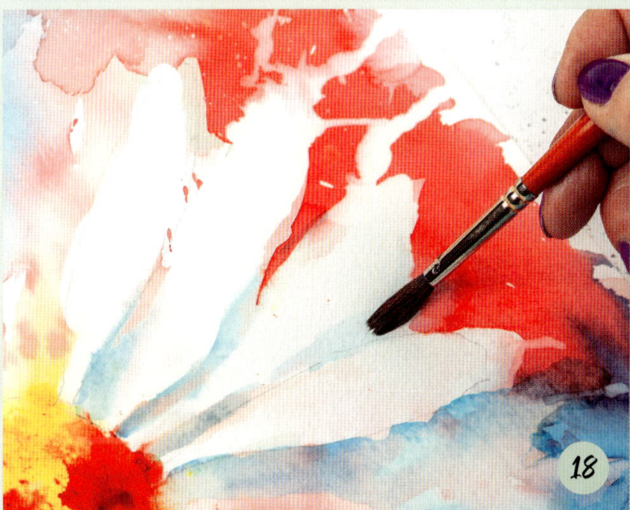

Tip

It's exciting to use a hairdryer to blow the wet bleach into the dry wash for a subtle effect.

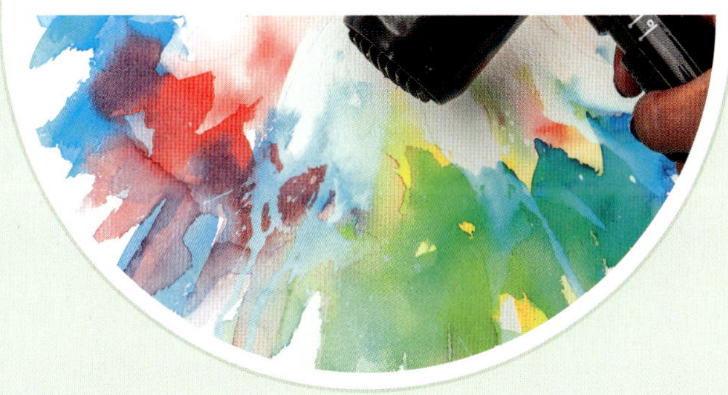

16 Use the belly of the old brush to gently pull out the bleach solution. You can tap the bleach water off the brush to give a spatter effect.

17 Using a clean brush, wet the orange in the centre of the flower and sprinkle a bit more orange powder into the wet area.

18 Using the turquoise and a brush, apply a light shadow wash on some of the petals, especially the ones that are sitting underneath the others so that the top petals appear to stand out. Let this dry.

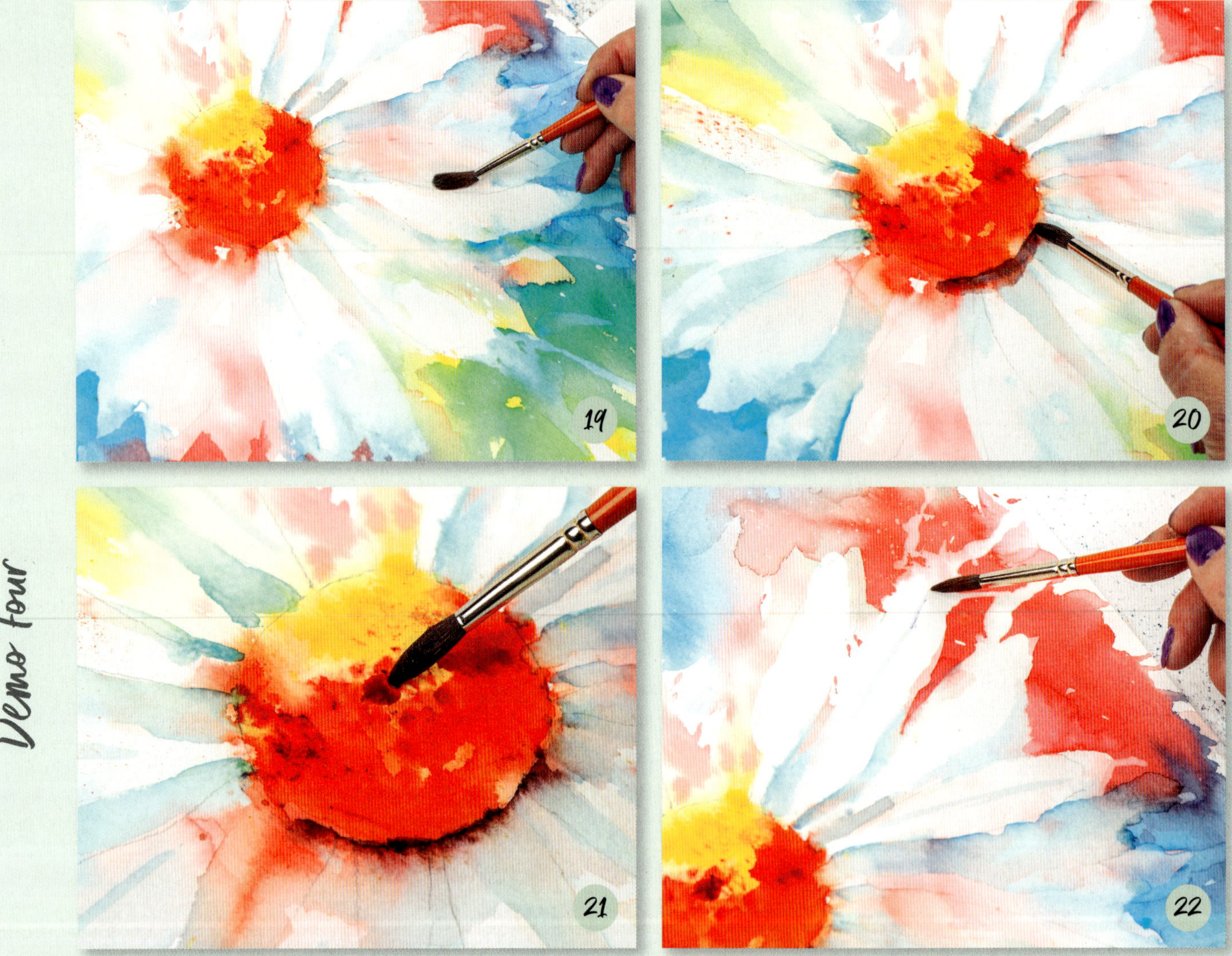

19 Work your way round the flower using the same technique to emphasize the petals and make them look separate.

20 Make a wash of crimson and turquoise combined and use it to add a linear shadow under the centre of the flower. Use the brush to soften the line so it blends into the white petals.

21 Using the crimson, add a dot to the centre of the flower.

22 Using watered down turquoise and a brush, add subtle veins to the petals.

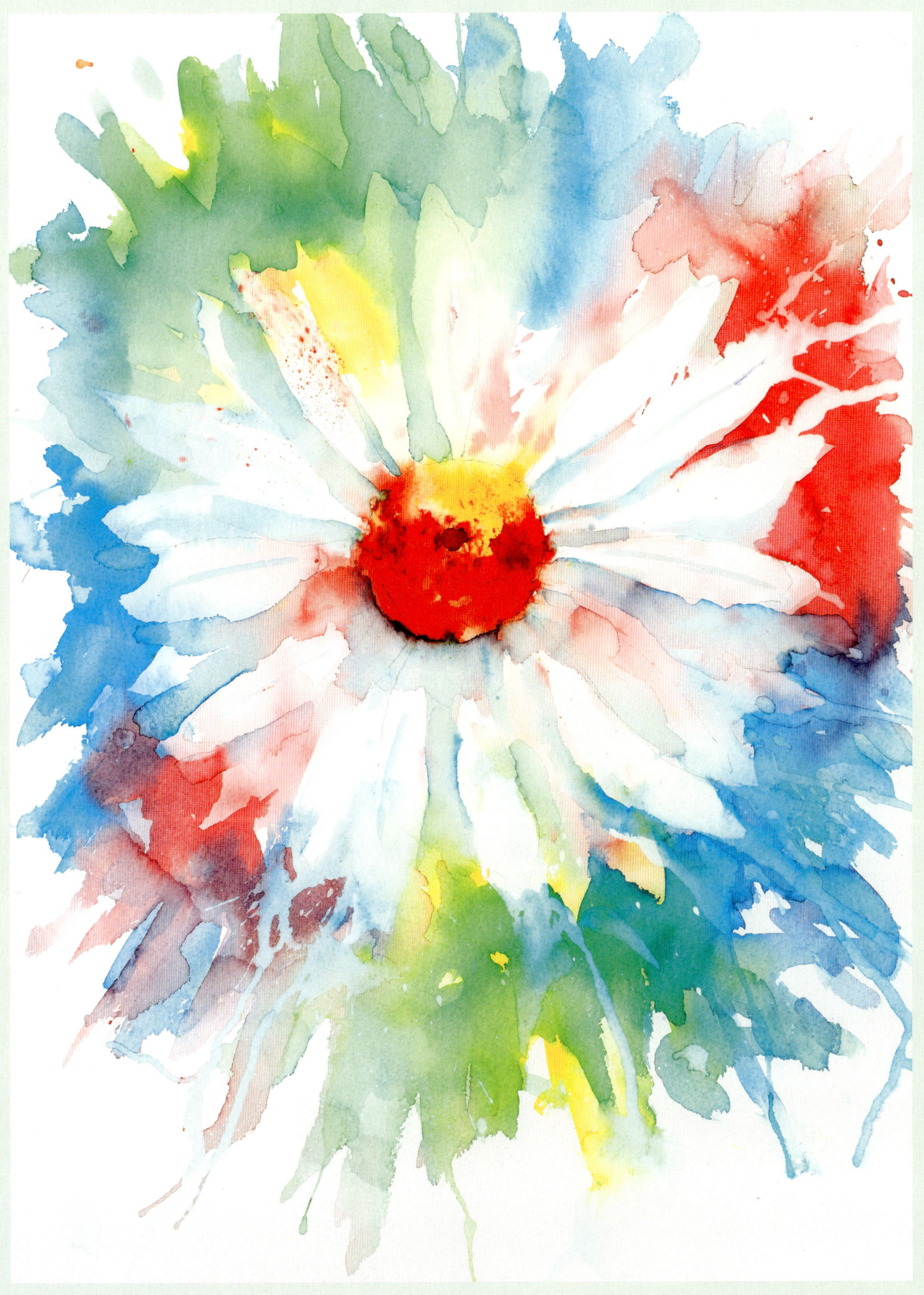
Demo four

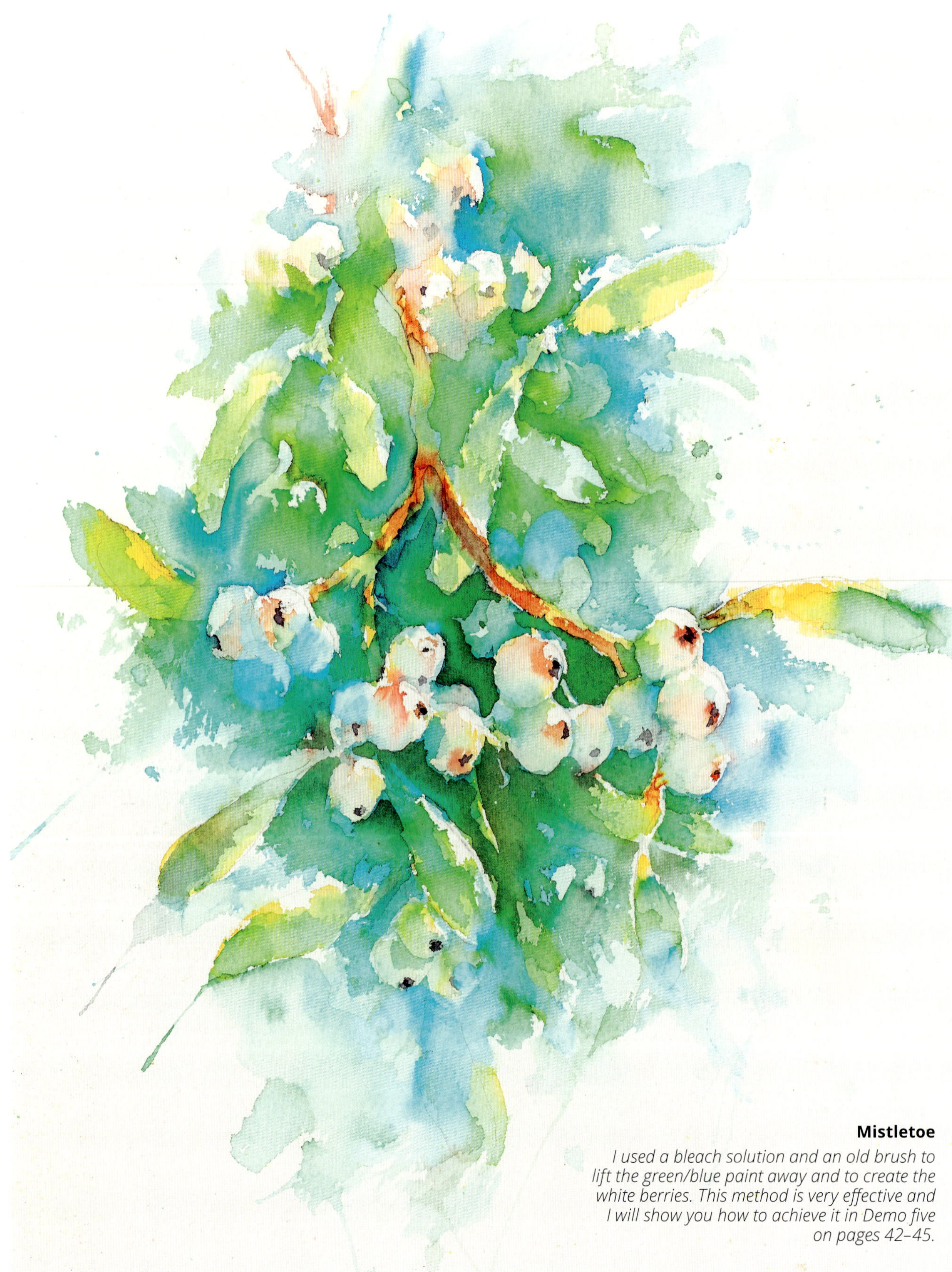

Mistletoe

I used a bleach solution and an old brush to lift the green/blue paint away and to create the white berries. This method is very effective and I will show you how to achieve it in Demo five on pages 42–45.

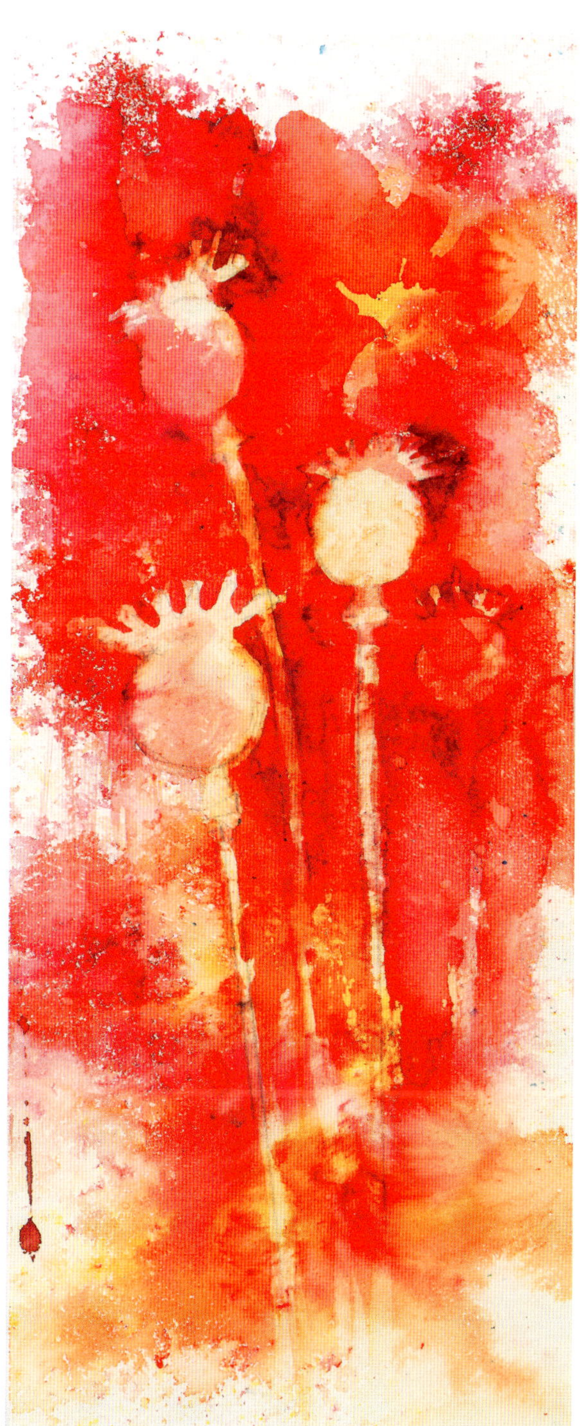

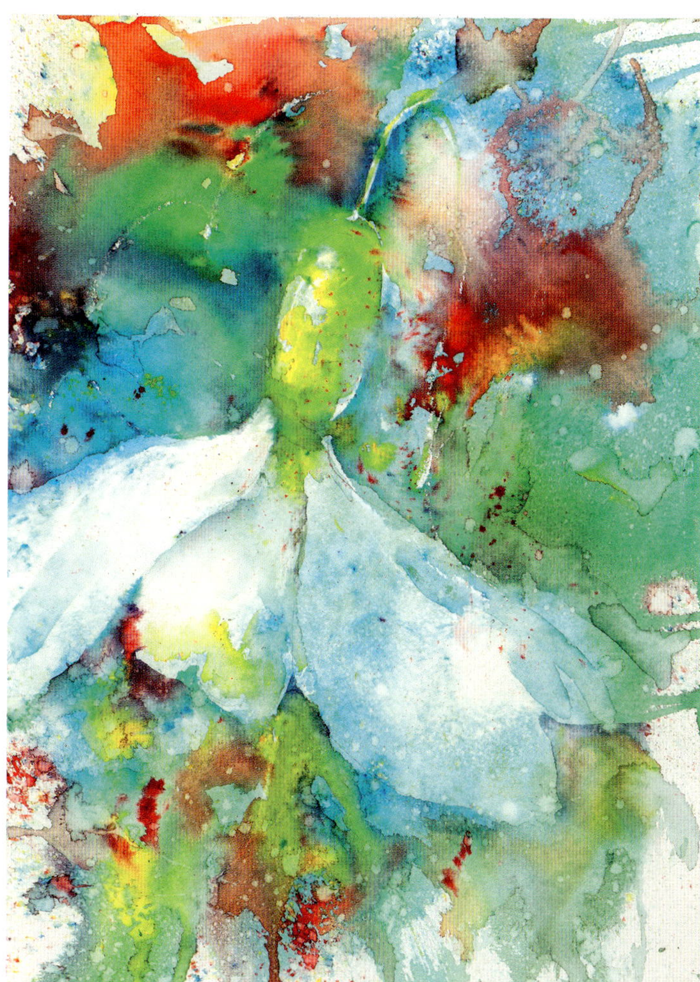

Snowdrop

To give more sparkle and light to the snowdrop I lifted out areas of the petals with a bleach and water solution.

Poppy Seed Heads

I covered the whole of the paper with a colourful Brusho wash then used a bleach solution to lift away the poppy seed head shapes.

Demo five

Line and Brusho wash

I am a big fan of the line and wash method when painting with Brusho. I start by drawing out my subject matter lightly in pencil first. I then use a black waterproof ink pen to draw over my pencil lines. Once the line drawing is dry I can then apply either a wash of Brusho or use my sprinkle and spray method to create bursts of colour within the ink line drawing, resulting in a lovely balance of line and Brusho colour working beautifully together.

What is fabulous about line and wash is that you don't need to keep your Brusho within the lines. The black outline serves to hold the painting together visually, giving it a framework. You can see this lovely technique used in the *White Duck* project on pages 52–59.

YOU WILL NEED

- Bockingford watercolour paper, Not surface 300gsm (140lb) quarter imperial (28 x 38cm/11 x 15in)
- 3B pencil
- Black waterproof pen
- Eraser
- Brusho paint: sea green, sunburst lemon
- Size 8 brush
- Old brush for bleach
- Spray bottle with 50% bleach, 50% water solution
- Jug of clean water
- Ramekin with clean water for bleach
- Scrap paper
- Kitchen paper

Steps

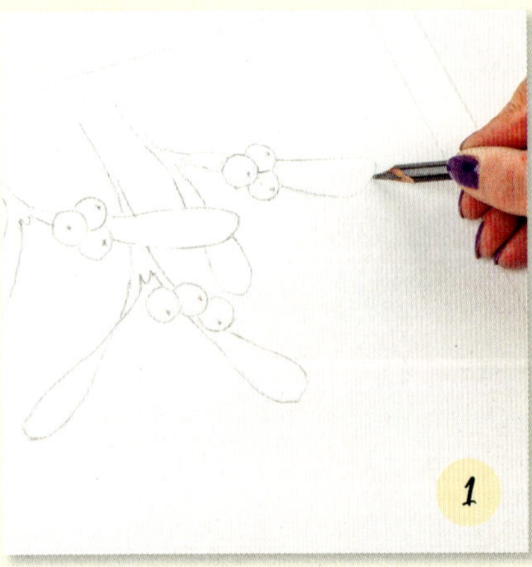
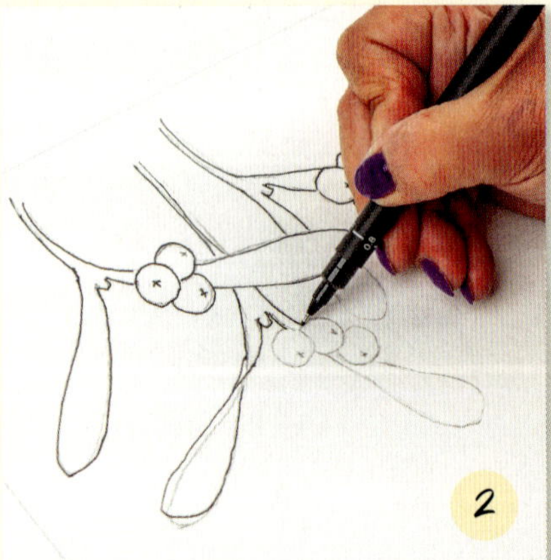
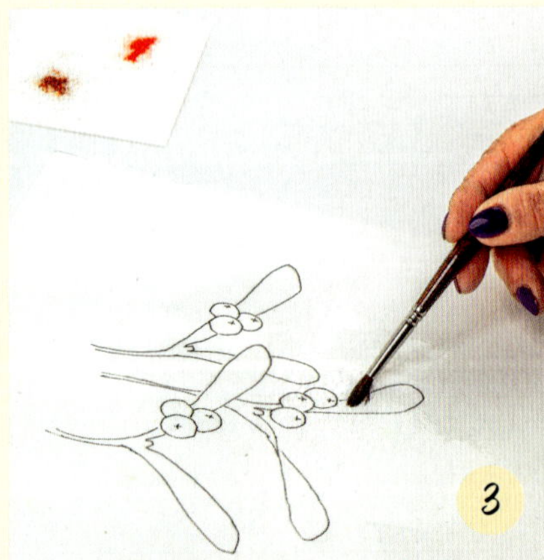

1 Sketch out the shape of the mistletoe onto your paper using a soft pencil.

2 Using a black waterproof pen, go over your pencil drawing.

3 Sprinkle sea green and sunburst lemon Brusho on a scrap of paper, using it as a palette. Wet the whole paper, but leave a couple of berries dry.

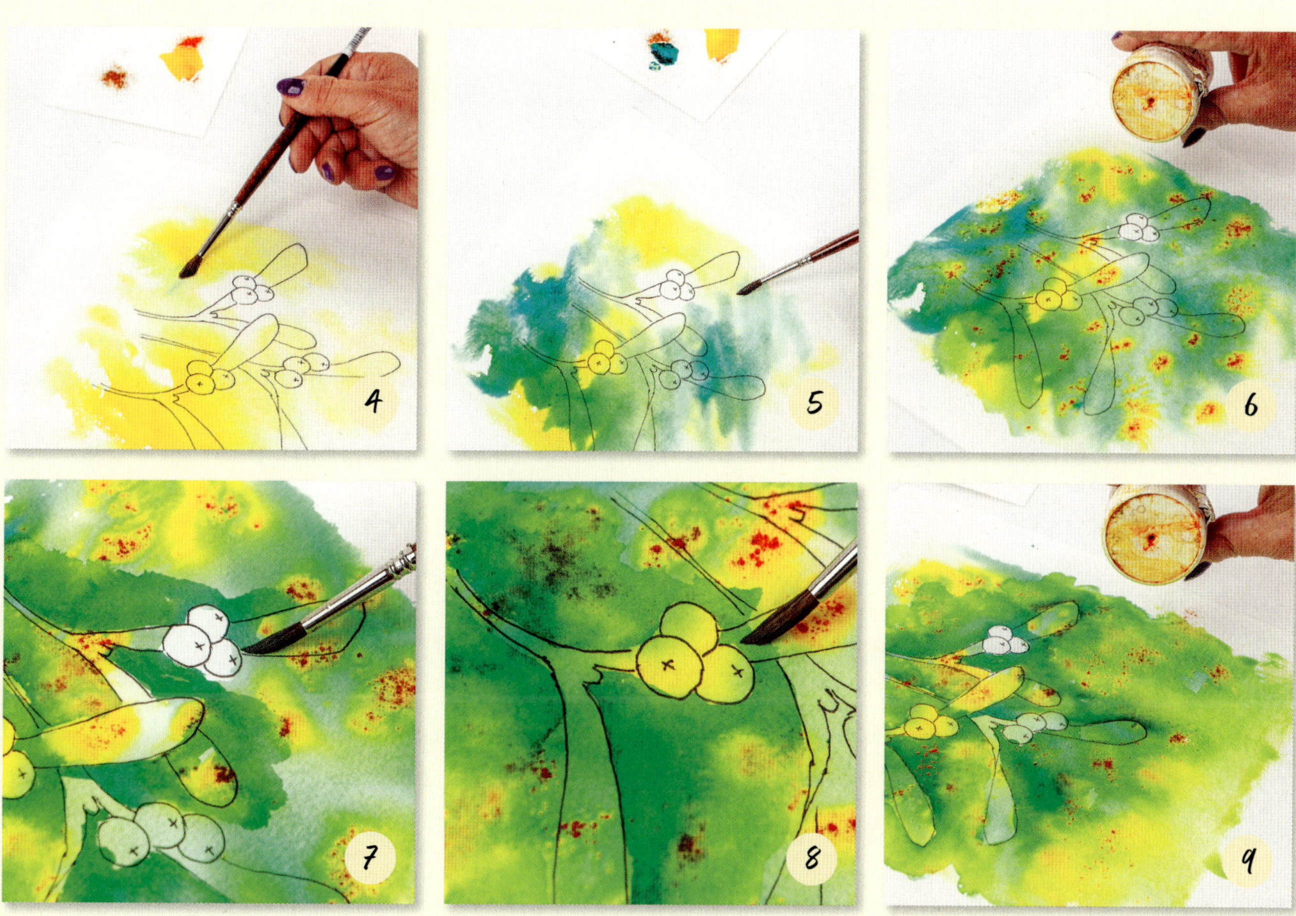

4 Pick up the sunburst lemon powder on your wet brush and paint all over the page, leaving the dry berries as white paper.

5 Do the same with the sea green, allowing the colours to mix together.

6 Sprinkle sunburst lemon into the washes on the painting to give texture. Allow to dry.

7 Using the sea green wash, paint around the shapes to include negative painting. The wash will also reactivate the yellow. This knocks back the background and makes the berries and leaves pop.

8 Where a leaf overlaps another one, paint across the top leaf to create a shadow underneath. Allow to dry.

9 Sprinkle more sunburst lemon around the edges of the paper to create more texture.

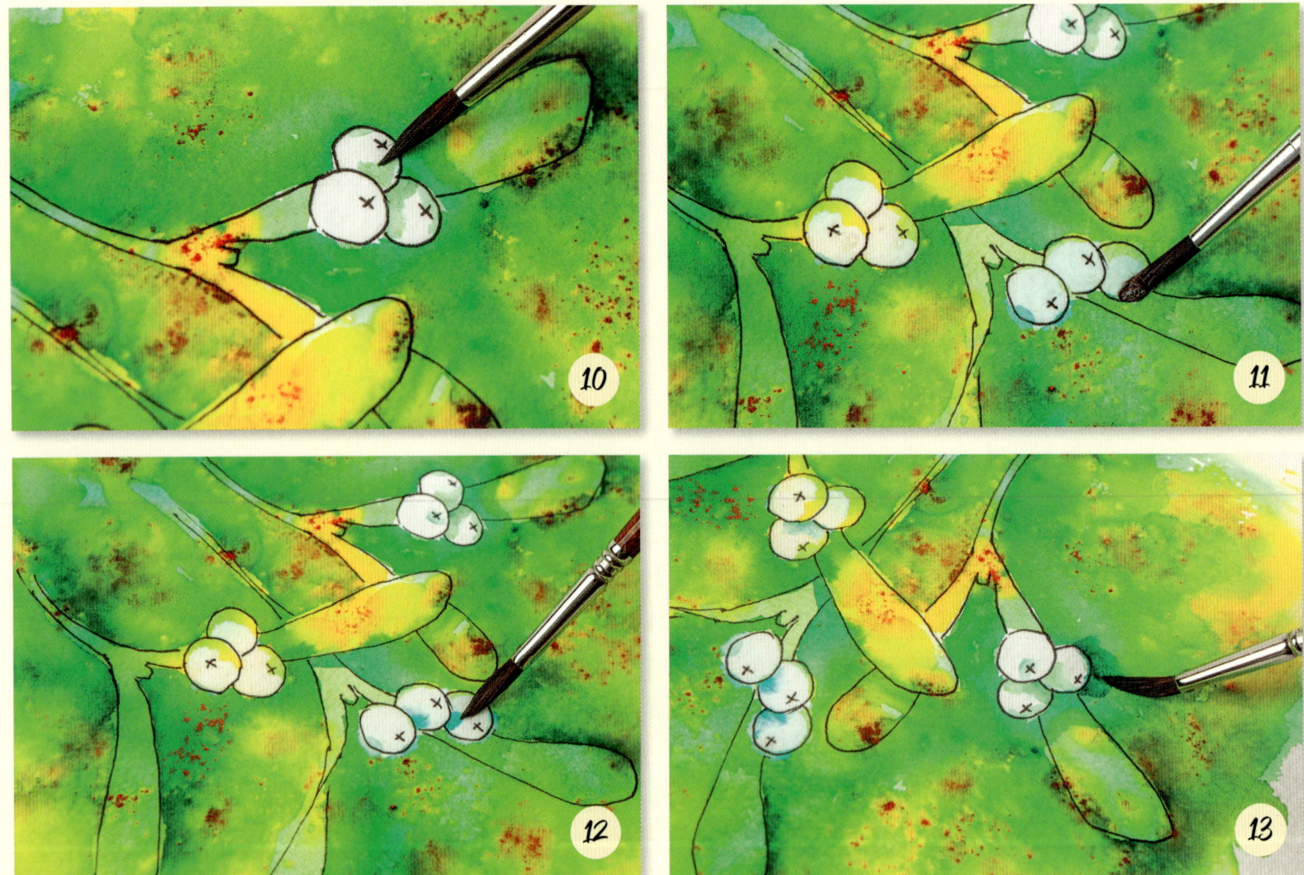

Demo five

10 Use the sea green wash to introduce a hint of a shadow underneath the exposed berries.

11 Spray bleach into a palette. Using an old brush, apply bleach to the berries on the left, then the berries at the bottom. Allow to dry.

12 Take the sea green wash and add a subtle shadow between the group of berries on the left and at the bottom.

13 Add darks under the berries, then soften with your brush. This helps the berries to jump out.

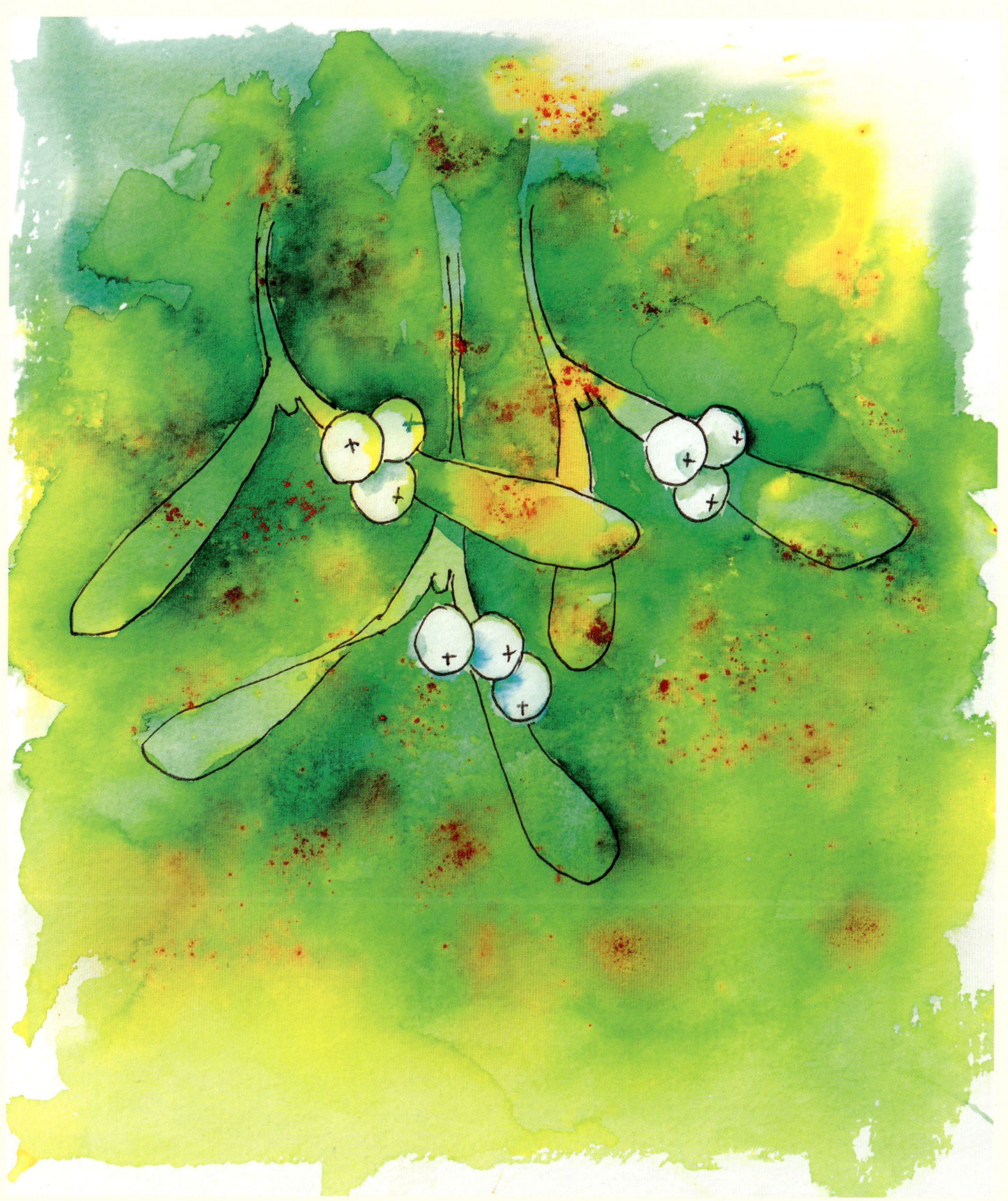

Mistletoe

*As you can see, using the line and wash technique creates a
very different mistletoe painting to the one on page 40. The
addition of pen makes it much bolder and more striking. This
demo would make a lovely Christmas card.*

USING BLACK BRUSHO

I would never dream of using black watercolour paint as I prefer to mix my own dark colours. However, the black Brusho is probably one of my favourite Brusho colours because it is not just black! It is a magical colour that is made up of lots of different coloured pigments that can cheekily sneak onto your painting when you are not looking! When it is sprayed with water you will see reds, blues and even yellows shine through. It really shows how beautiful black Brusho is. You can see this technique used in the *Cottage in the Snow* project on pages 108–115.

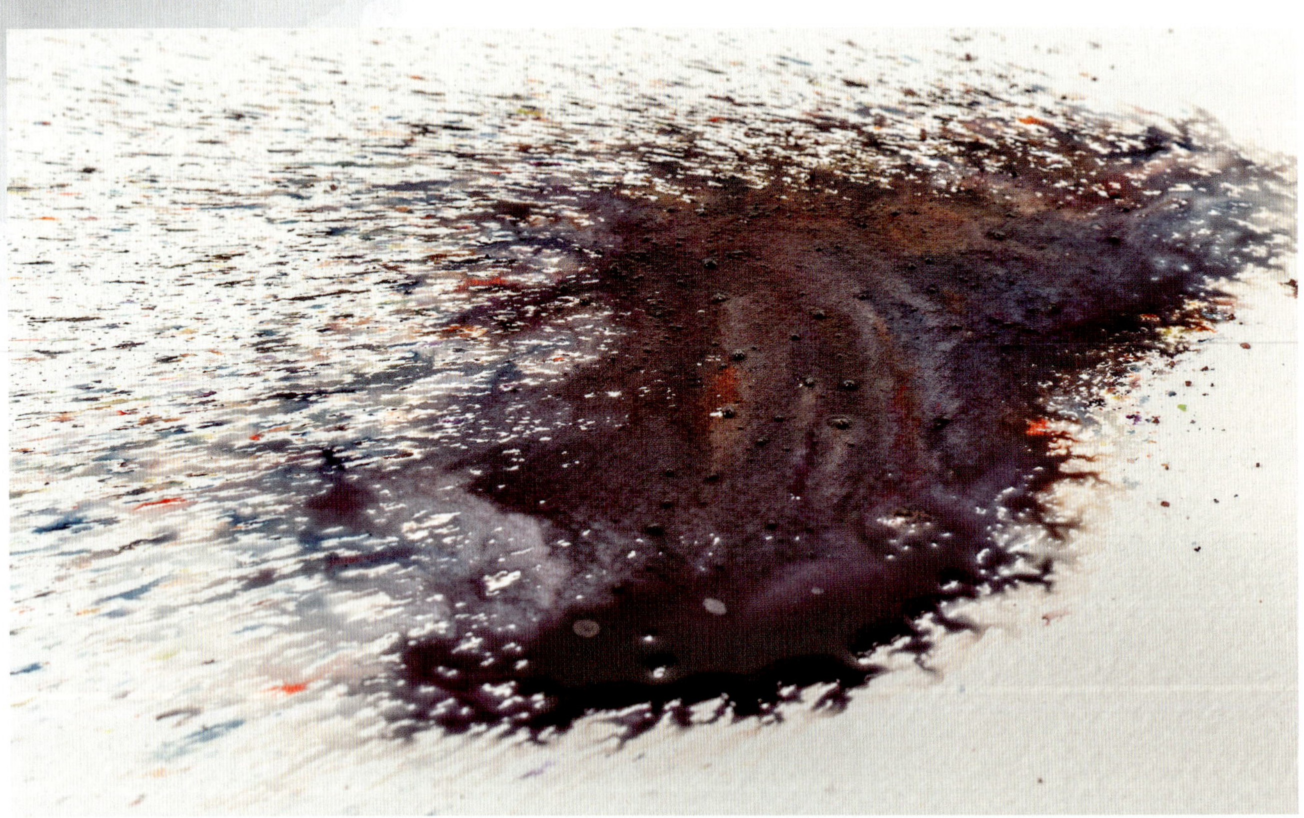

Using black Brusho

This cheeky little blackbird is a perfect choice to showcase the beautiful black Brusho with the help of a little yellow. The colourful sprinkles help to suggest that he has just had a wash in a puddle and is having a good shake and of course keeping his eye on the little bumblebee.

YOU WILL NEED

- Bockingford watercolour paper Rough surface 300gsm (140lb) quarter imperial (38 x 28cm/ 15 x 11in)
- 4B pencil
- Eraser
- Black waterproof pen
- Brusho paint: black, sunburst lemon
- Size 8 brush
- Spray bottle with water
- Wax crayon or candle wax
- Palette or scrap of paper
- Kitchen paper

Steps

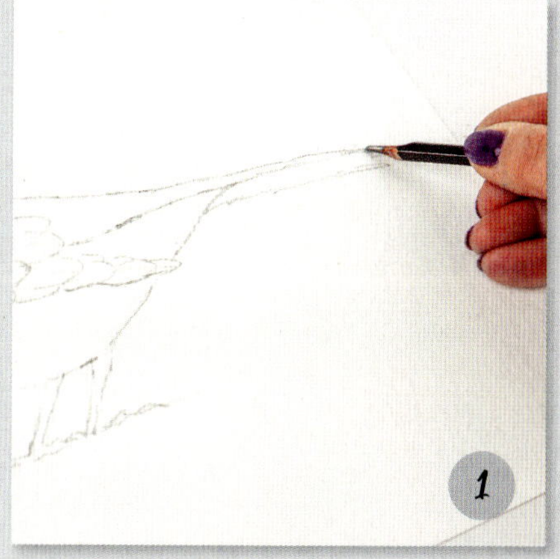

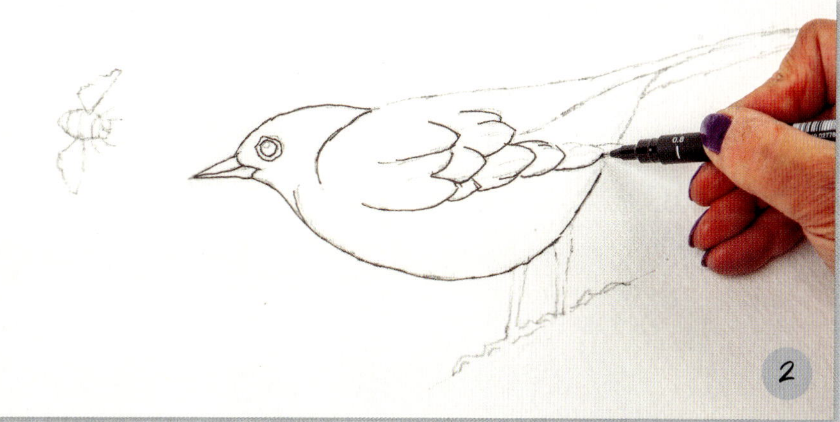

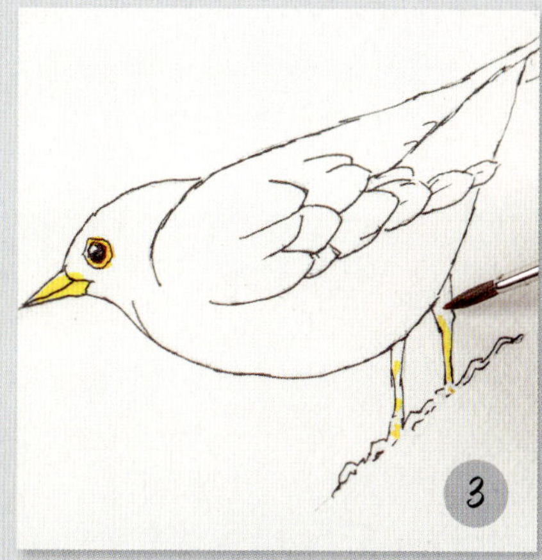

1 Sketch out the shapes of the blackbird and bee onto your paper using pencil.

2 Using a black waterproof pen, go over your pencil drawing. Once the pen is dry, use an eraser to remove the pencil lines.

3 Mix a small amount of sunburst lemon in a palette or scrap of paper and paint the yellow of the bird's eye, the beak, a touch around the legs and a section of the little bee. Wait for this to dry before moving on to the next stage.

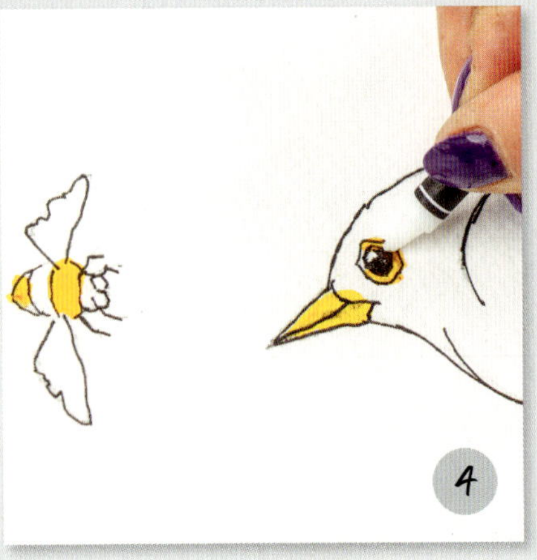

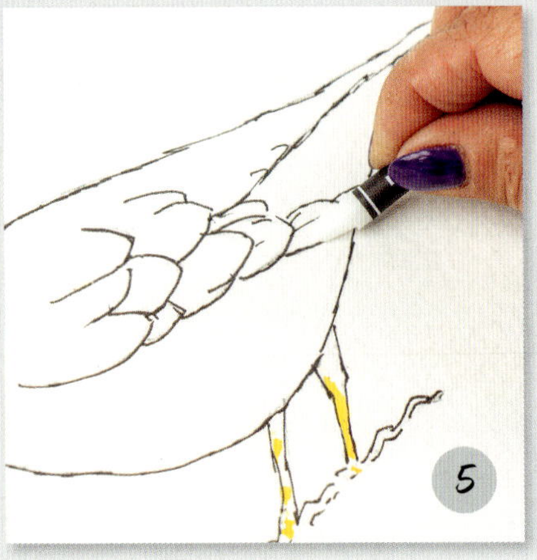

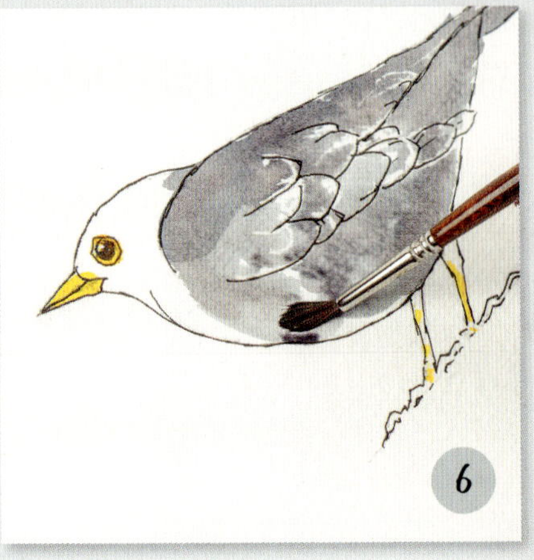

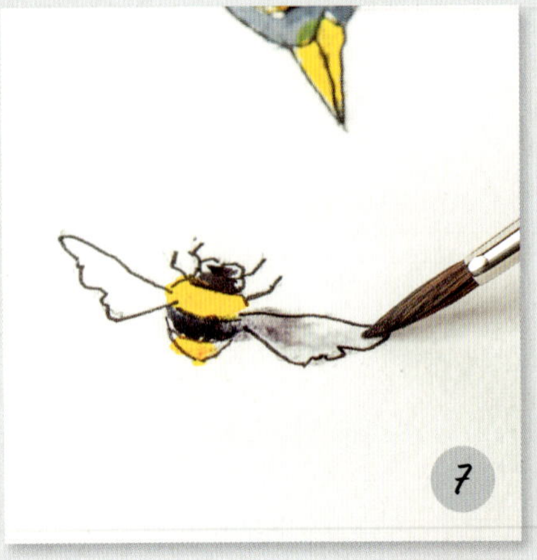

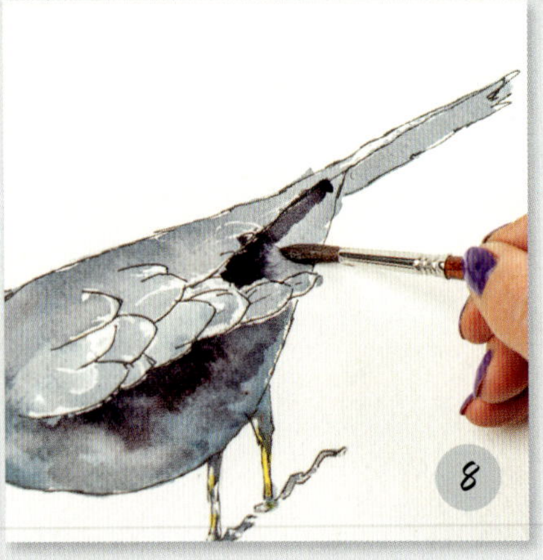

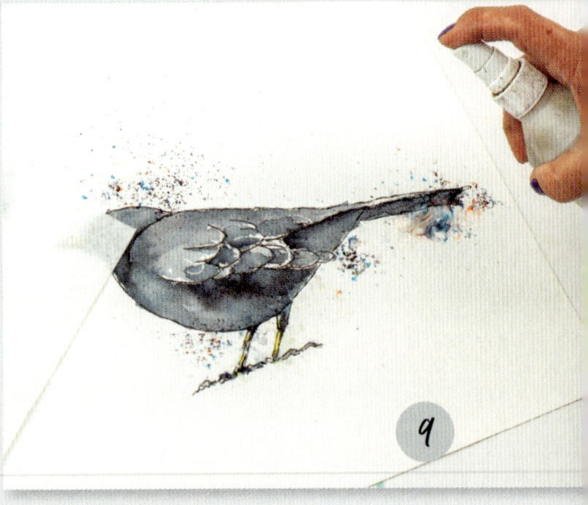

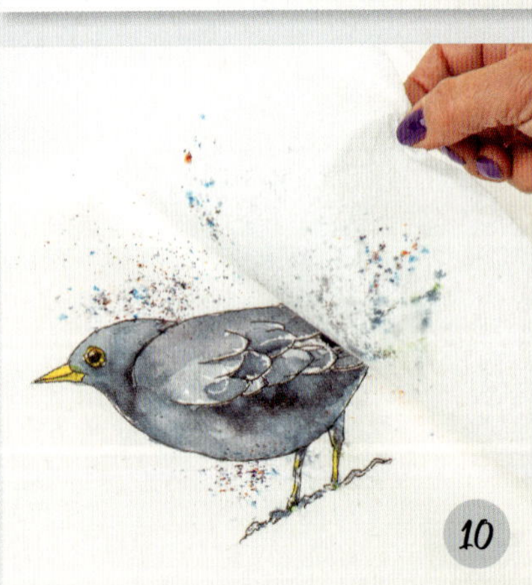

4 Apply wax resist over the yellow areas by placing the wax over the top of the dry yellow wash.

5 Apply the wax to the feather areas and in the tail.

6 Mix a wash of black Brusho in your palette and apply as a flat wash to the bird shape covering the body and head. Blend with your brush for a smooth wash and allow to dry. Don't worry if you go outside the lines.

7 Add black to the bee's body. Clean your brush. Paint over the wings with your wet brush, allowing the black to run into the bee's wings.

8 Using a darker wash of the black, paint in the dark under the wing, tail, head and legs. This will help to highlight the wax that was applied earlier. Soften the wash by adding water and dragging the brush down. Allow to dry.

9 If you're happy with the overall result, you can put your brush down. However, I'm feeling brave and want to take it a step further! I place a piece of kitchen paper over the blackbird's head to preserve the yellow and then gently sprinkle a little black pigment onto the paper and around the blackbird. I spritz the powder using water in a spray bottle.

10 Lay kitchen paper over the bird to absorb any excess water.

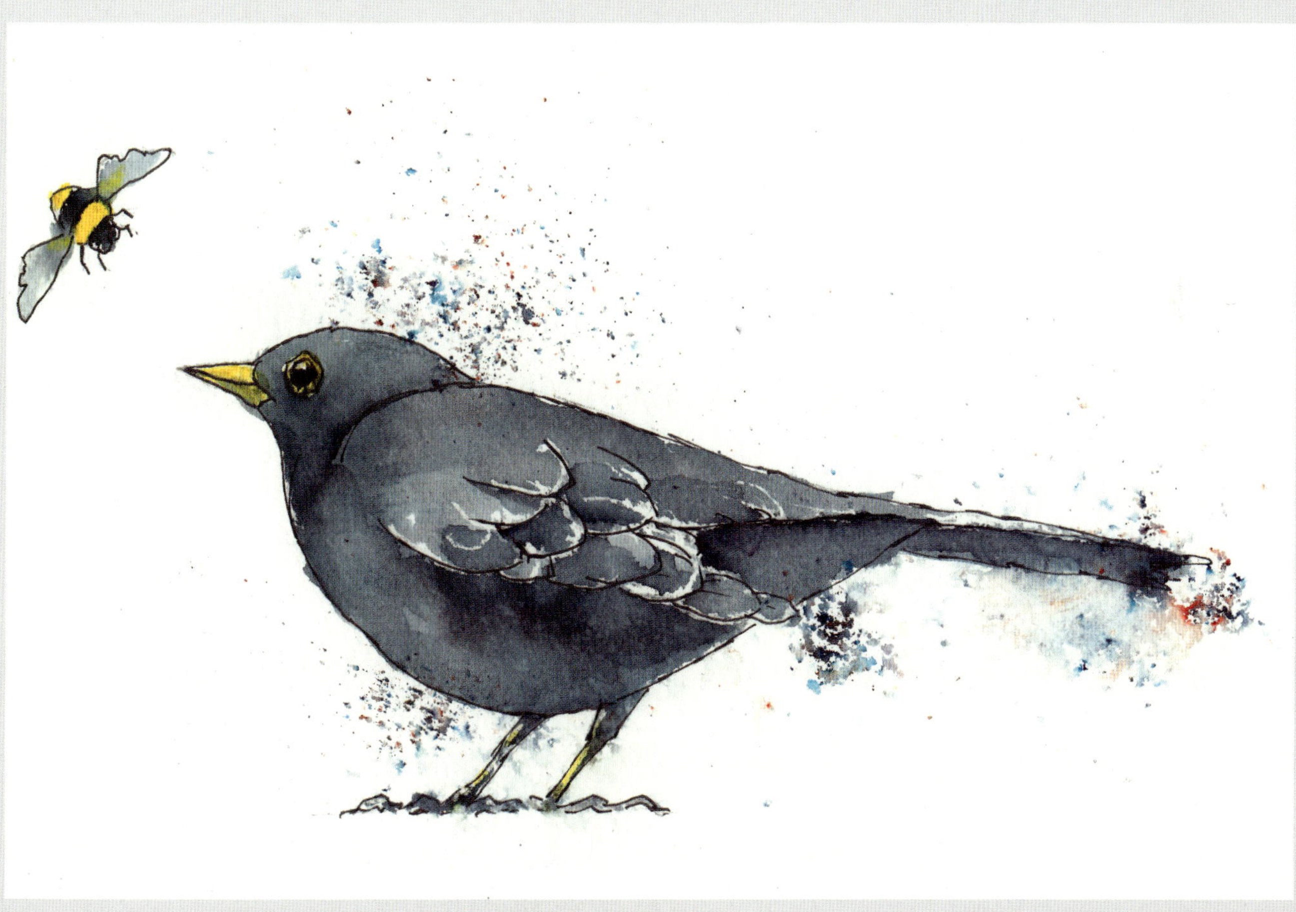

Demo six

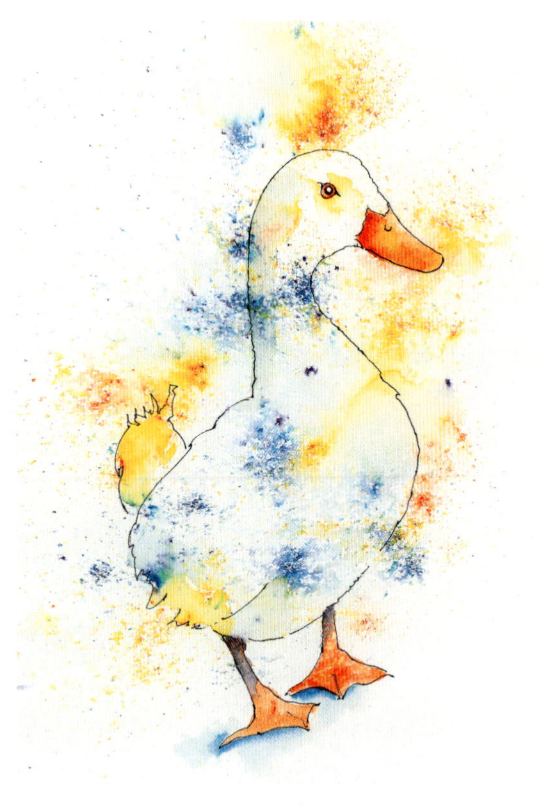

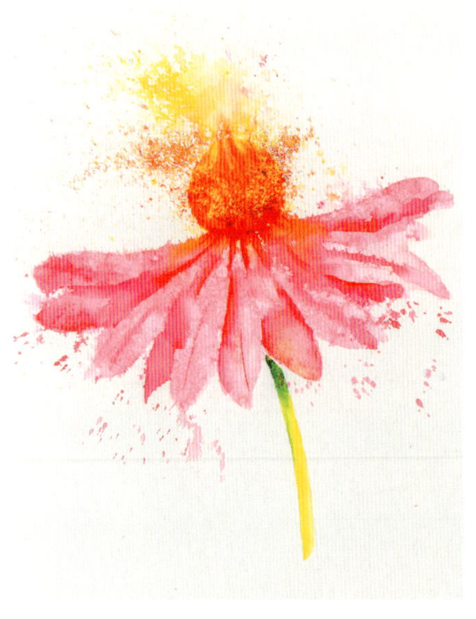

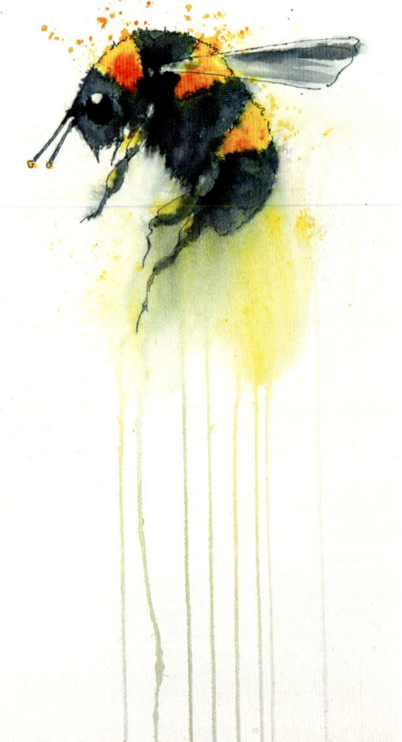

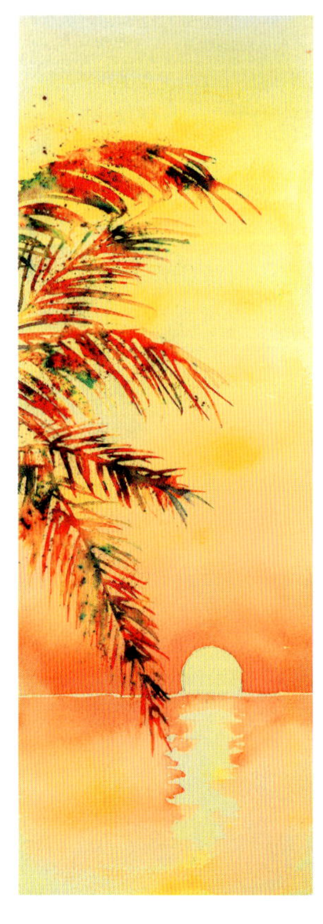

Your masterpieces will naturally look different to mine and that is absolutely fine. With Brusho you can create works of art that are totally personal to you.

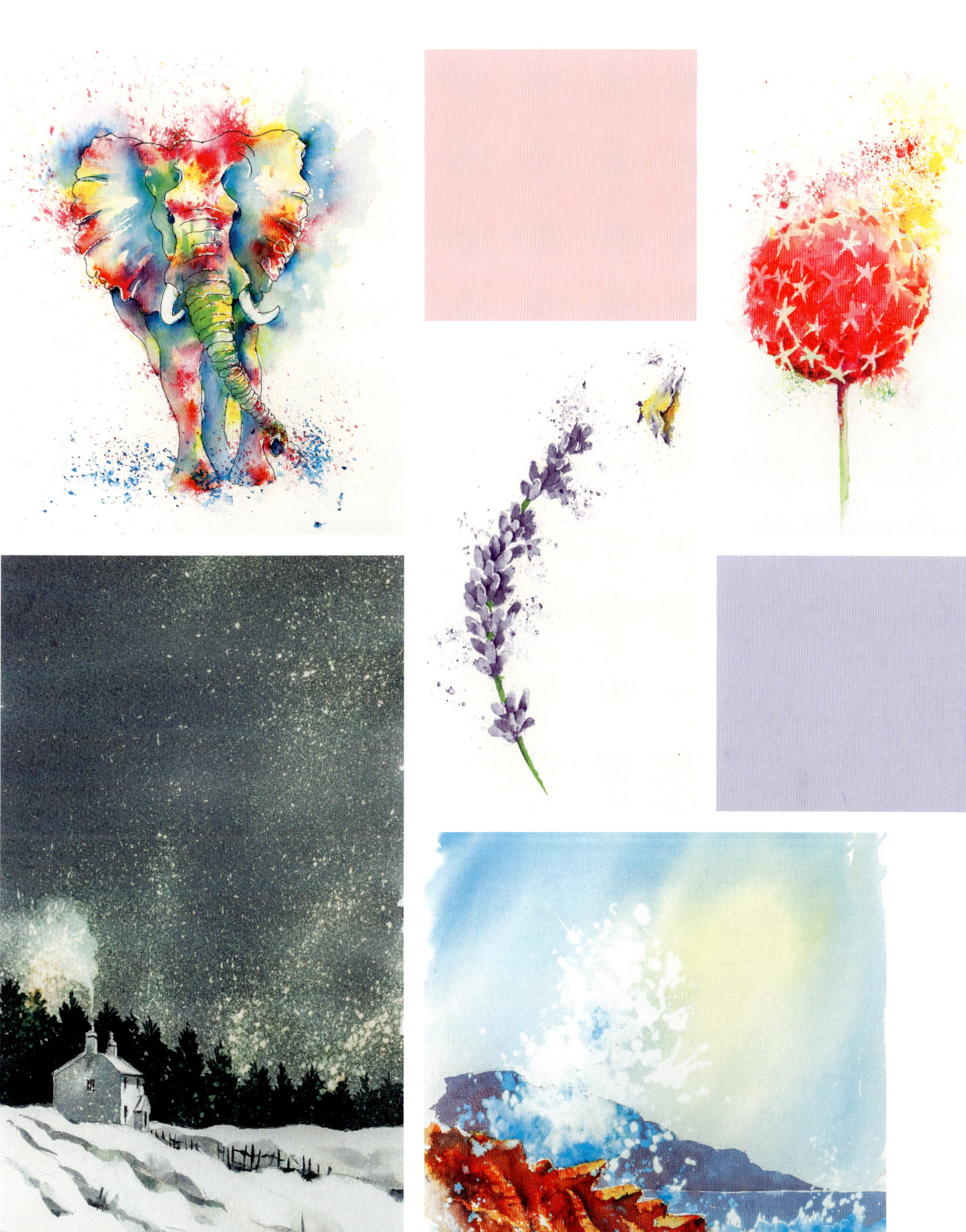

White Duck

This super colourful Brusho duck is a lovely project to start with, especially if you are new to Brusho. It uses the sprinkle and spray method that we learnt on pages 15–16. We will start by creating a strong linear ink drawing before sprinkling Brusho onto the paper and spritzing with the spray bottle to create lots of lovely explosions of colour. We will also smooth out the Brusho colour to create small sections of colourful wash as shown on page 16.

Adults and children or grandchildren will love having a go at this project it is so accessible.

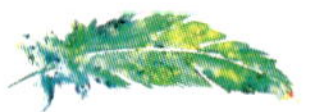

YOU WILL NEED

· Bockingford watercolour paper
300gsm (140lb) Not surface,
half imperial (38 x 56cm/15 x 22in)
· 3B pencil
· Eraser
· Black waterproof pen
· Brusho paint: gamboge, ultramarine blue, orange
· Size 8 round brush
· Spray bottle with water
· Jug of clean water
· Palette or scrap paper
· Kitchen paper

Tip

Make sure that the ink pen you use is permanent – you don't want the black ink to run when you spray water onto it.

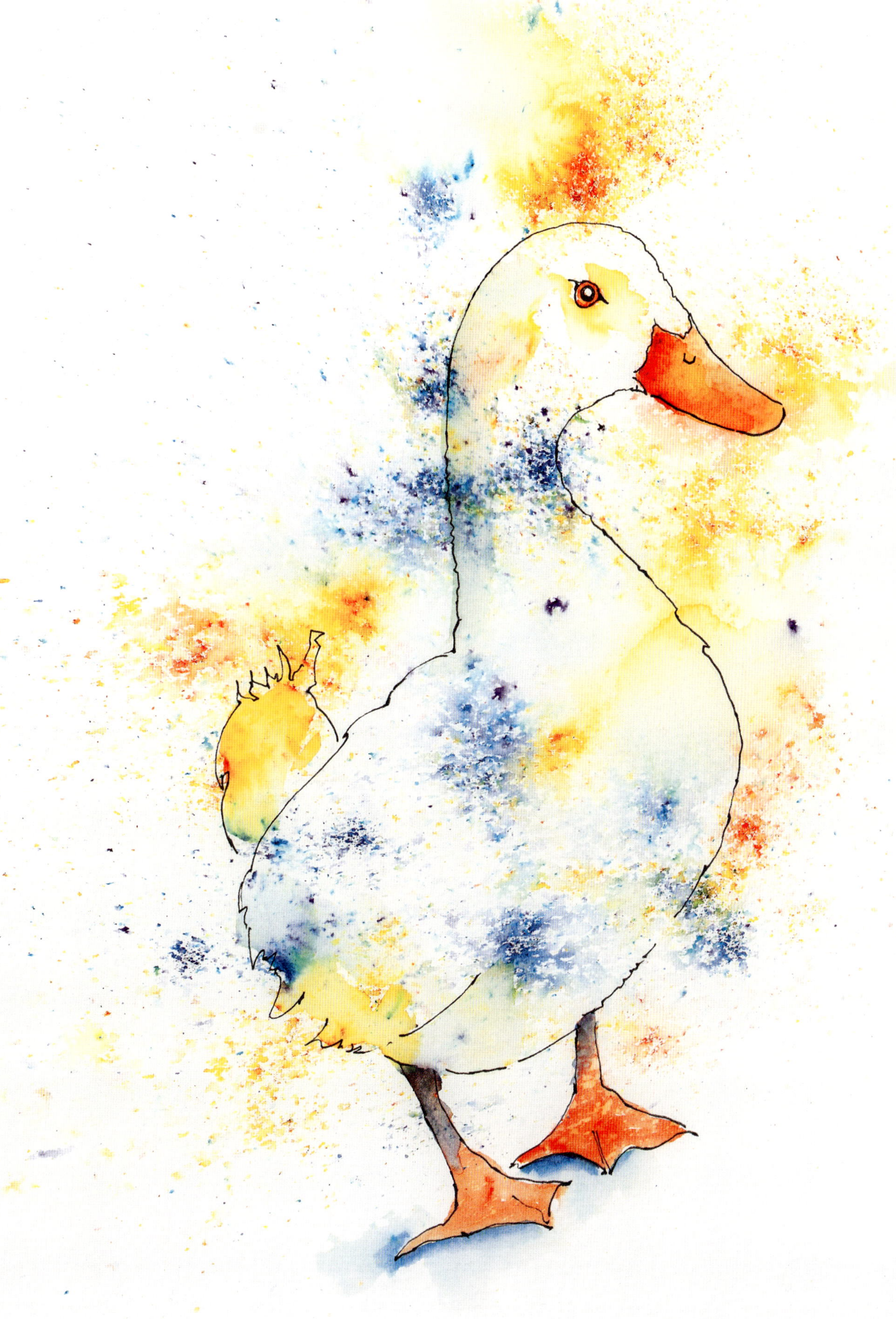

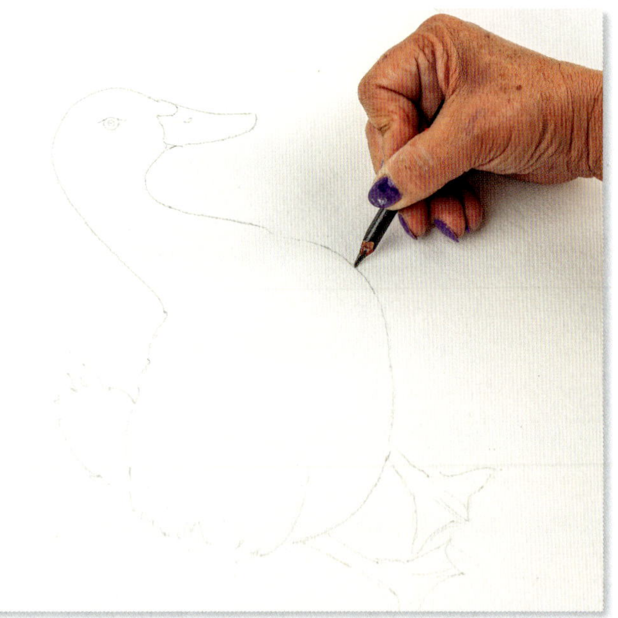

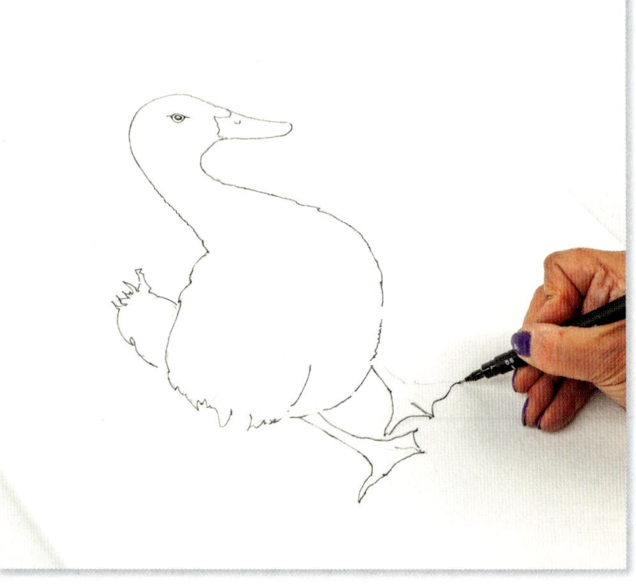

1 Using pencil, draw a simple outline of the duck without any details.

2 With your black waterproof pen go over your pencil drawing using simple quirky lines to suggest the shape of the duck. You can also darken the duck's eye, remembering to leave a small highlight. Make sure your ink line is dry before moving on to the next stage. Use an eraser to remove the pencil lines.

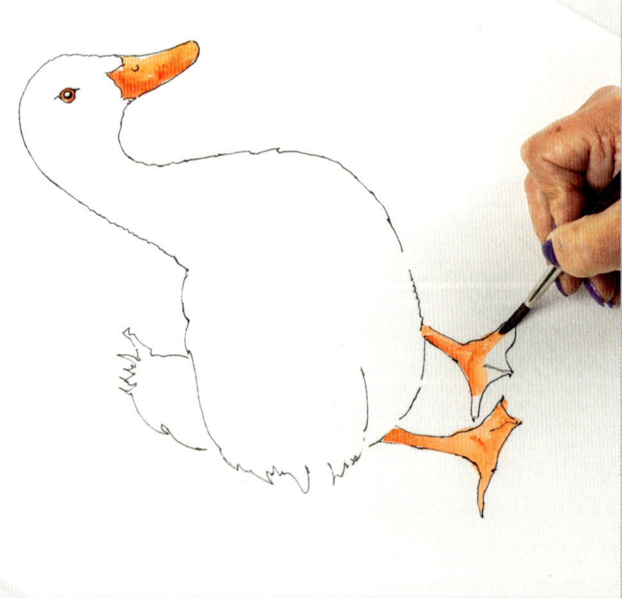

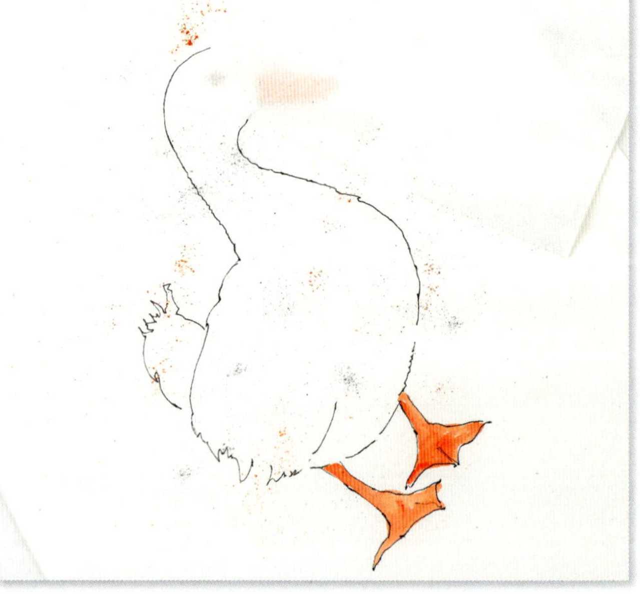

3 Mix the orange Brusho in a palette with water, or on a scrap of paper. Use your brush to paint in the eye, beak and feet. Allow this to dry.

4 Now for the fun bit! Cover the eye and beak with a piece of kitchen paper to preserve the colour. Work your way around the bird, randomly sprinkling gamboge, ultramarine blue and orange into the shape of the duck, letting some of the colours jump outside your drawing. Remember that Brusho really does go a long way, so try not to be too enthusiastic with sprinkling.

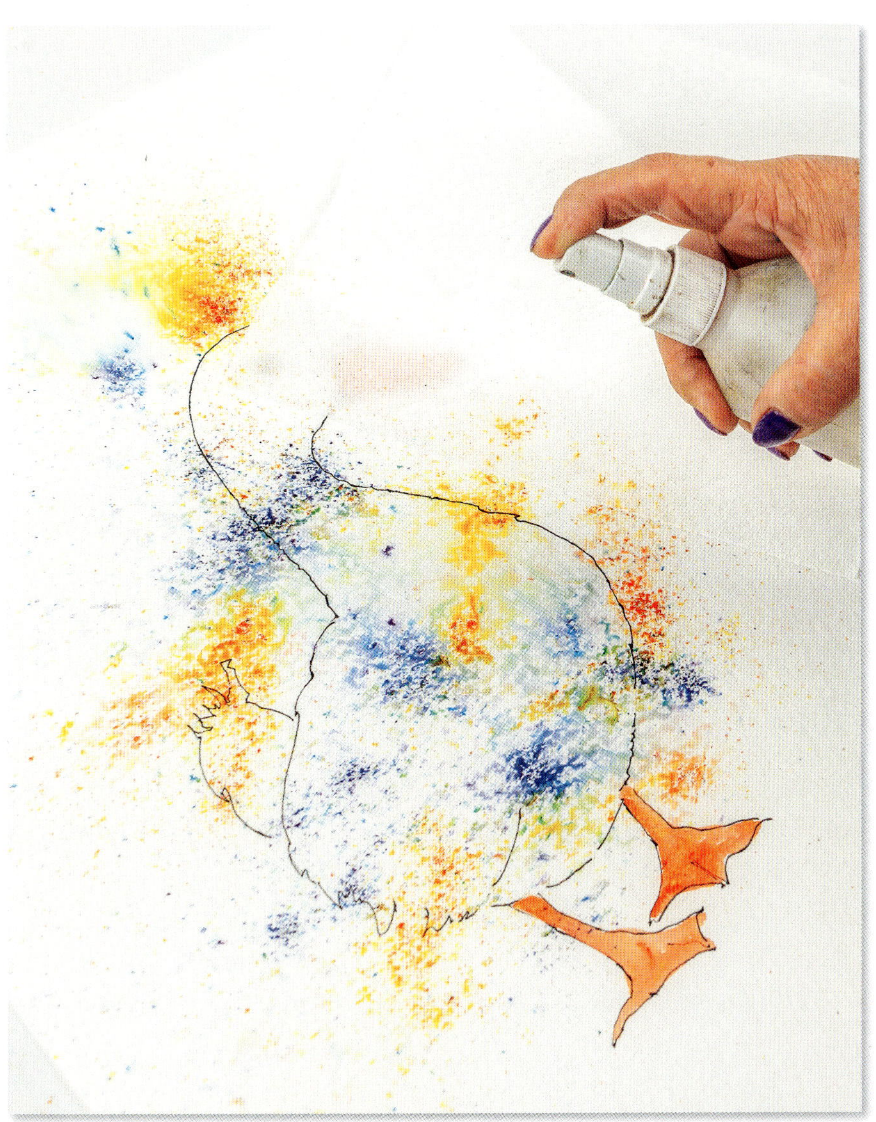

5 Starting at the top of the page, spray clean water onto your painting and watch the colours explode before your eyes. I always enjoy this bit!

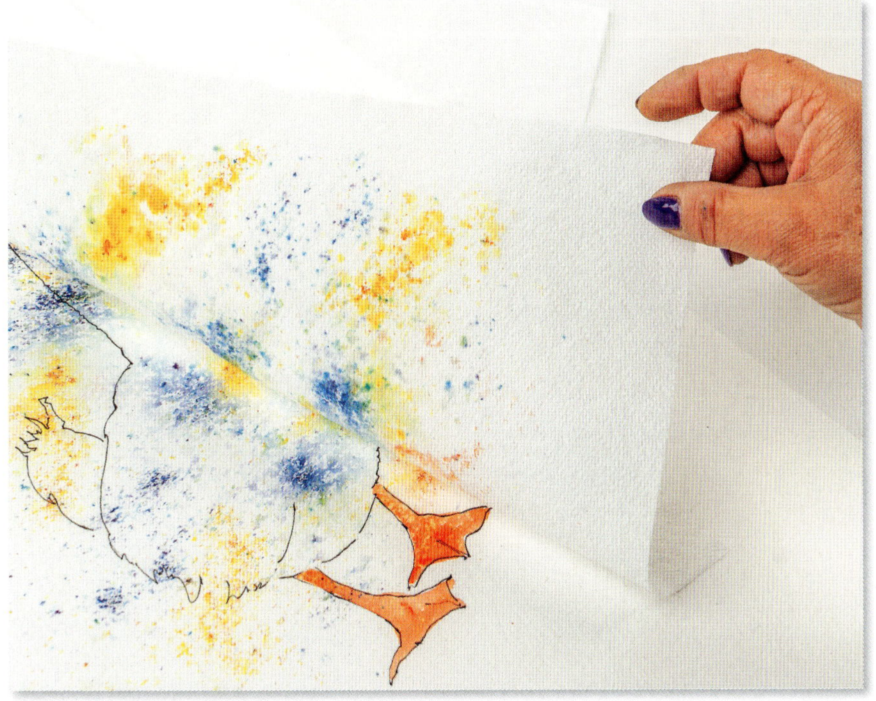

6 Dab with kitchen paper to soften the colour if needed.

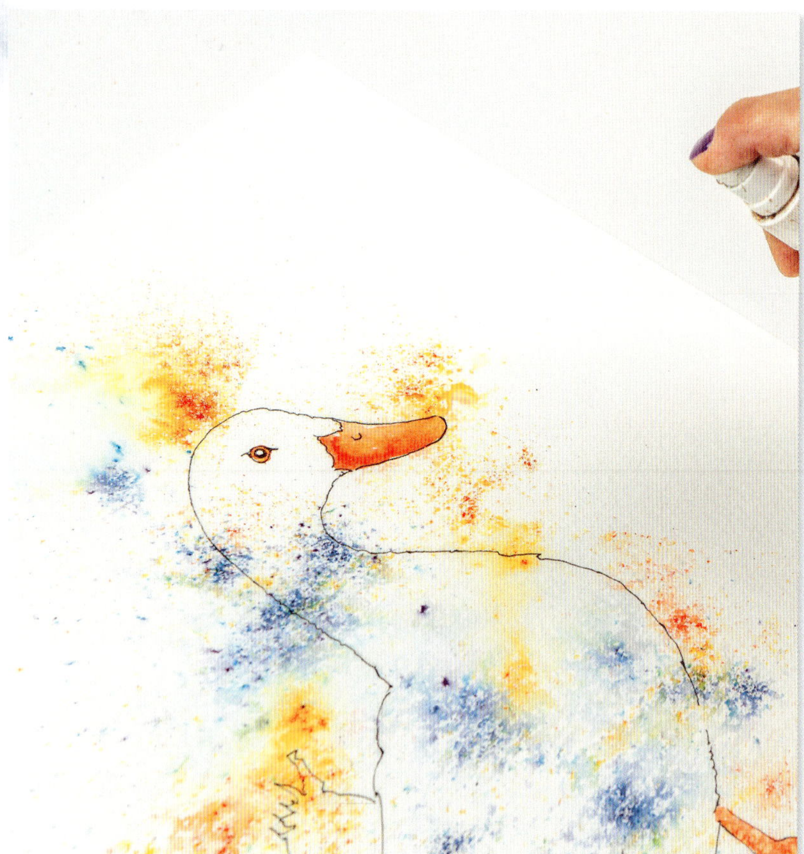

7 Sprinkle a little gamboge around the beak area and spray it so the wash of colour balances with the rest of the painting.

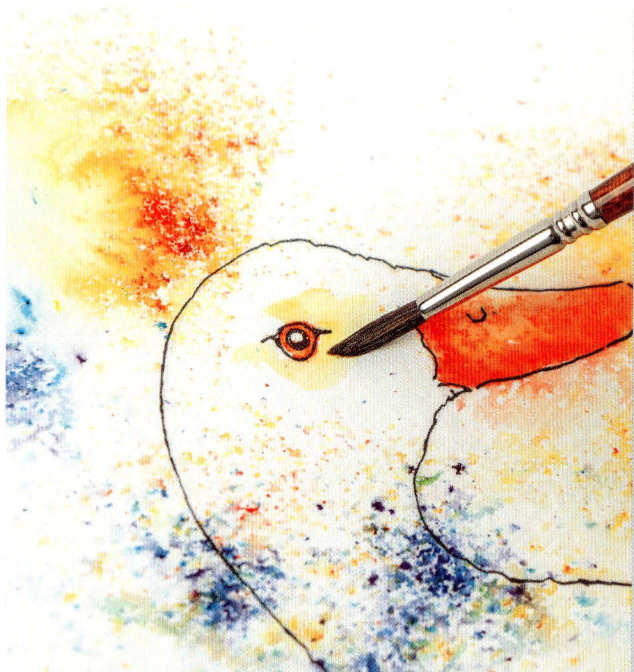

8 With a wash of gamboge on a scrap of paper as a palette, add a little colour around the eye with your brush.

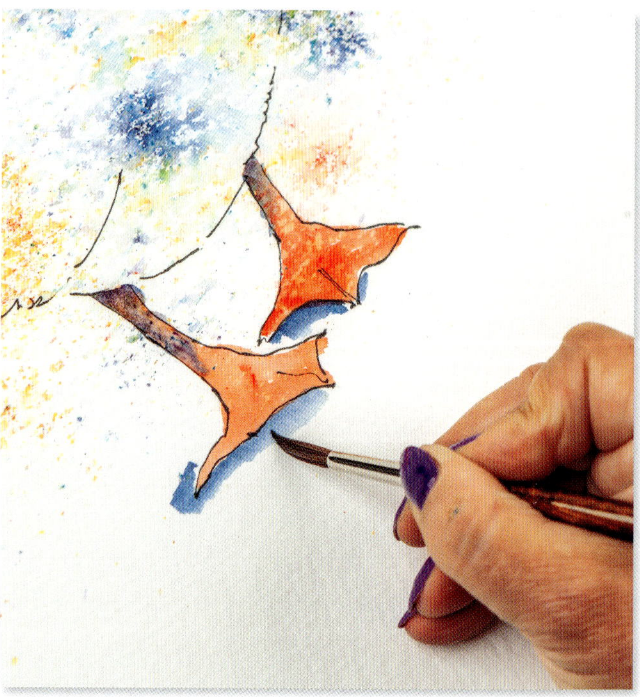

9 Use some of the ultramarine wash on your scrap paper to paint in a little shadow onto the legs underneath the body and a hint of a shadow on the ground surrounding the feet. This helps anchor him to the ground.

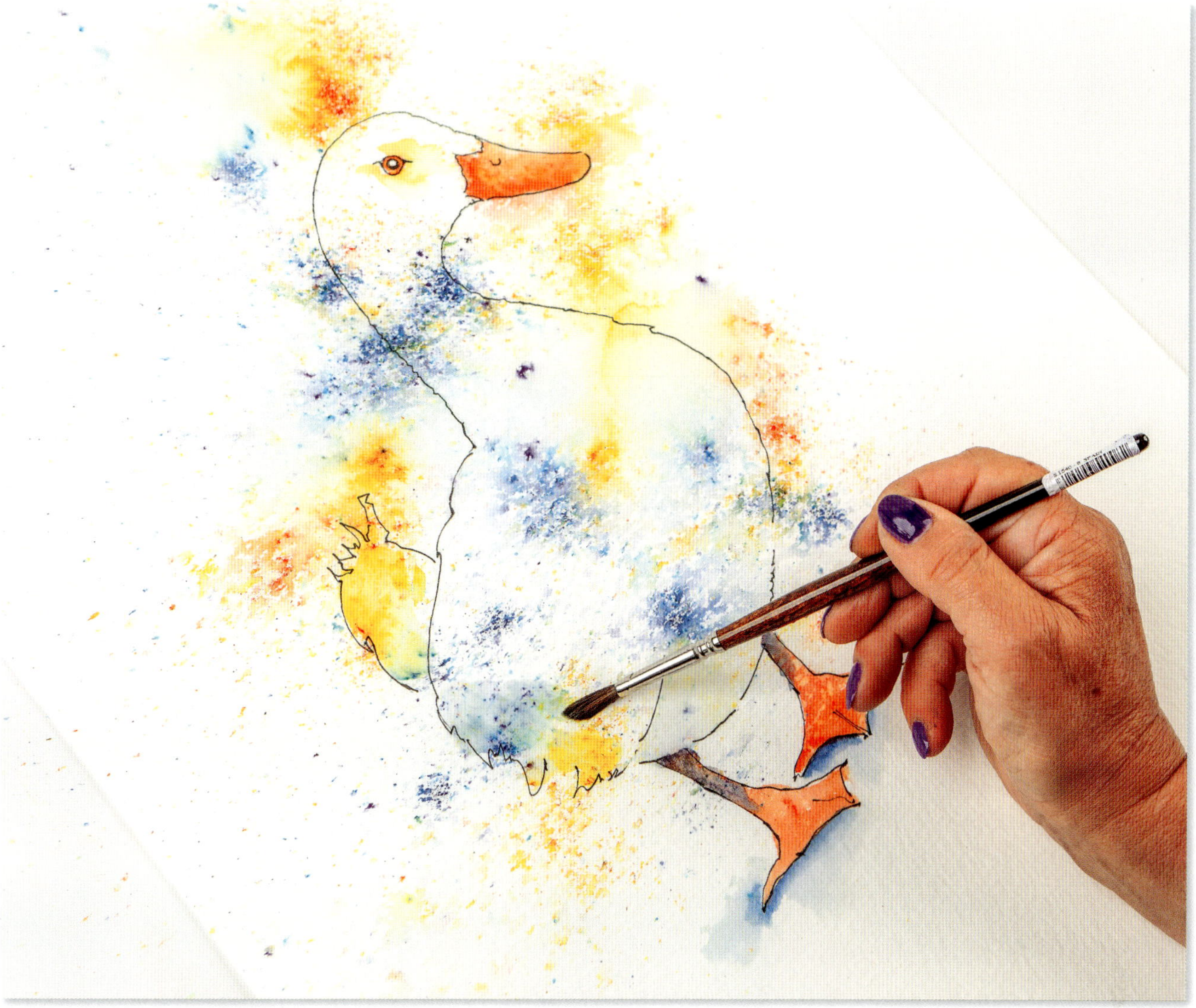

10 Soften a few washes by reactivating the paint with a wet
brush and clean water. I have done this on the wing
areas, the tummy and the back of the neck.

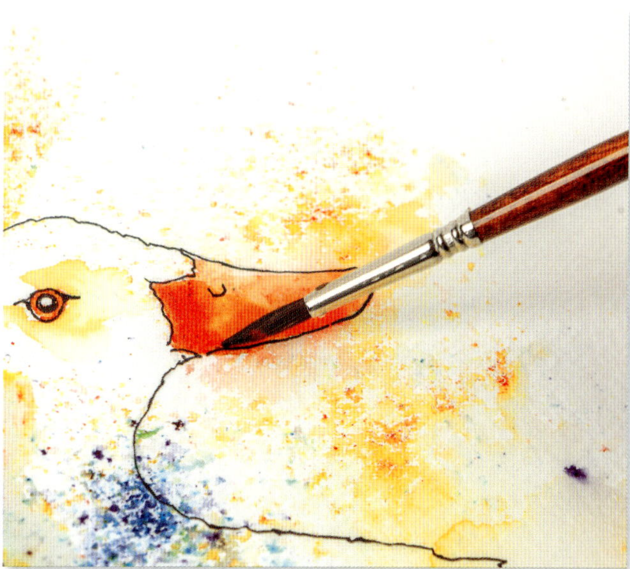

11 Use an orange wash to darken the beak
at the top.

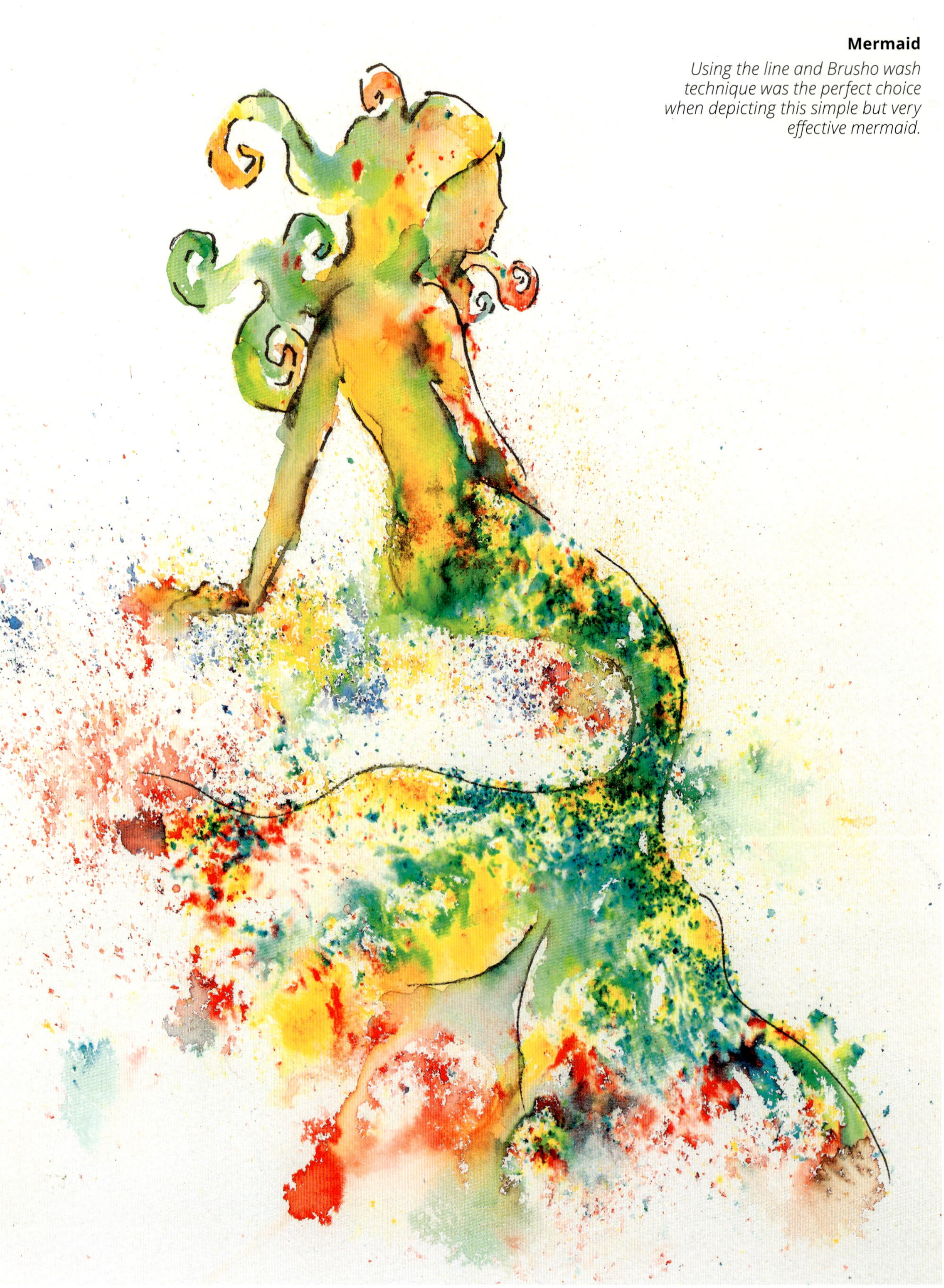

Mermaid

Using the line and Brusho wash technique was the perfect choice when depicting this simple but very effective mermaid.

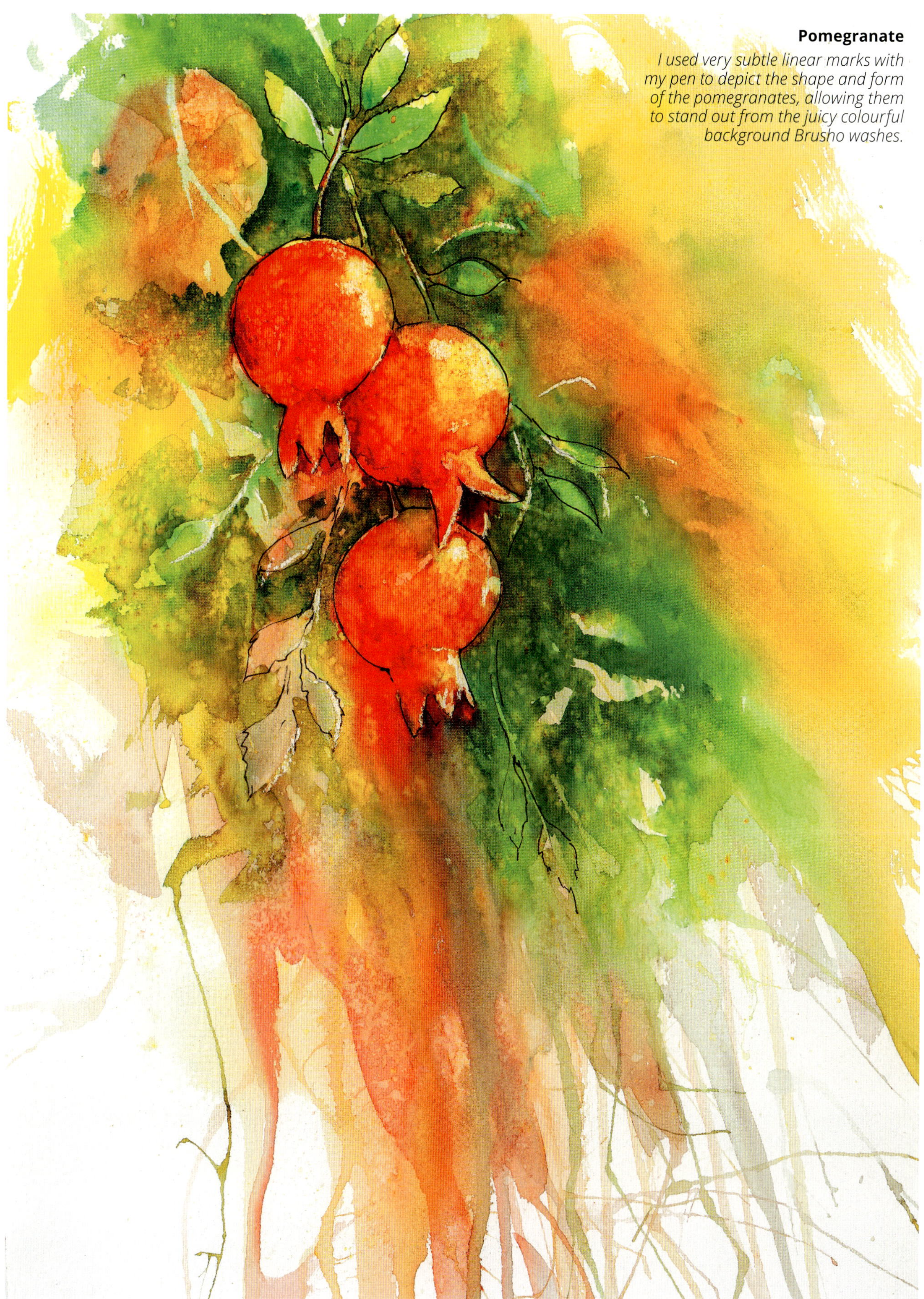

Pomegranate

I used very subtle linear marks with my pen to depict the shape and form of the pomegranates, allowing them to stand out from the juicy colourful background Brusho washes.

Ballerina

Capture the essence and poise of this graceful dancer with Brusho
and wax resist. All that lovely Brusho sprinkled texture helps to convey
the flowing movement of the ballerina as she melts from one move
to another.

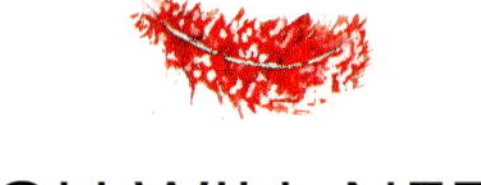

YOU WILL NEED

· Bockingford watercolour paper
300gsm (140lb) Not surface,
quarter imperial (28 x 38cm/11 x 15in)

· 3B pencil

· Eraser

· Brusho paint: sunburst lemon and alizarin crimson

· Size 8 brush

· Spray bottle with water

· Wax crayon or candle wax

· Kitchen paper

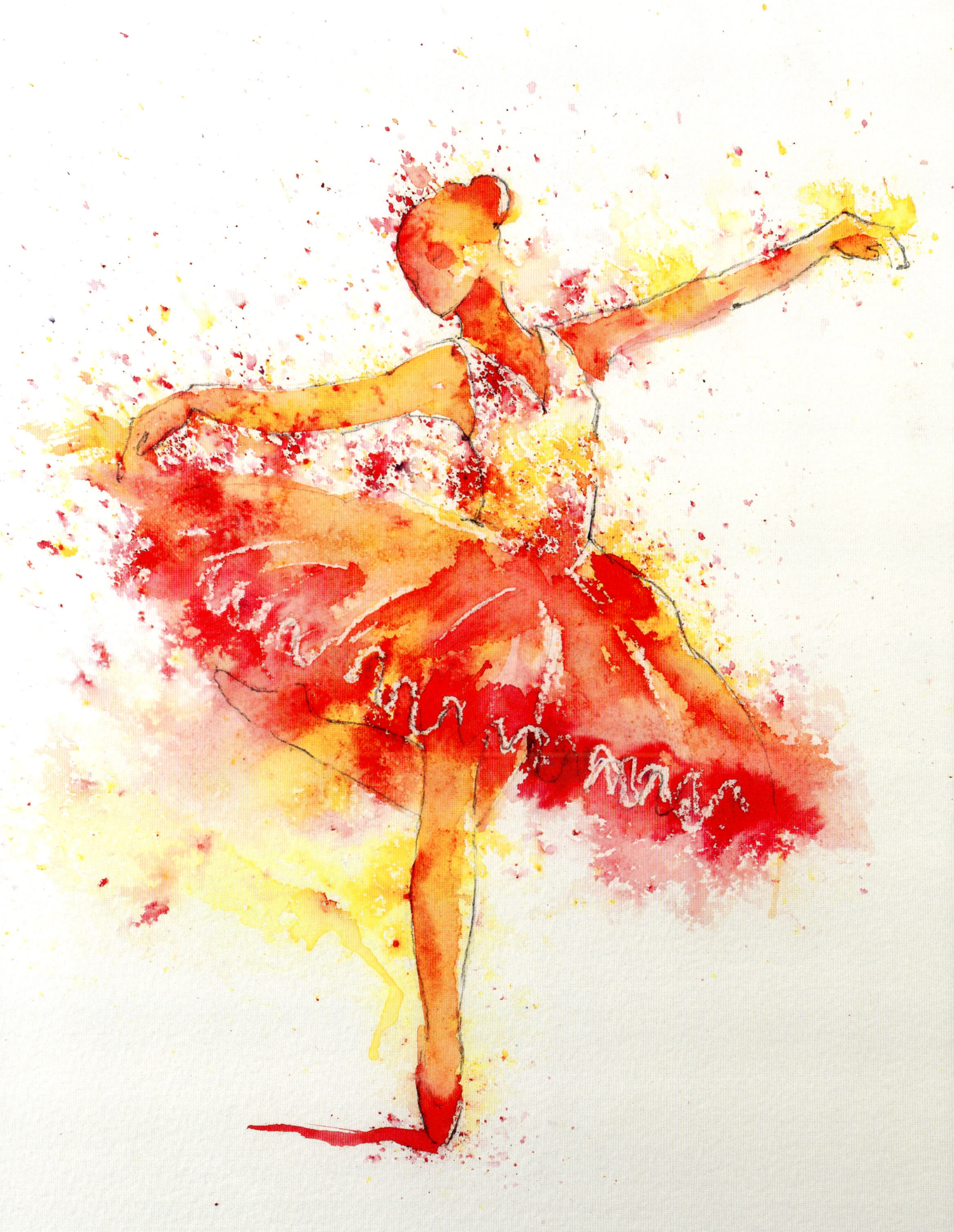

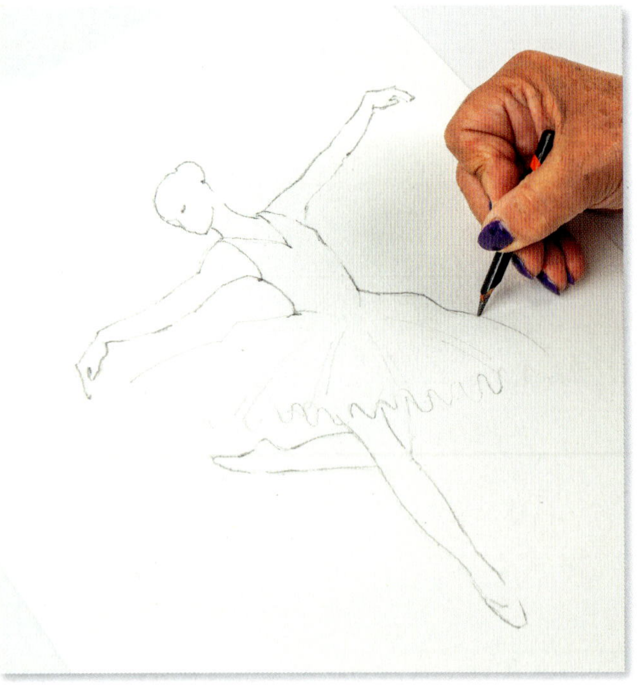

1 Using pencil, sketch a simple outline of the dancer. Do not include details like facial features – we want to capture the moment, rather than paint a portrait.

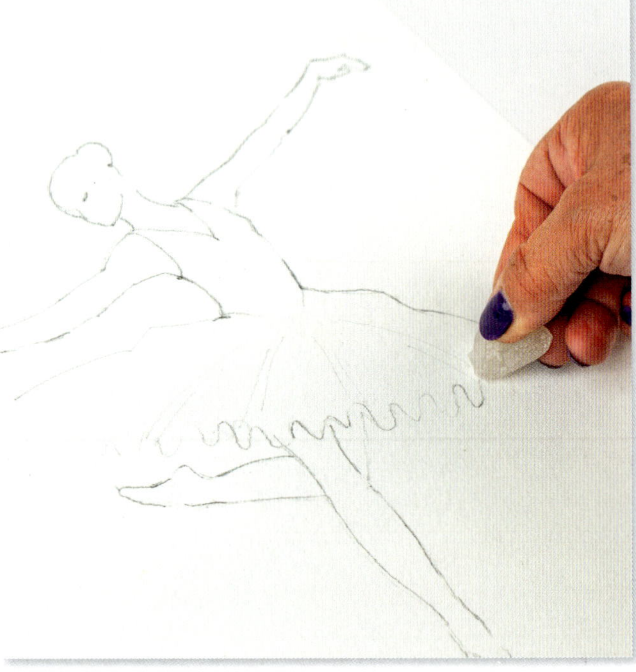

2 Apply wax to the areas you want to preserve: the arms, legs and a swirl of wax into the skirt of the tutu to suggest the fabric.

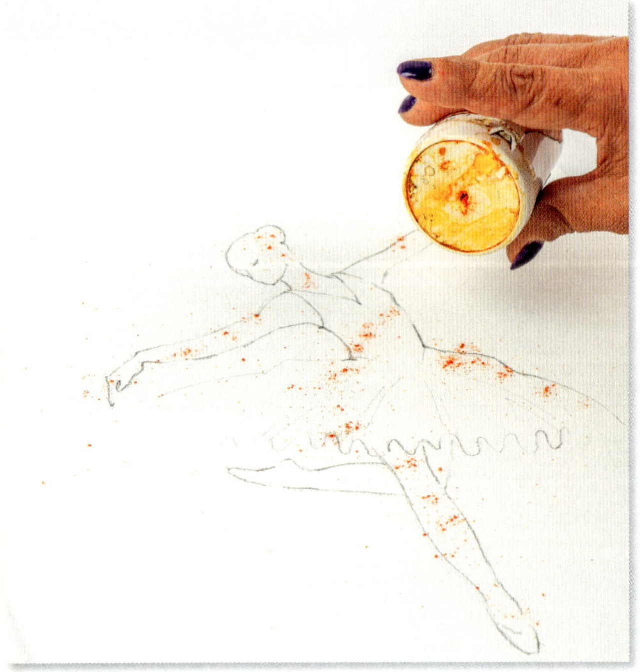

3 Sprinkle the sunburst lemon onto your dancer. You don't have to keep within your drawing: a few sprinkles around the dancer will suggest movement.

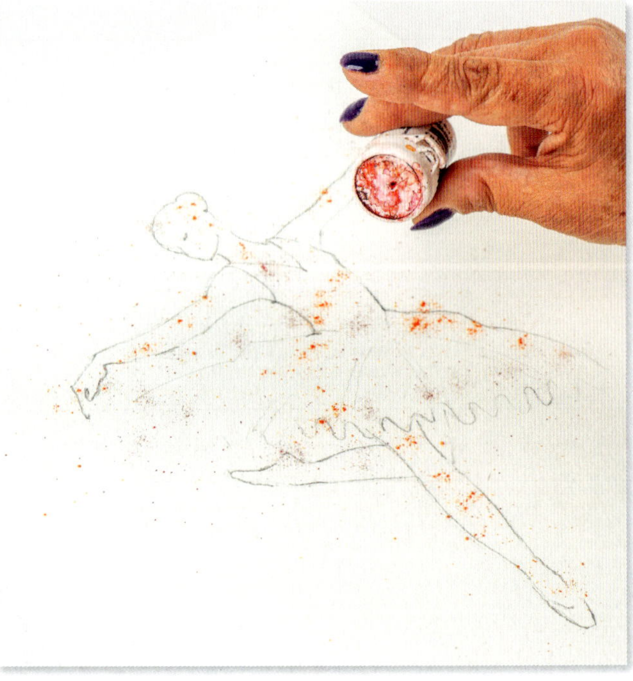

4 Sprinkle the alizarin crimson onto your dancer.

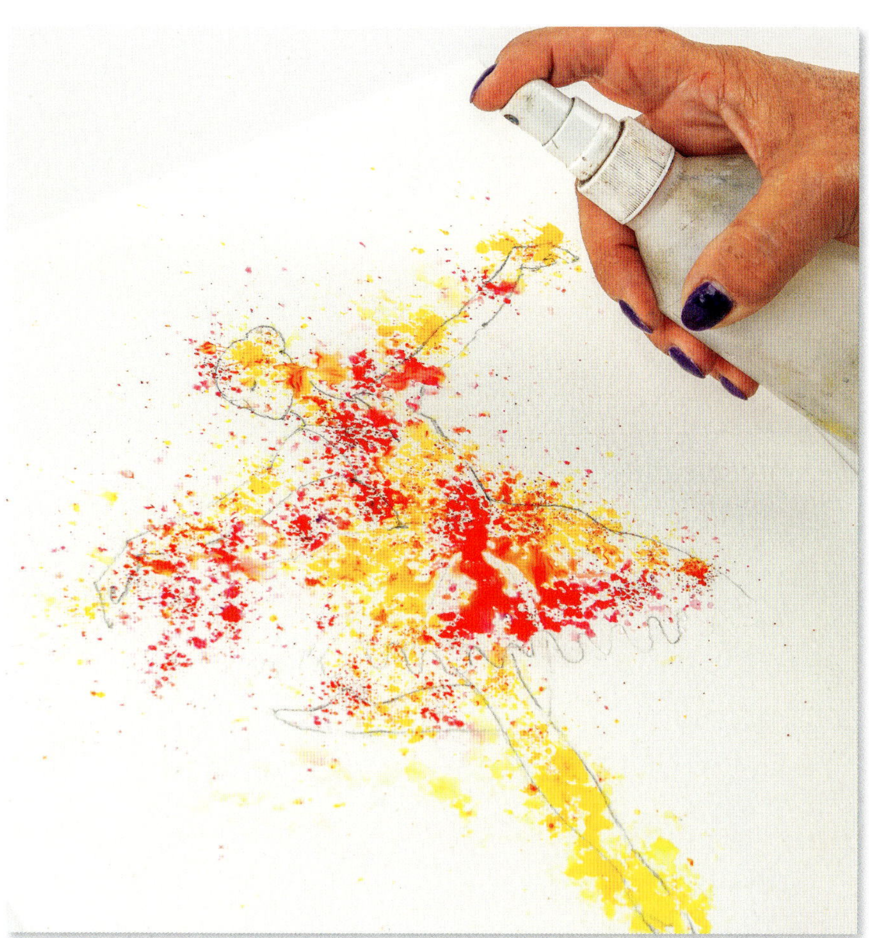

5 Spray with your water bottle to activate the colours.

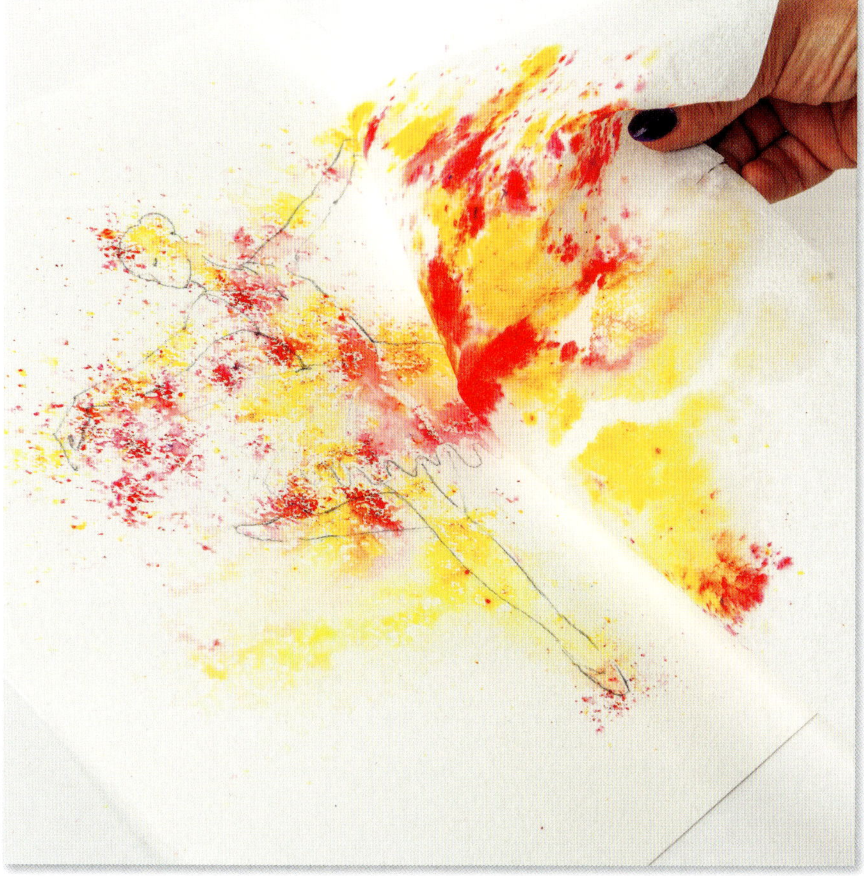

6 Dab with kitchen paper or a clean cloth if needed. Allow this to dry.

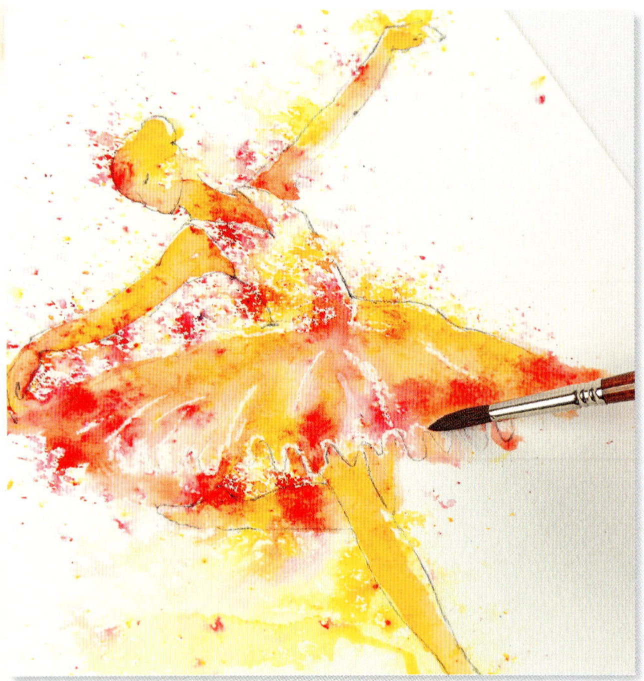

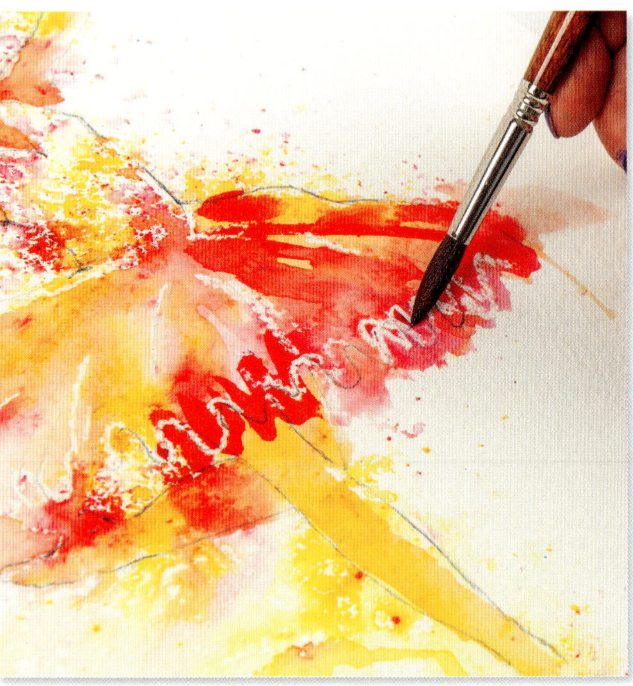

7 With a clean brush, start to smooth out some of the textured washes, particularly on the dancer's upper body, tights and tutu. Allow to dry.

8 You can add more washes of colour if your painting needs it. I add more alizarin crimson around the folds of the tutu skirt in the creases where the wax was applied. Smooth out with your brush. Let this dry.

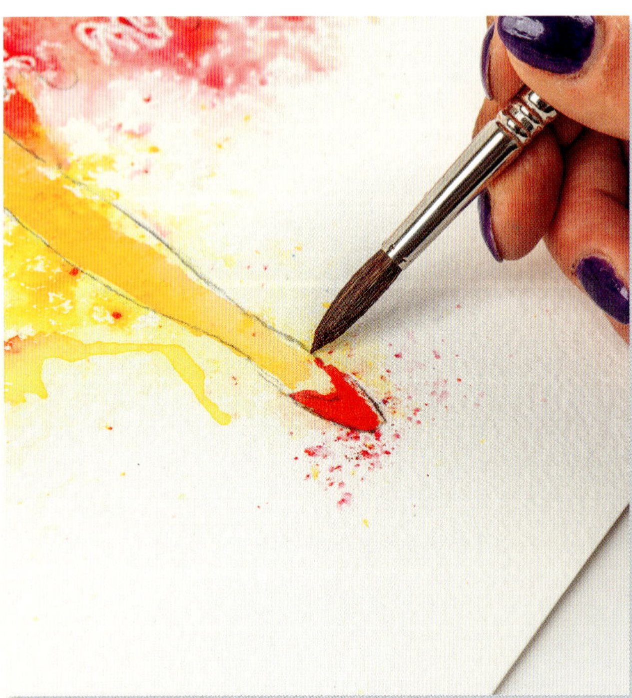

9 I also add the same wash to the ballet shoes.

Tip

If you have overspinkled your powder, and feel that your painting would benefit from a few bleached-out areas, you can lift away areas of colour, remembering to use your old brush.

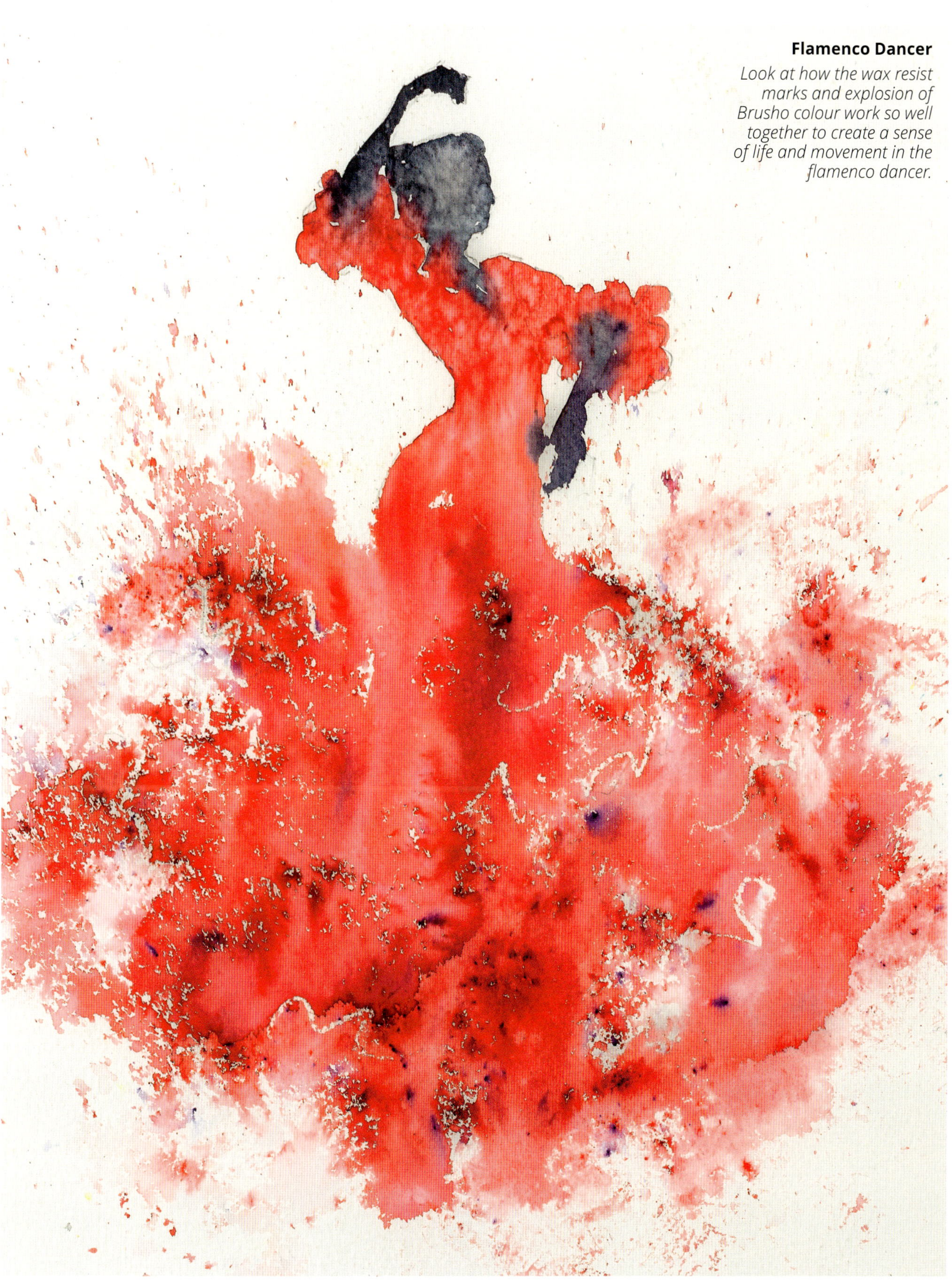

Flamenco Dancer
Look at how the wax resist marks and explosion of Brusho colour work so well together to create a sense of life and movement in the flamenco dancer.

Echinacea

Let me show you how to paint this beautiful echinacea flower,
(sometimes known as 'coneflower' because of its cone-shaped middle).
It is this central area that is perfect for depicting with our colourful
Brusho crystals that will explode from the centre of the flower.

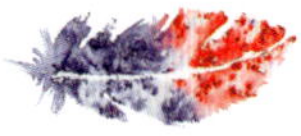

YOU WILL NEED

· Bockingford watercolour paper
300gsm (140lb) Not surface,
half imperial (38 x 56cm/15 x 22in)

· 3B pencil

· Eraser

· Brusho paint: sunburst lemon, orange, alizarin crimson,
ultramarine blue

· Size 12 brush

· Spray bottle with water

· Jug of clean water

· Palette

· Kitchen paper

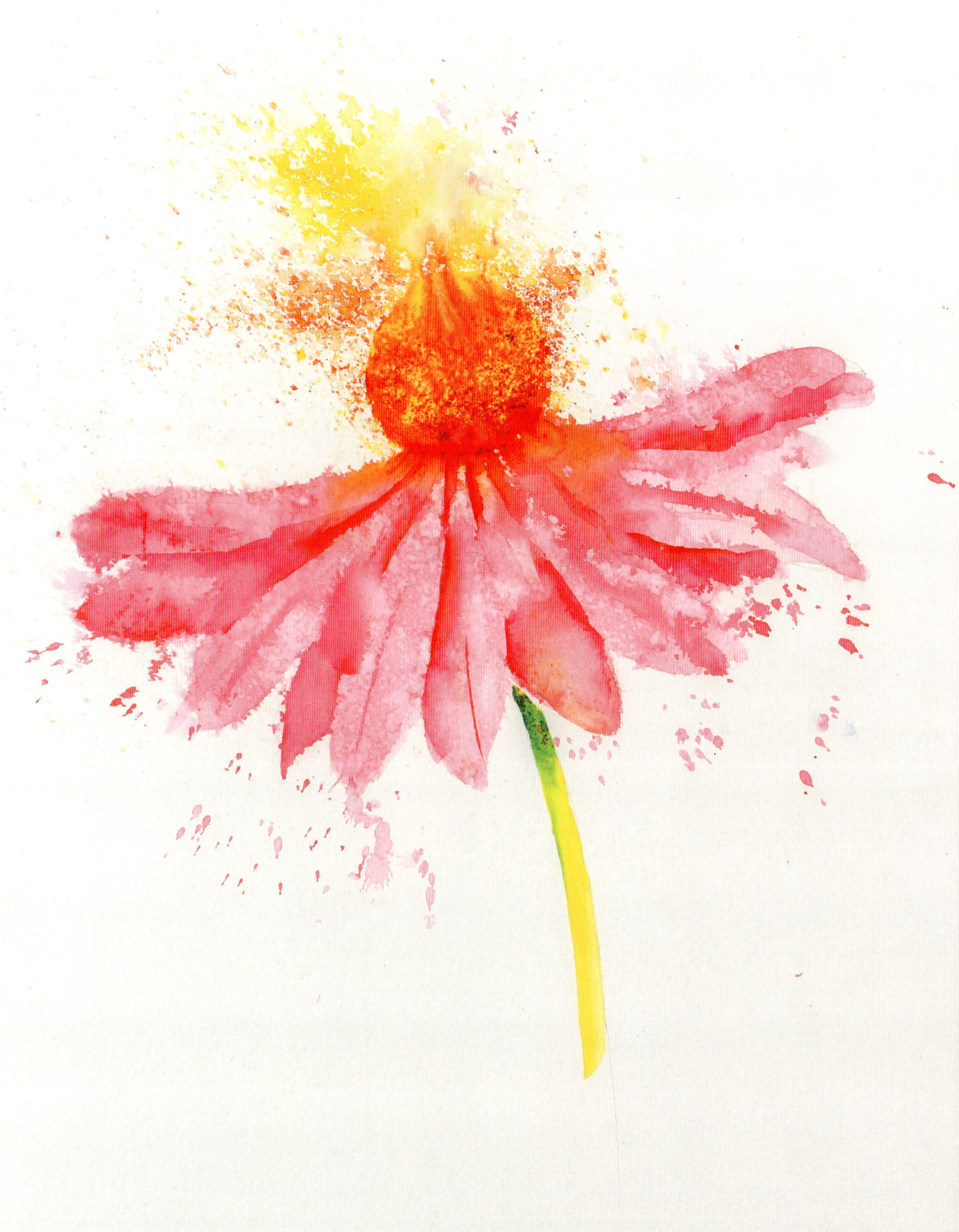

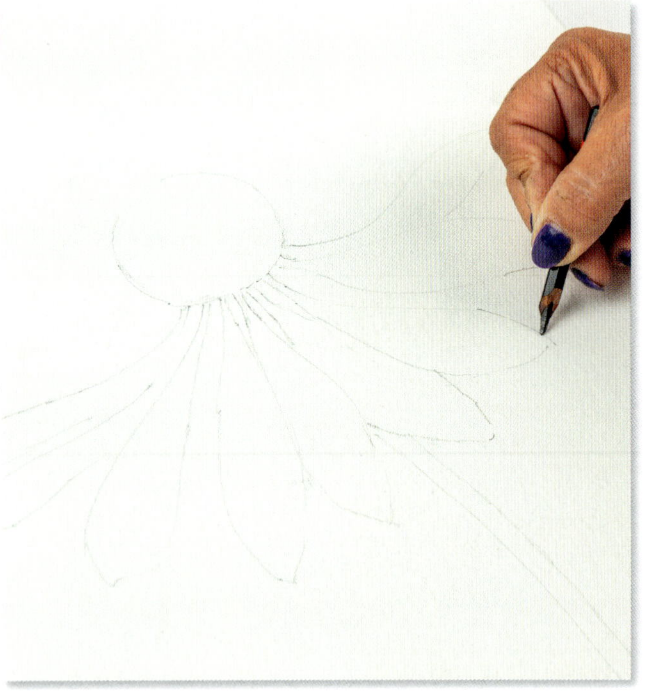

1 Using a soft pencil, draw a simple outline of the flower, keeping details to a minimum.

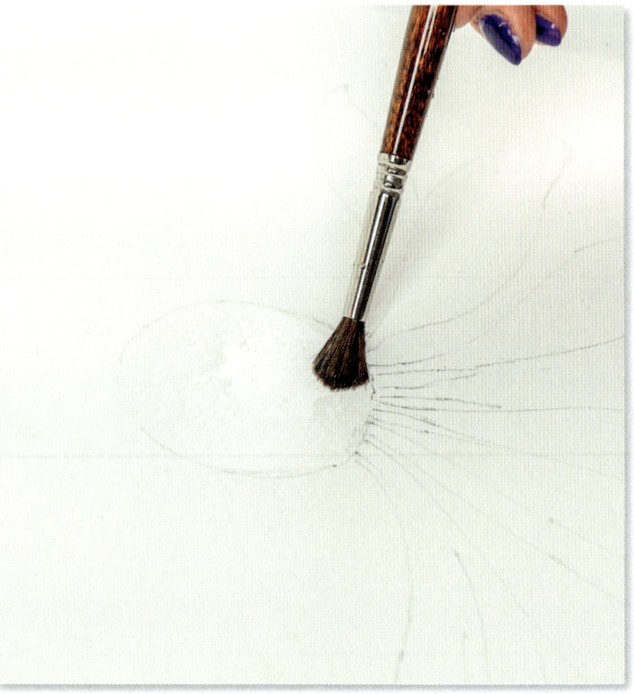

2 With your brush, wet the cone shape.

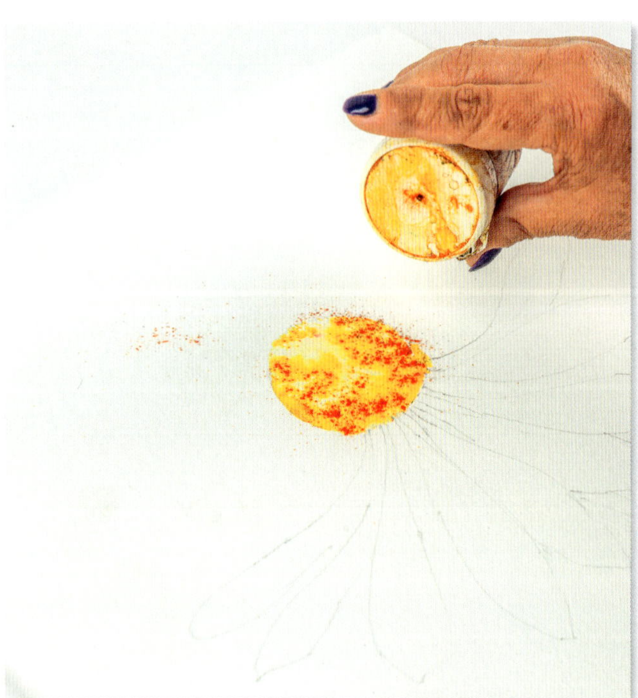

3 Sprinkle sunburst lemon into the wet area.

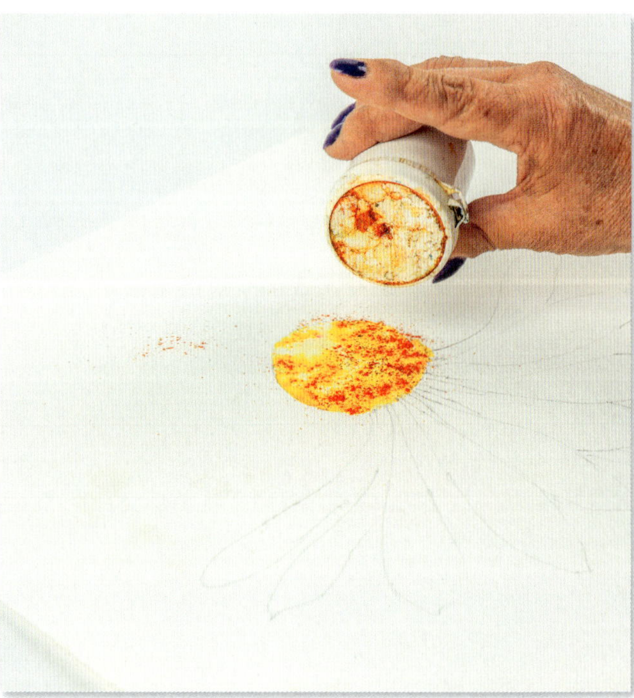

4 Next, tap out the orange powder around the edges, allowing it to fall outside the pencil lines.

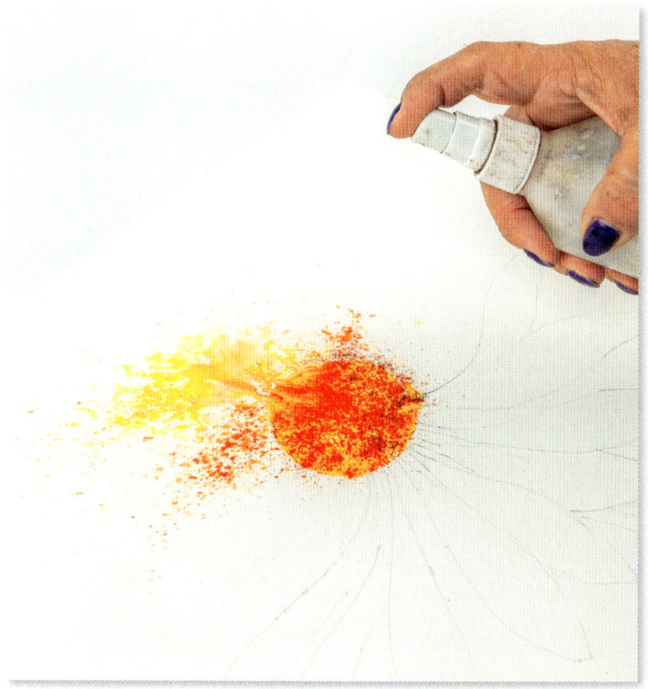

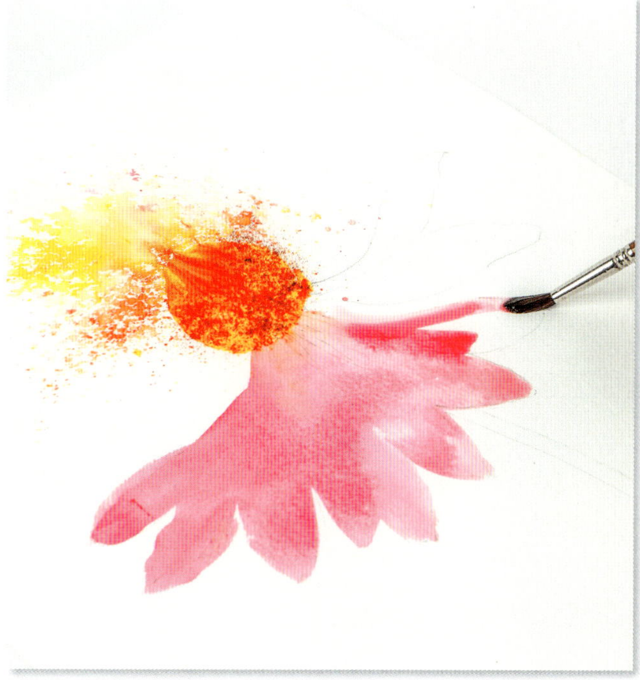

5 Spray the cone shape with water and watch the colours explode outside of the shape. Allow to dry.

6 Mix a light wash of alizarin crimson in your palette and suggest loose colourful petals that radiate from underneath the cone shape. Don't worry about keeping within the pencil lines.

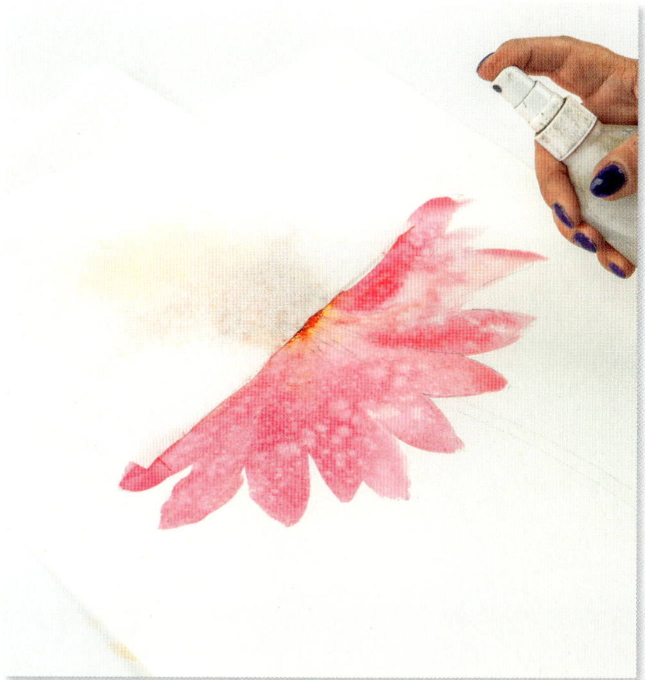

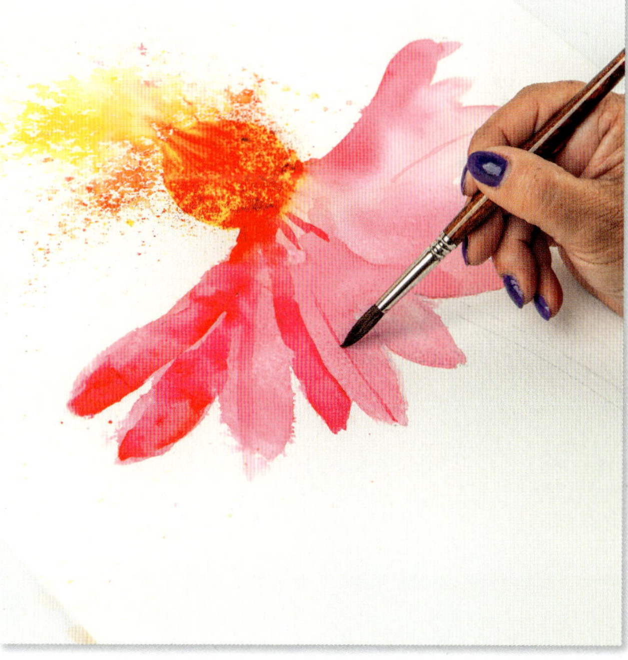

7 Mask off the cone shape with kitchen paper to preserve its colour and spritz the petals to give them a little texture. Allow to dry.

8 Mix a darker wash of alizarin crimson in the palette and start to paint darker petals especially underneath the top petals, giving the illusion that they are underneath and in shadow.

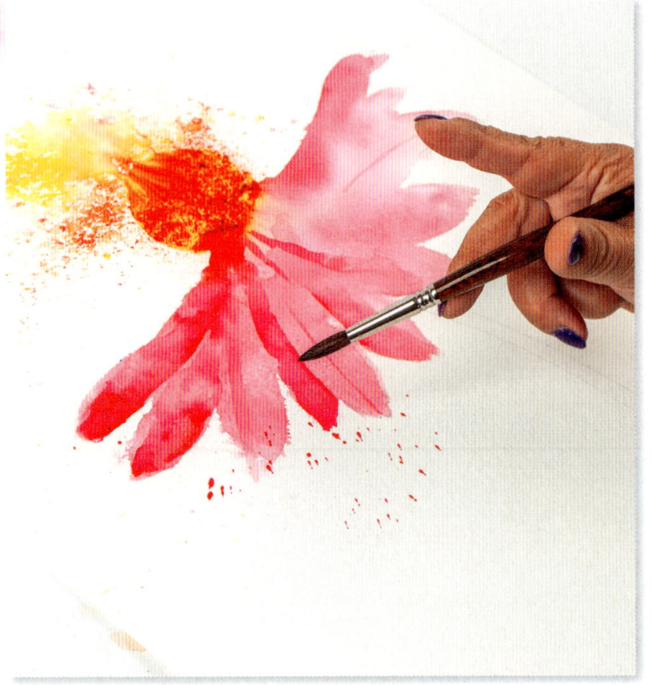

9 Tap your brush to allow a spattering of colour.

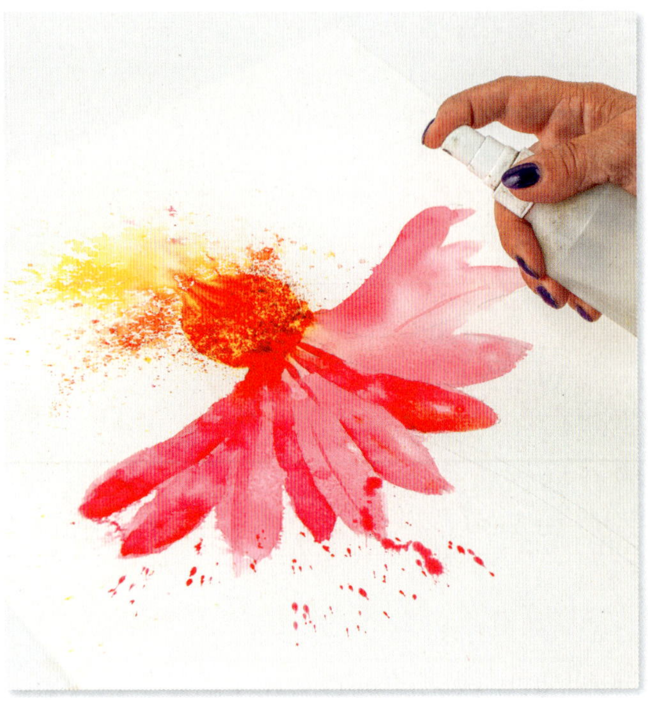

10 Spritz your work if you wish. This will reactivate some of the Brusho crystals.

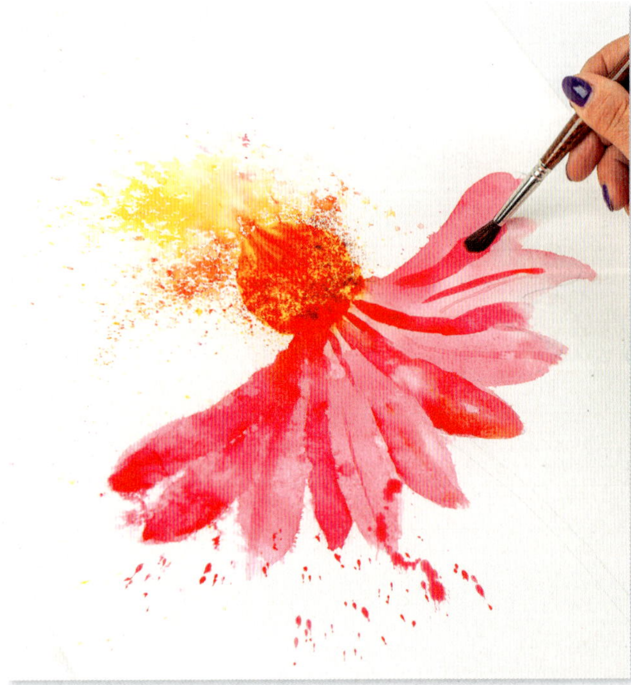

11 Continue accentuating the petals by painting darker areas.

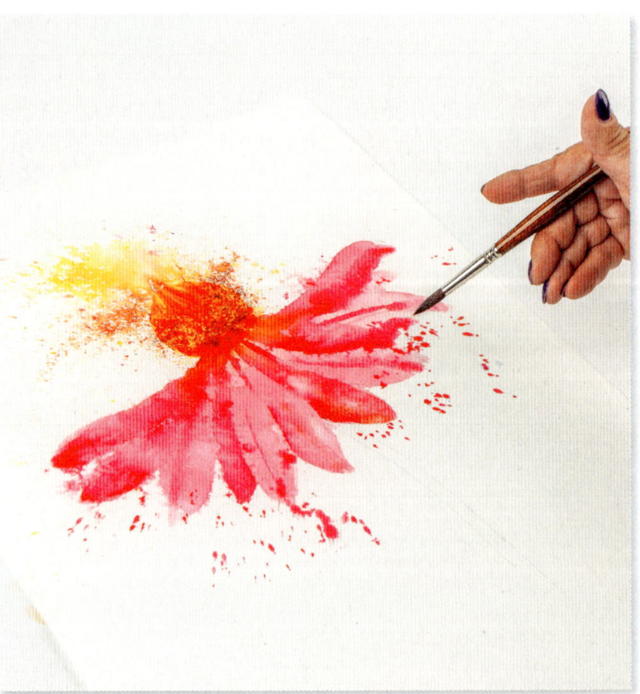

12 Spritz your work again and then spatter more of the alizarin crimson wash under the flower petals.

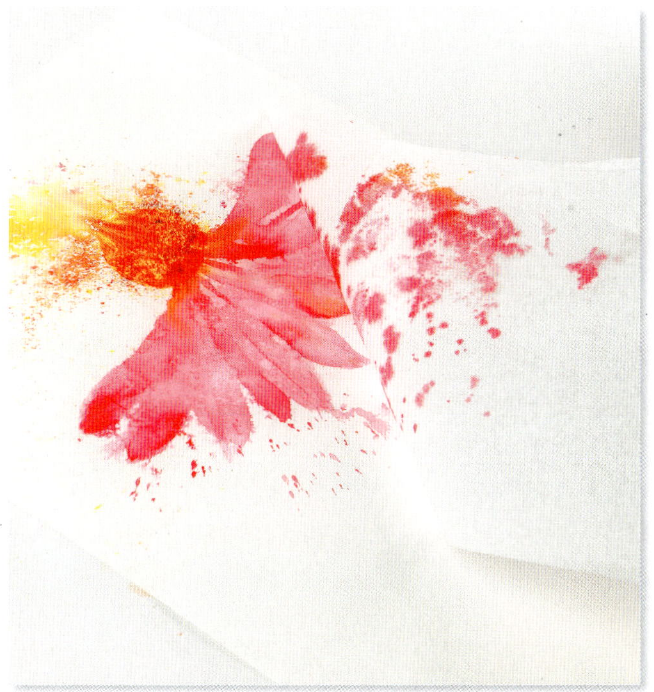 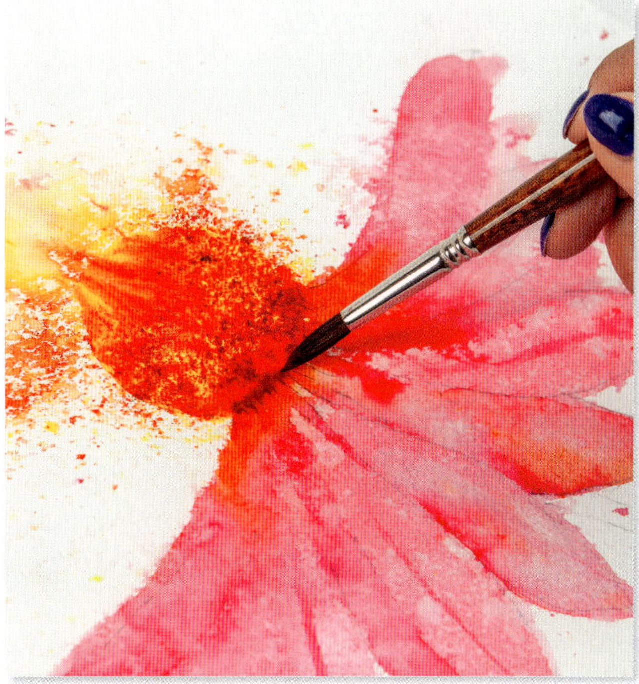

13 Blot your painting to remove excess water. If you feel you haven't got enough Brusho powder, add more at this stage.

14 Using a wash of alizarin crimson and the size 12 brush, darken where the cone shape meets the petals.

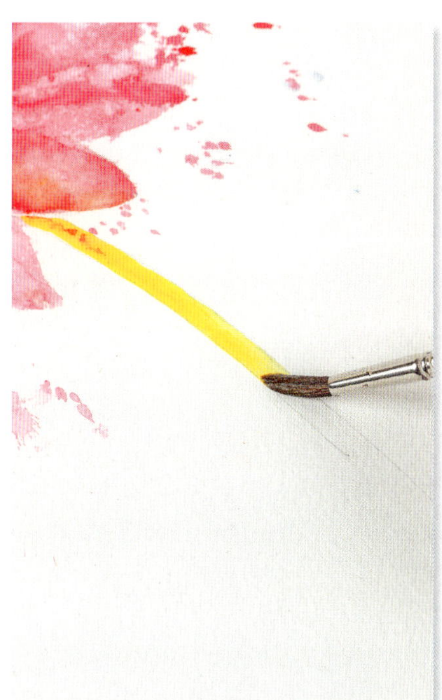 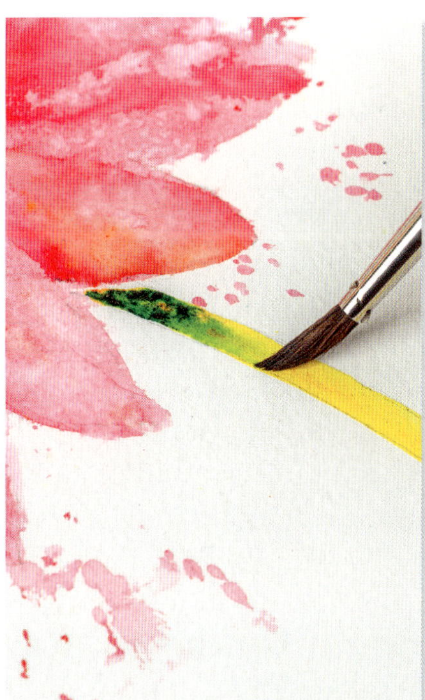 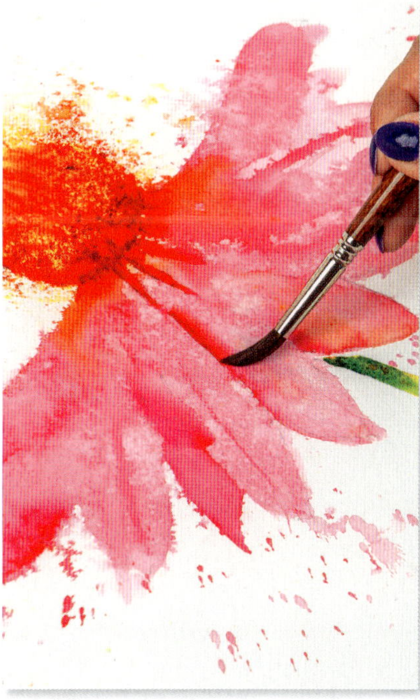

15 Using a small wash of sunburst lemon in the palette, paint the stem area working from the top to the bottom.

16 While this is still wet, introduce a touch of the ultramarine blue to suggest a shadow on the stem. Let it gently run down.

17 Reinforce some of the darks on the petals. Use your size 12 brush to drop in a hint of alizarin crimson.

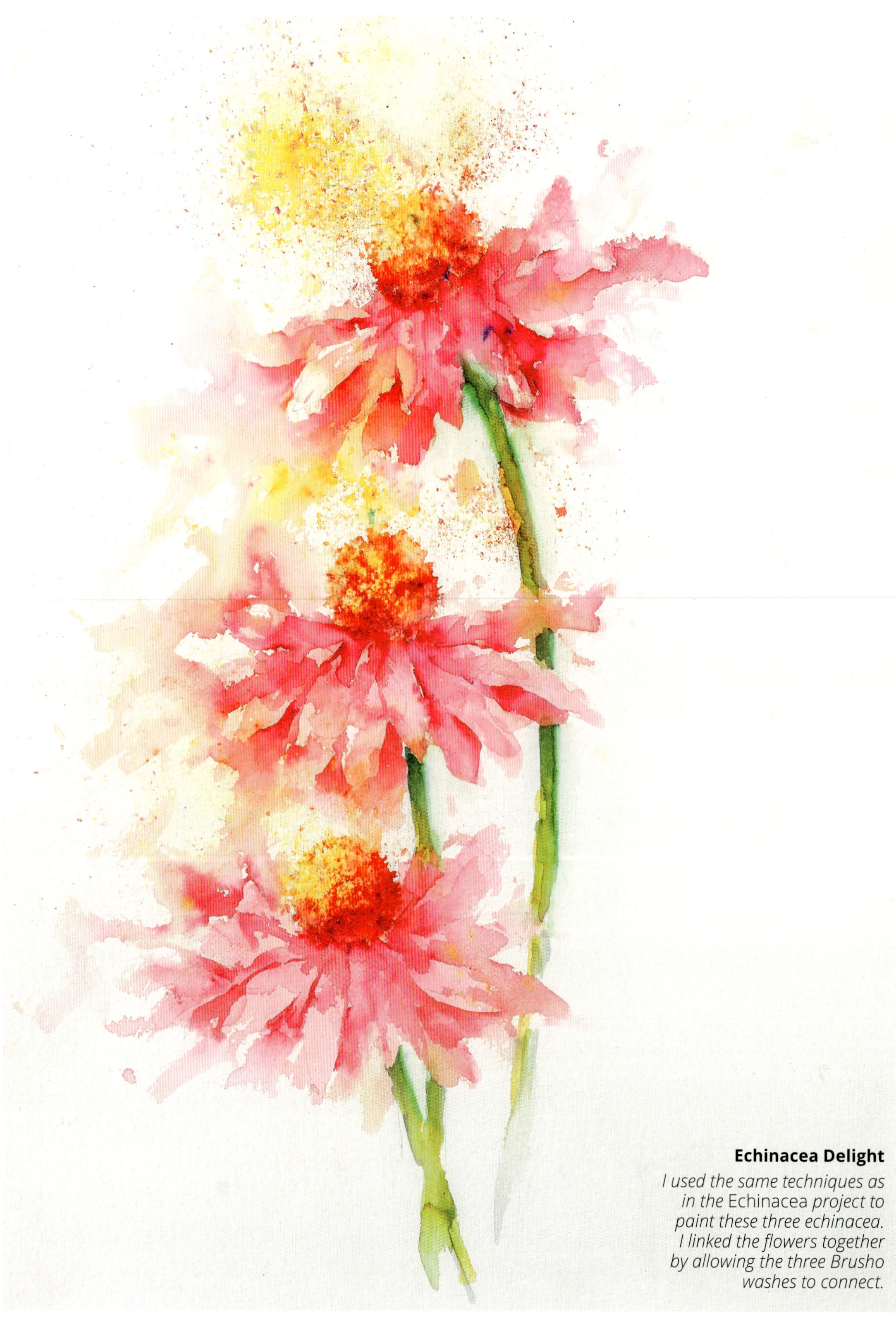

Echinacea Delight
I used the same techniques as in the Echinacea *project to paint these three echinacea. I linked the flowers together by allowing the three Brusho washes to connect.*

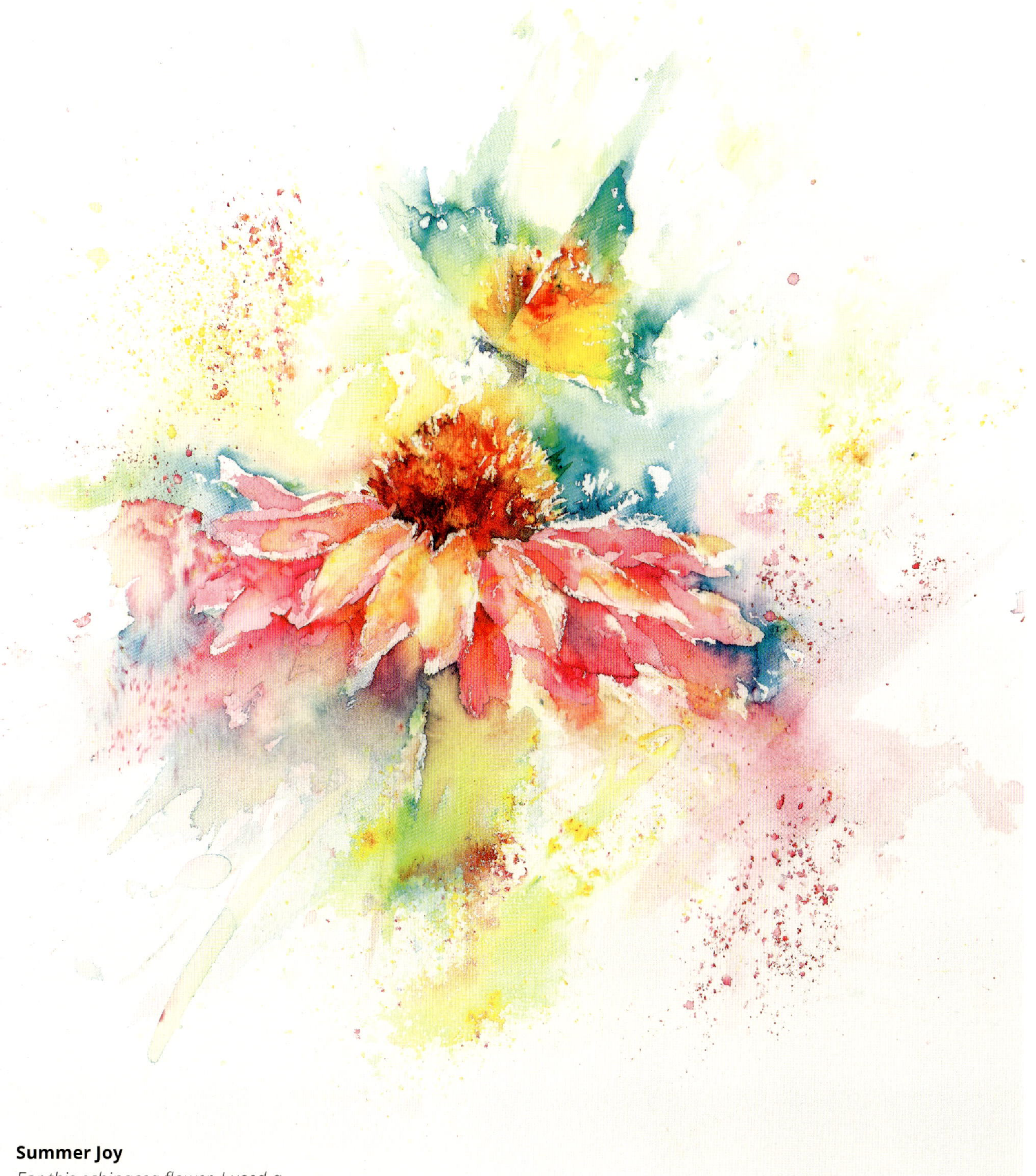

Echinacea

Summer Joy

For this echinacea flower, I used a little wax resist to emphasize the petal shapes. The inclusion of the lovely butterfly helps to bring the painting to life.

Bumblebee

Bees are very important pollinators and the unsung heroines of the natural world. This project is dedicated to this amazing insect by capturing it in flight in a loose colourful style with Brusho. We can paint this fuzzy bumblebee using just three Brusho colours.

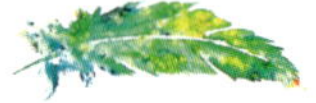

YOU WILL NEED

· Bockingford watercolour paper
300gsm (140lb) Not surface,
half imperial (38 x 56cm/15 x 22in)

· 3B pencil

· Eraser

· Black waterproof pen

· Brusho paint: sunburst lemon, brilliant red, black

· Size 8 brush

· Spray bottle with water

· Kitchen paper

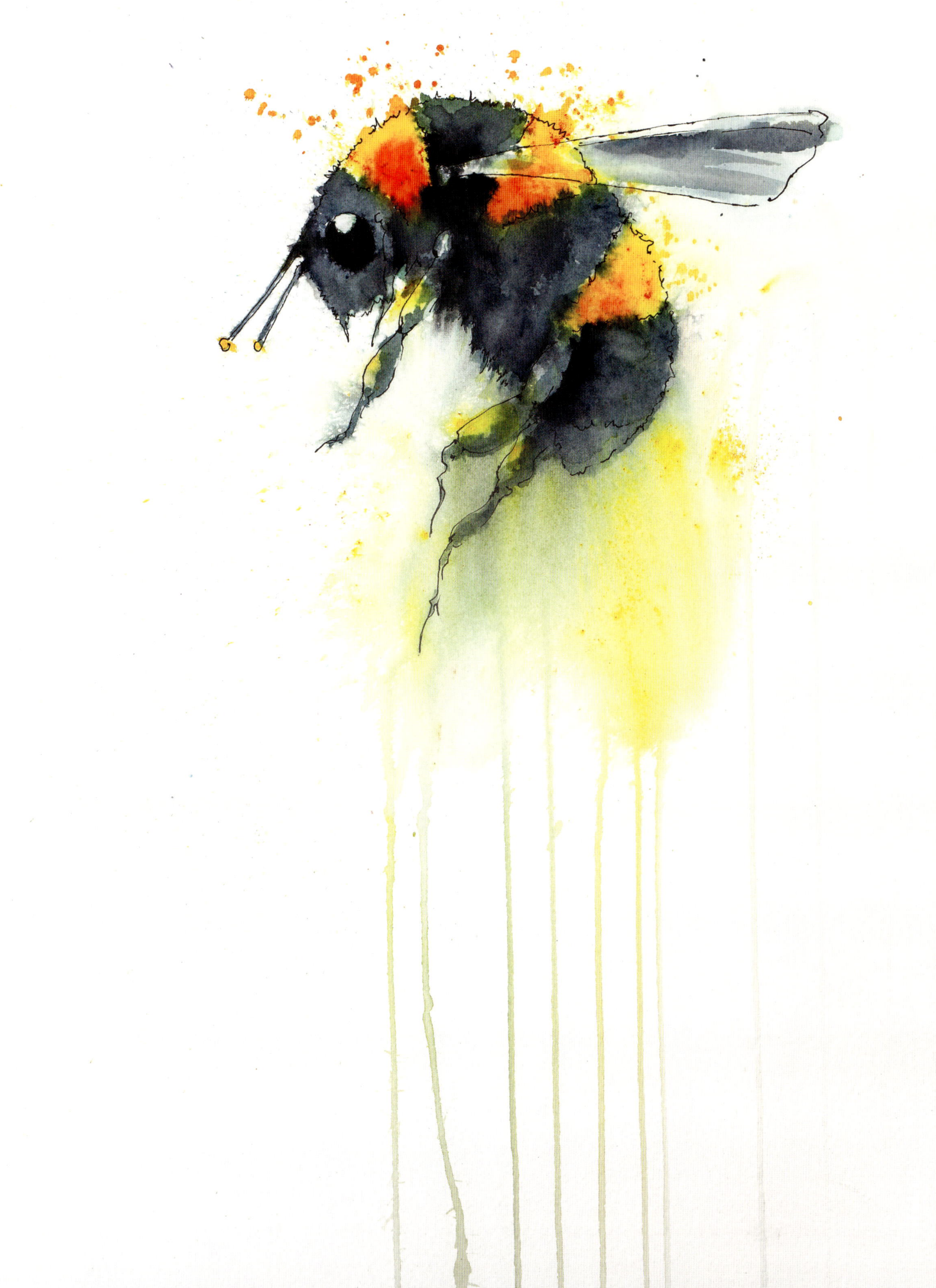

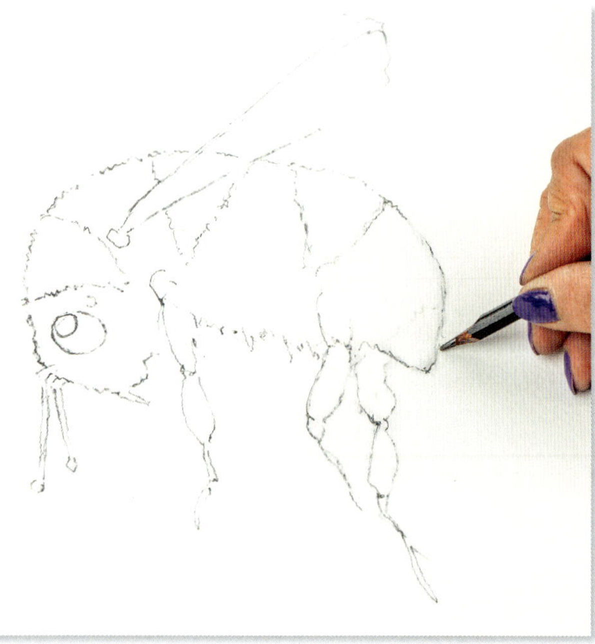

1 Using a soft pencil, start with a nice loose drawing, keeping details to a minimum.

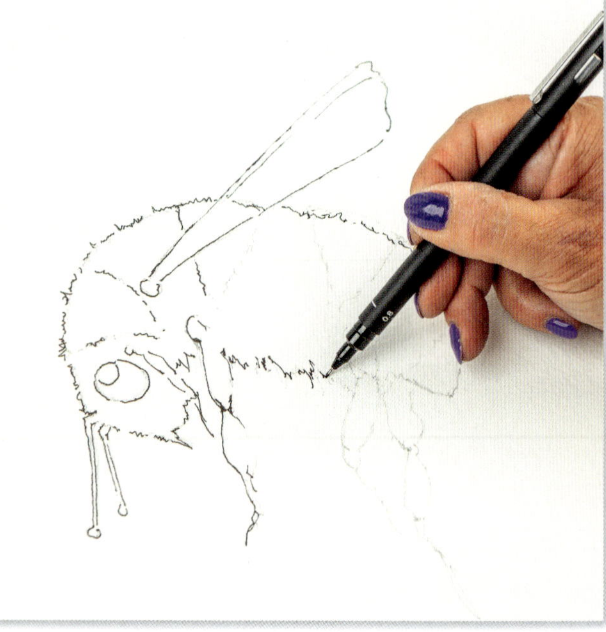

2 Using a black waterproof pen, go over your pencil drawing. Once the ink is dry, use an eraser to remove the pencil lines.

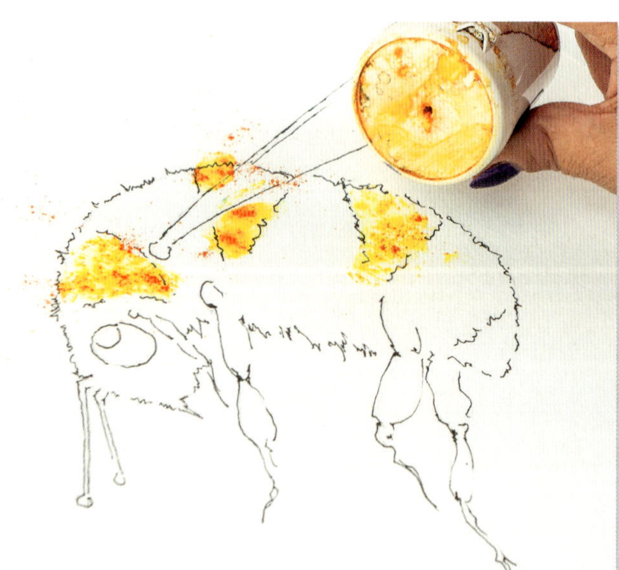

3 Wet the areas of paper that you want to be yellow and sprinkle the sunburst lemon into this area. Don't worry if the yellow decides to jump out of this area – in fact, these little areas of colour can be spritzed later on to create a bit of life and movement. Add some yellow to the legs to suggest the pollen the bee has collected.

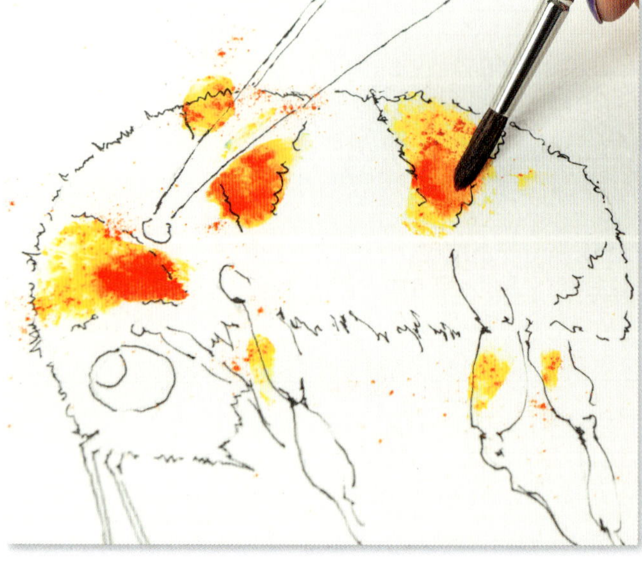

4 Drop a touch of the brilliant red wash into the yellow while the yellow wash is still wet.

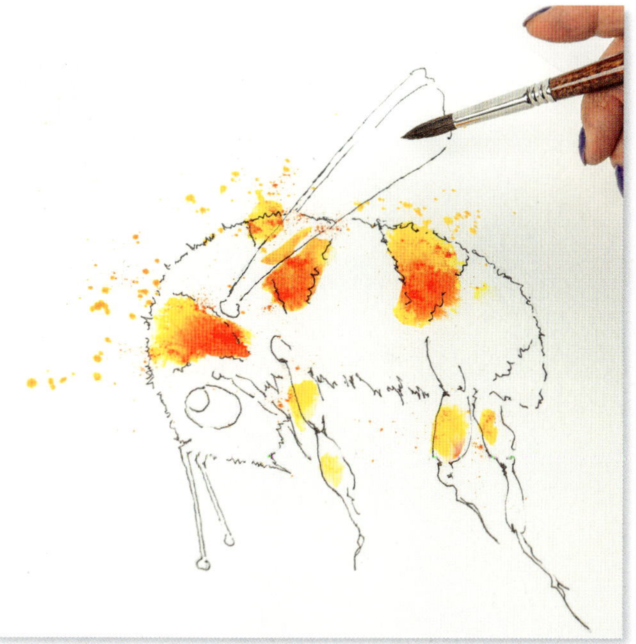

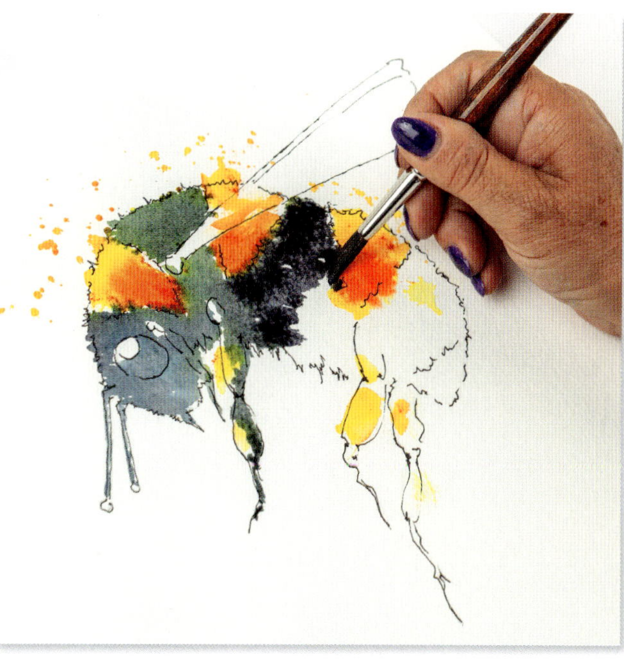

5 Using the same yellow wash, tap a few spatters at the top of the bumblebee to indicate lots of pollen flying around. Allow to dry thoroughly.

6 Make a black wash in the palette and paint the black areas of the bee, starting with the head and working around and down the body, painting around the yellow areas. Leave the white highlight of the eye area blank – you can wax it if you like. We will make this much darker at a later stage. Leave the wing area blank.

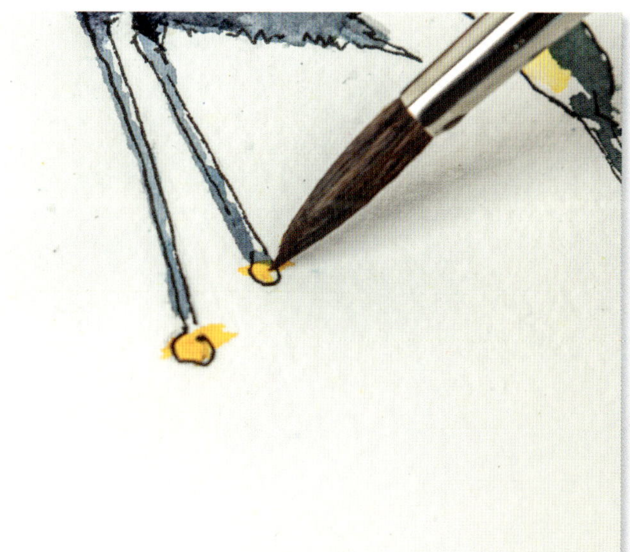

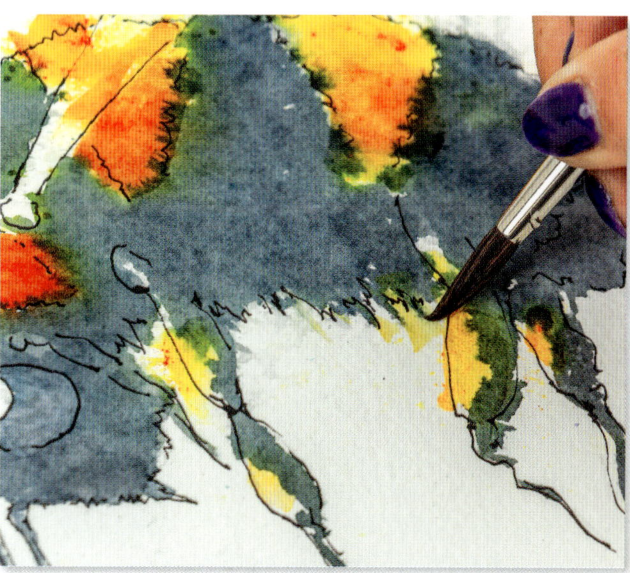

7 Add in a yellow dot to each of the antennae with your sunburst lemon wash.

8 Use the point of your brush to pull out some little shapes to give your bee a fuzzy appearance. Don't worry about keeping your paint within the lines. The advantage of a line and wash painting is that the lines hold the painting together visually even if the paint creeps outside.

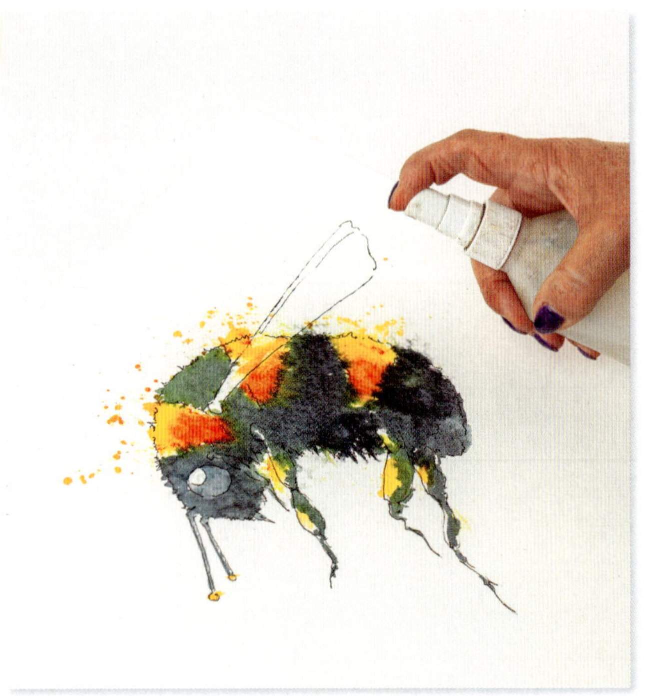

9 Spritz your bee with water.

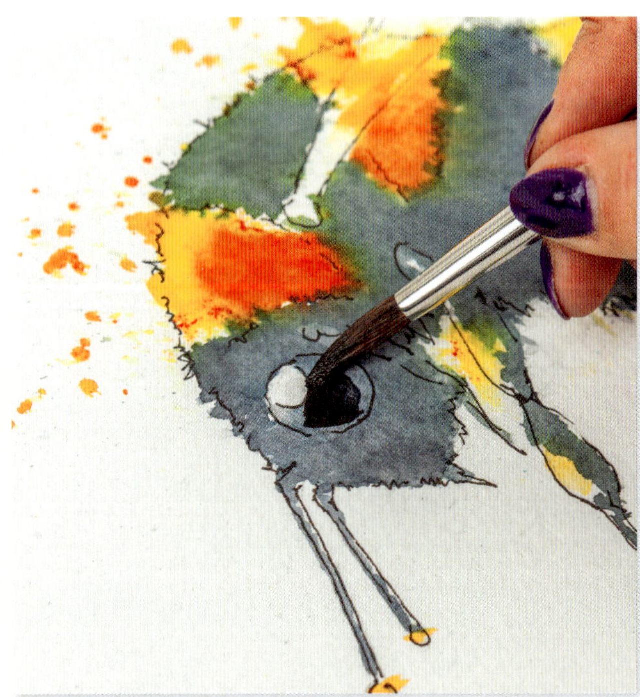

11 Using a black wash, add details starting with the eye. Make this darker than the black body colour so it will stand out, but remember to keep a little white highlight.

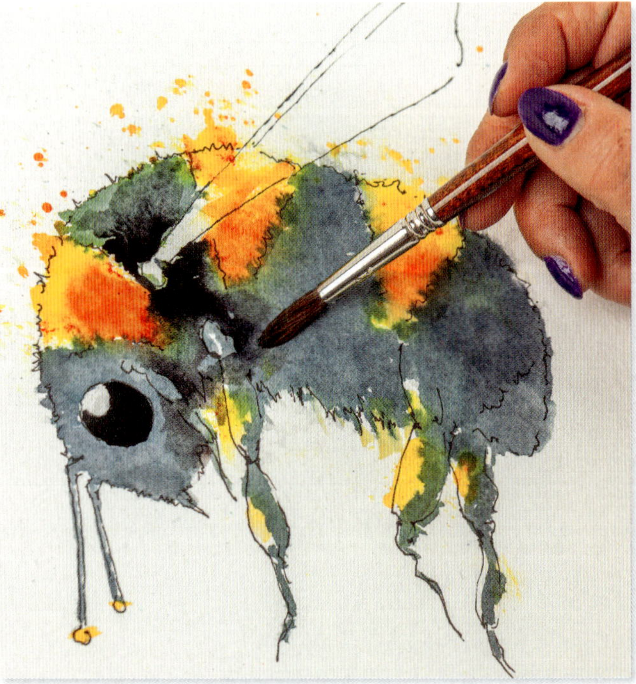

10 Blot with kitchen paper to remove any excess water.

12 Using the same black wash, darken some areas and then wet the area with your brush to blend the colour.

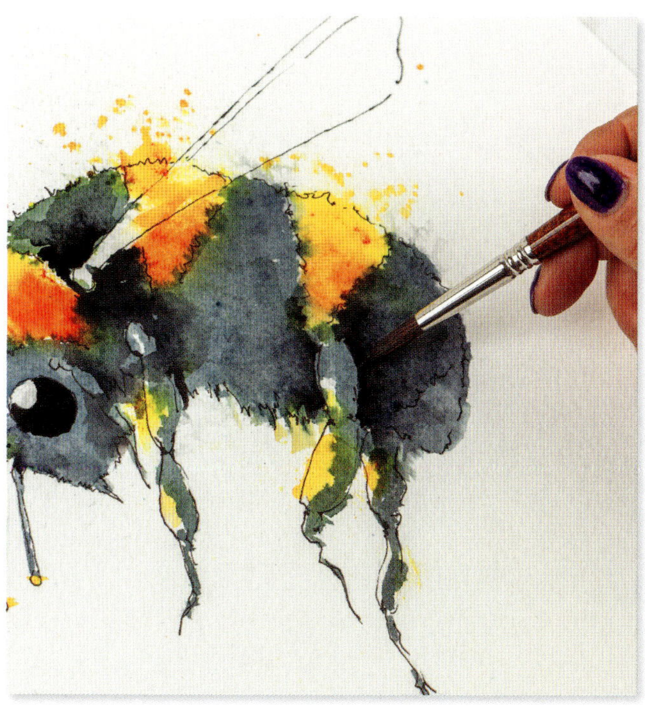

13 Continue building up the darker areas.

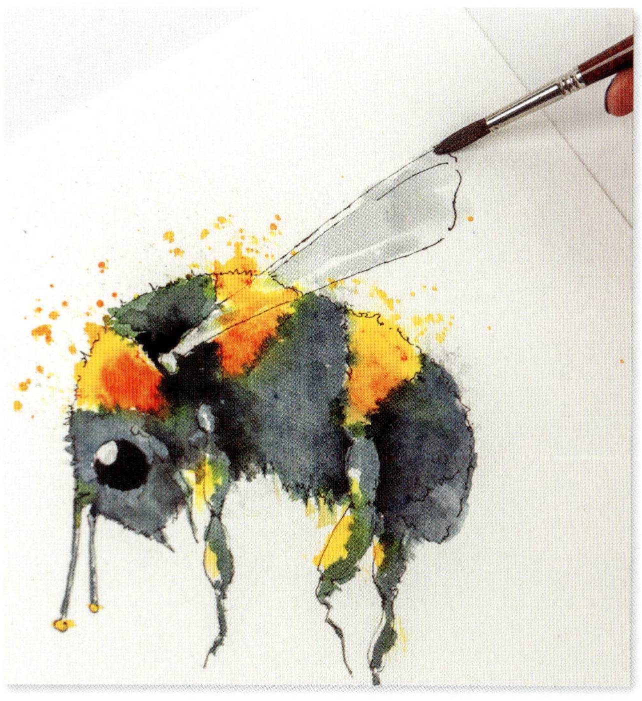

14 Add more water to your black wash to paint the lighter area of the wing. Let this dry.

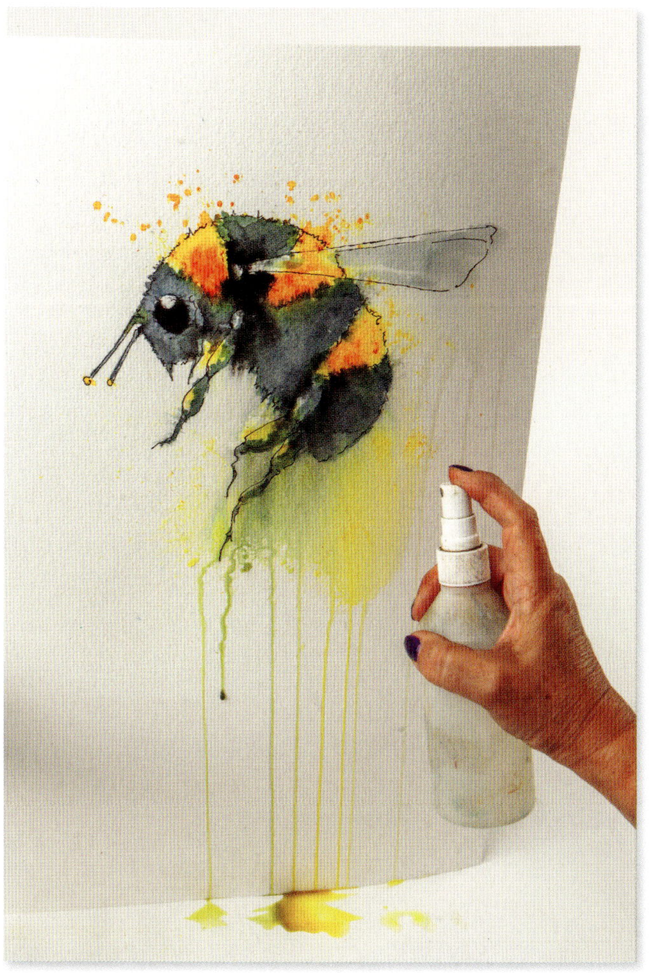

15 If you wish to add more yellow sprinkles around your bee, carefully tap out the sunburst lemon crystals around the bee's bottom and give them a spritz. Don't aim the spray at the bee's body, you don't want him to disappear! Remember to set your spray bottle to a fine mist rather than a direct spray. Hold the paper vertically, allowing the paint to run down the page. Allow to dry.

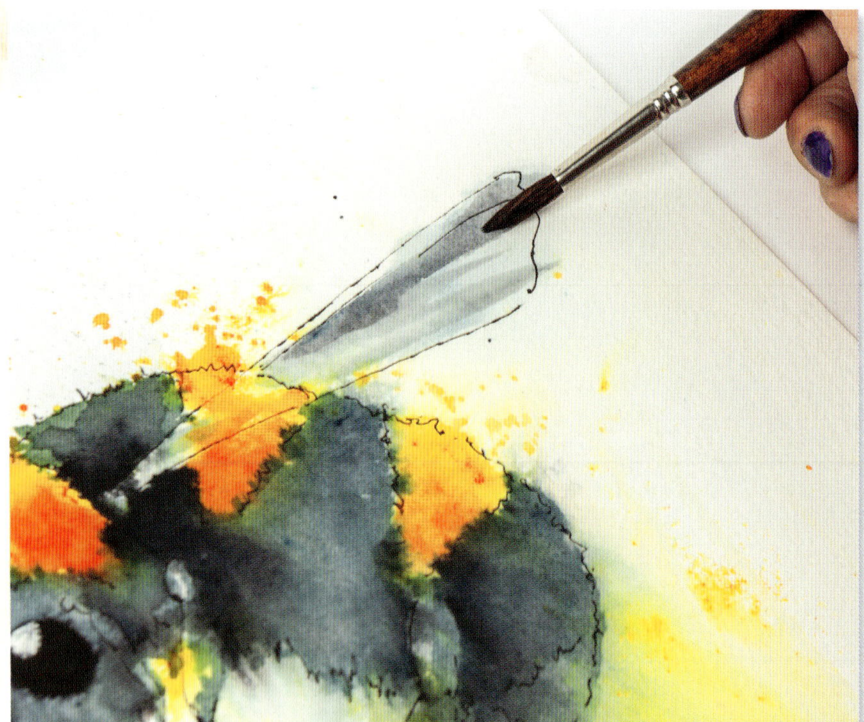

16 My bee needs more dark in the wing area. Use the black wash in your palette for this.

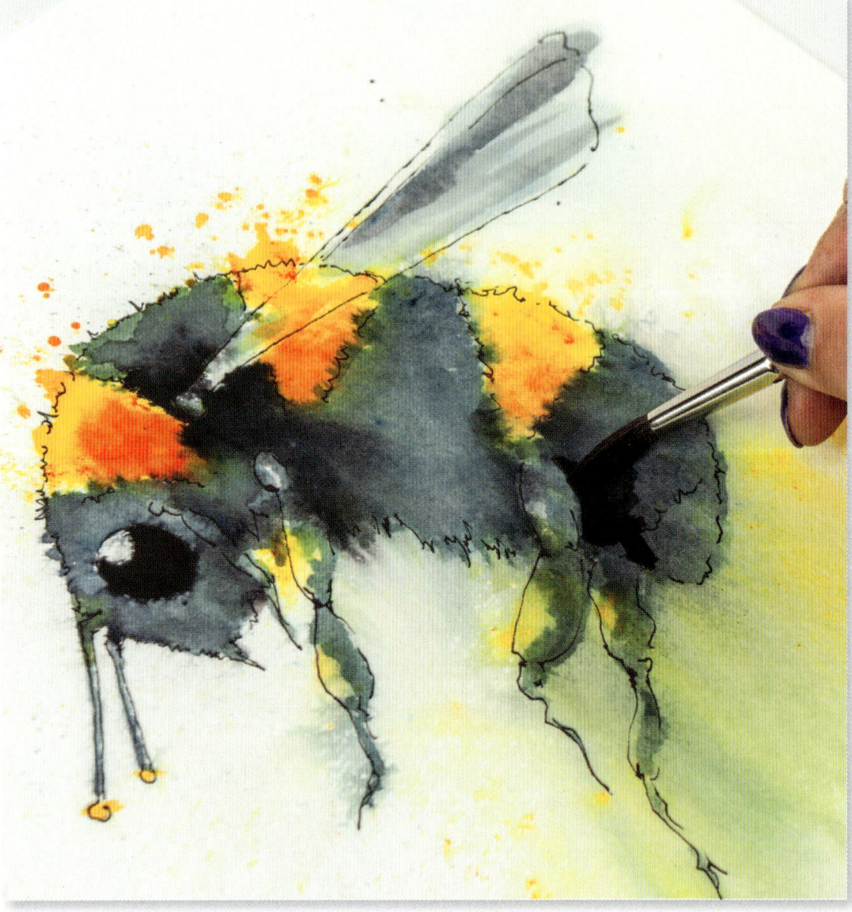

17 Use the wash to redefine any areas lost through zealous spritzing!

Polperro Harbour, Cornwall, UK

Brusho is a suitable medium for any subject matter including landscapes. This charming painting of Polperro Harbour is so well suited to the Brusho line and wash technique.

I applied my ink drawing first before adding Brusho washes of colour. The vibrant Brusho colour washes brought my drawing to life and I added a touch of my sprinkle and spray technique in the foreground to suggest the rocks, steps and harbour wall.

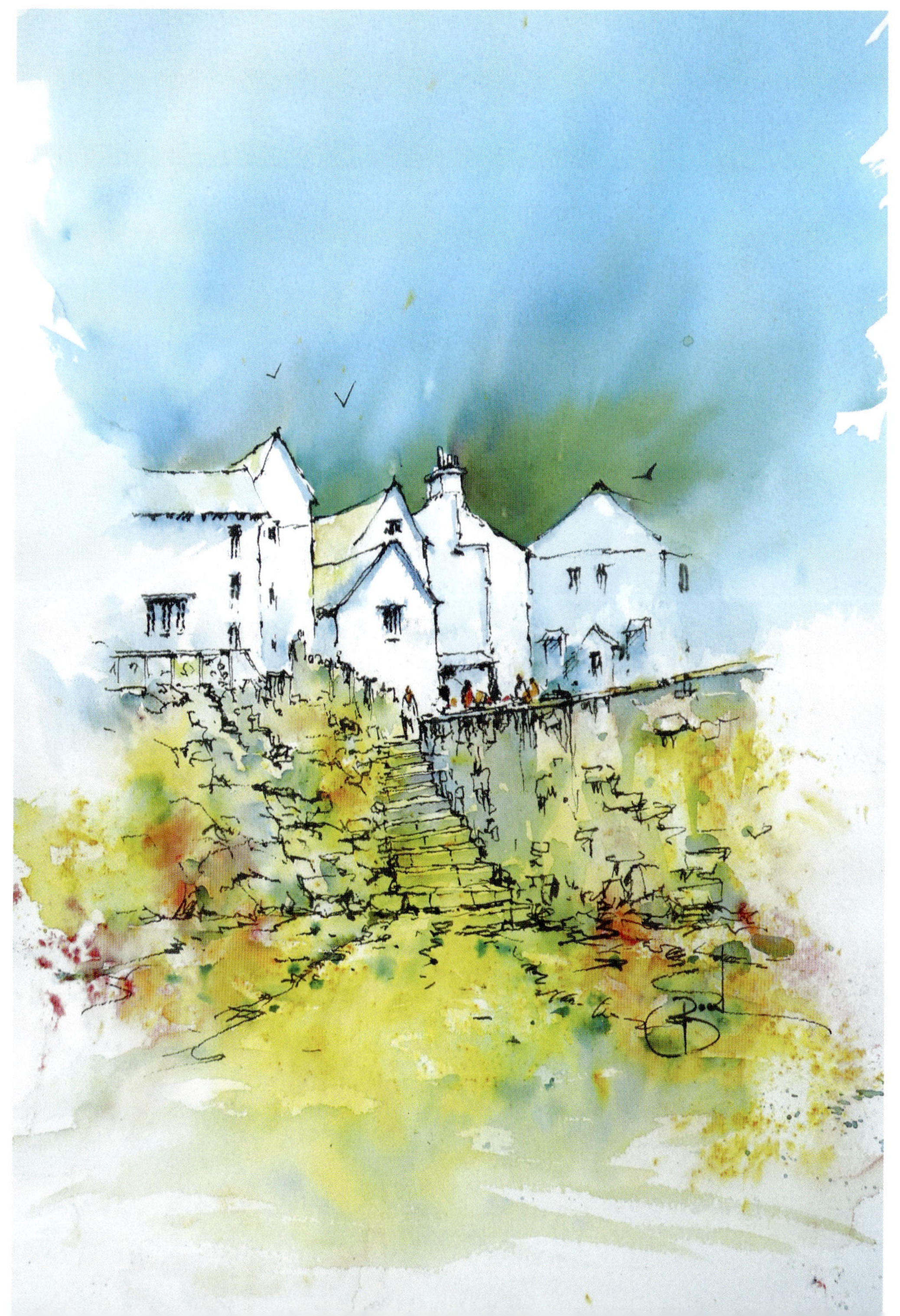

Palm Trees

Using Brusho allows us to paint a beautiful sunset with colourful palm trees. We will be using techniques you are now familiar with such as sprinkling Brusho onto wet paper and using smooth Brusho washes of colour, almost like a watercolour wash.

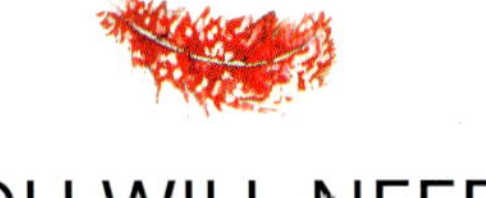

YOU WILL NEED

· Pad of Bockingford watercolour paper
300gsm (140lb) Not surface 14.8 x 42cm (5¾ x 16½in)

· 3B pencil

· Eraser

· Brusho paint: sunburst lemon, scarlet, ultramarine blue

· Size 8 brush

· Sword brush or rigger

· Jug of clean water

· Kitchen paper

Tip

It is very easy to become overenthusiastic and shake out far too much Brusho powder. Remember to tap out just a small amount of Brusho and wait for a few minutes. You can always add more if you think that your painting needs it.

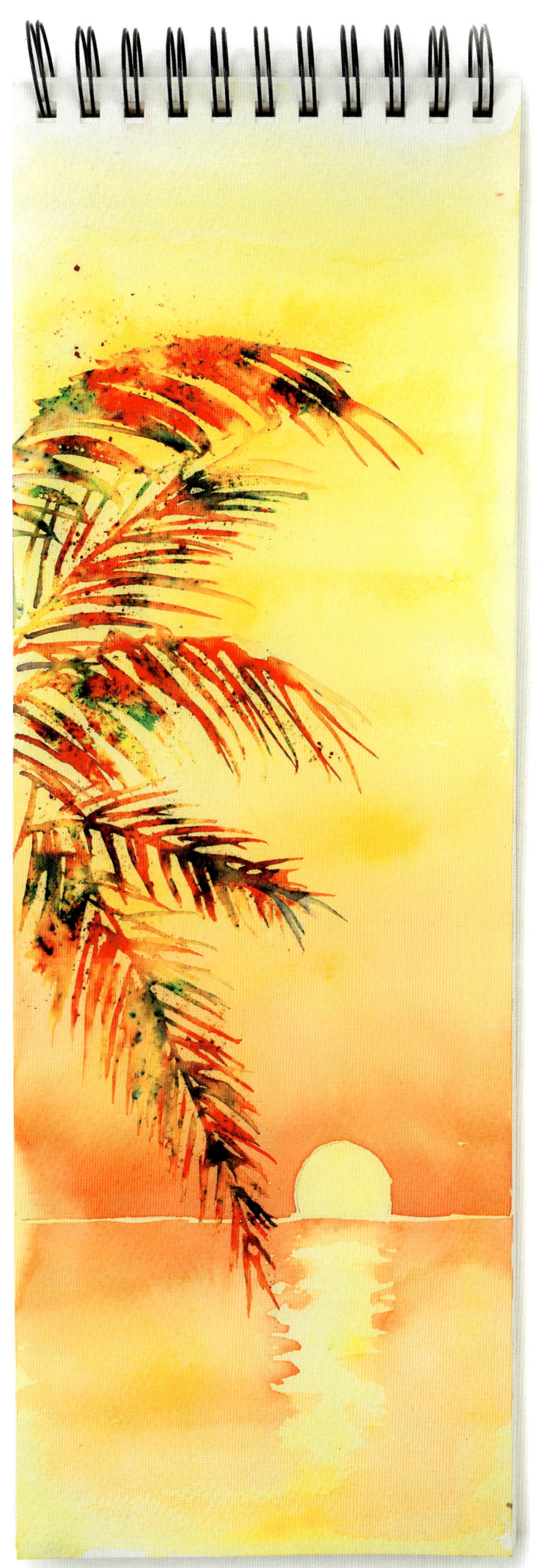

Palm Trees

1 Draw a simple pencil line for the horizon. Draw around a Brusho pot to create a semicircle above the horizon for the sun.

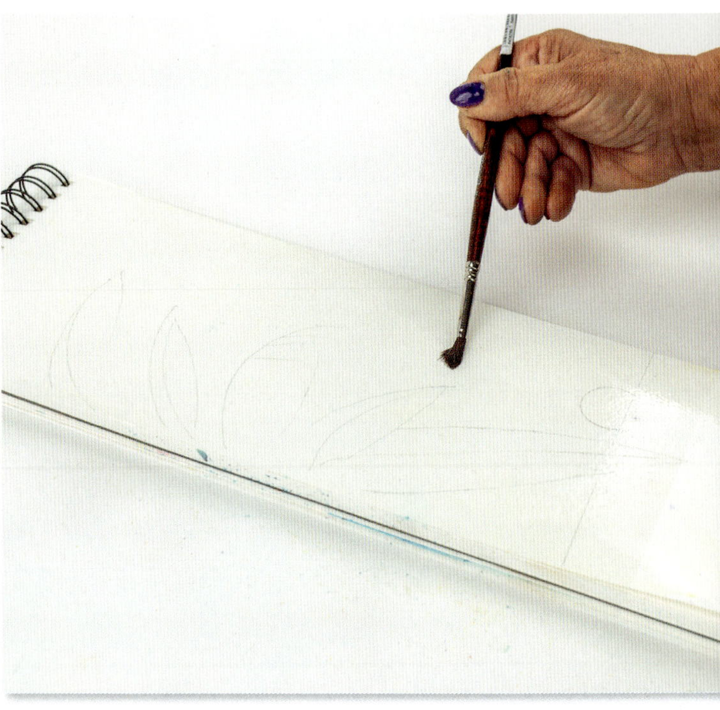

2 Basic shapes can indicate where you would like your palm tree fronds. It is impossible to sketch every frond, not to mention a lot of work! Using your size 8 brush or a spray bottle, wet the whole page with clean water.

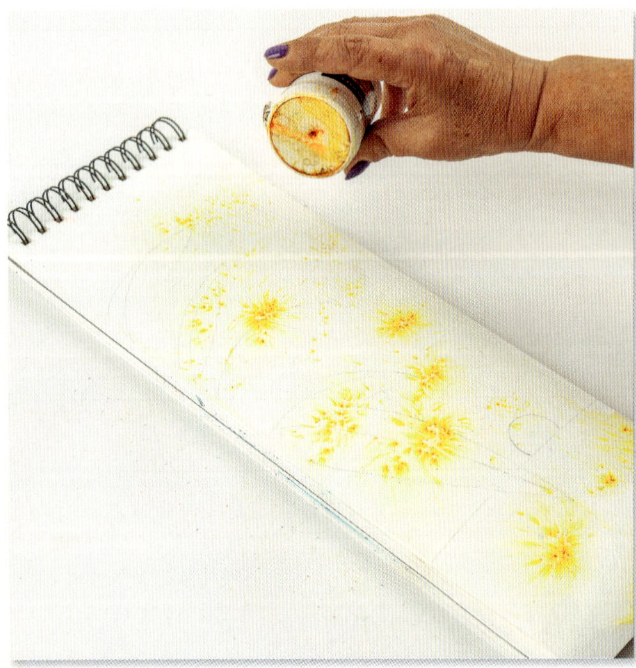

3 Sprinkle in the sunburst lemon.

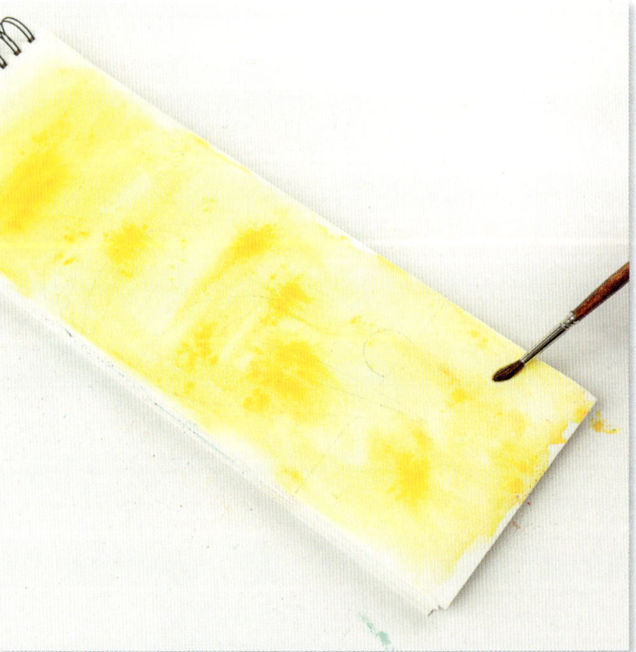

4 Smooth it in with your brush. Allow to dry.

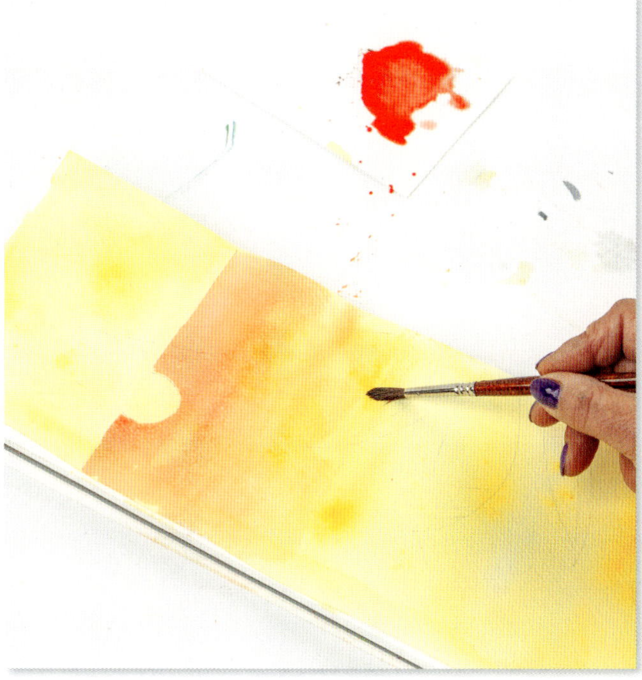

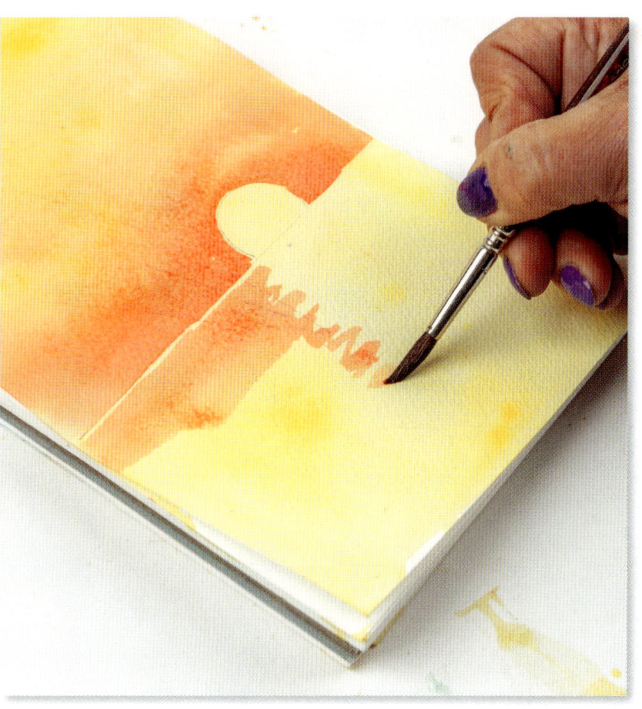

5 Rotate your pad. Mix a large watery wash of scarlet on your scrap paper. Starting at the horizon line, paint around the sun shape and soften the orange wash into the yellow sky by using a brush loaded with clean water to create a graduated wash.

6 Turn your pad back the right way. Leaving a slight gap below the horizon line, paint the reflection of the sunset using the scarlet wash and smooth it out with clean water on your brush. Allow to dry.

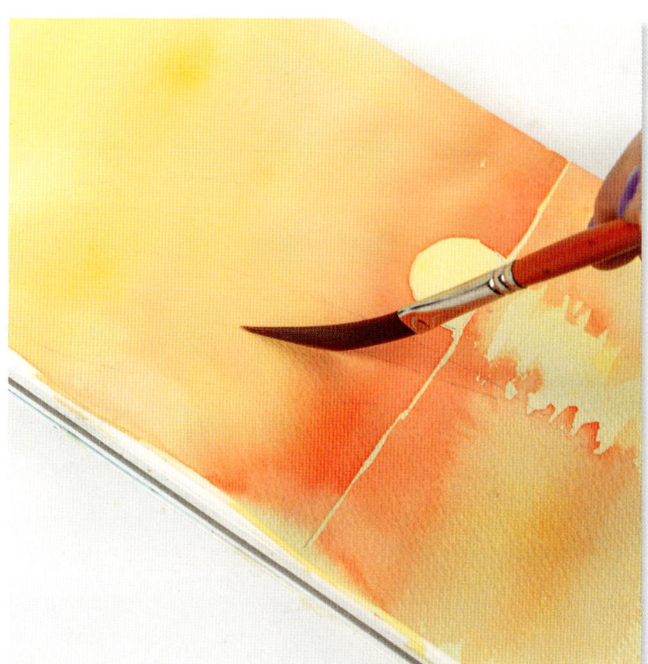

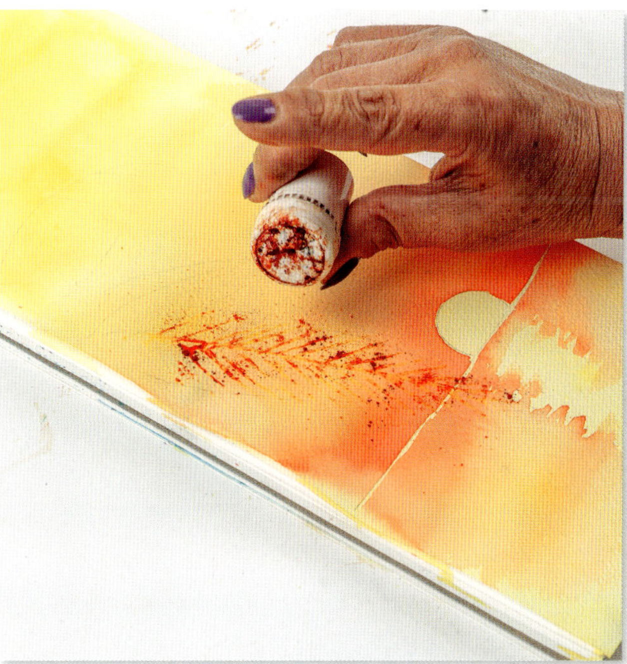

7 Now for the fun bit! Using your sword brush or rigger and clean water, wet the palm tree fronds starting at the bottom; just two to start with.

8 Sprinkle scarlet and sunburst lemon into this wet area. The colours should explode following the contours of the water.

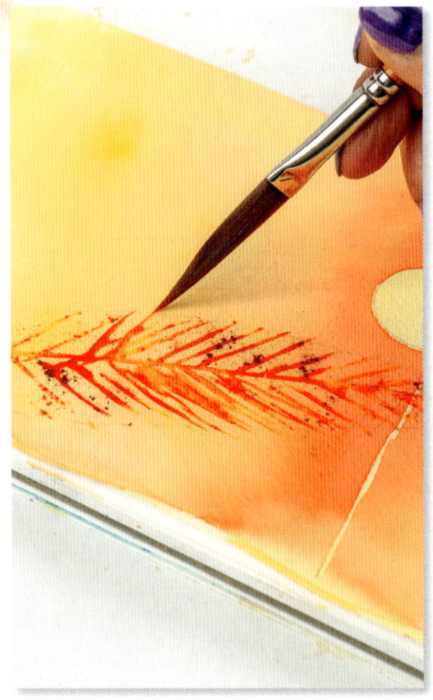

9 Use the tip of your wet brush to reactivate the paint.

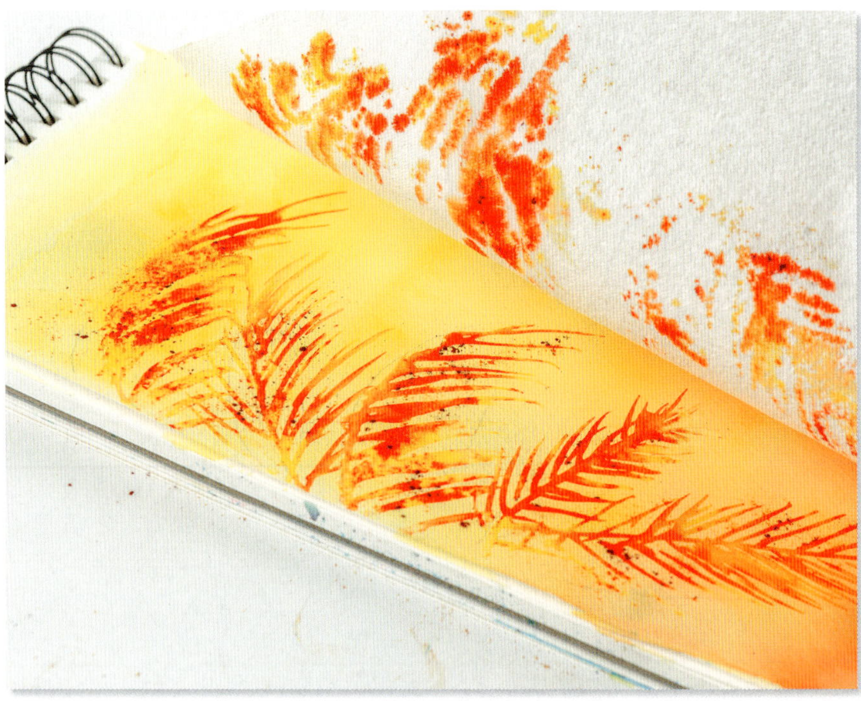

10 Blot your washes with kitchen paper.

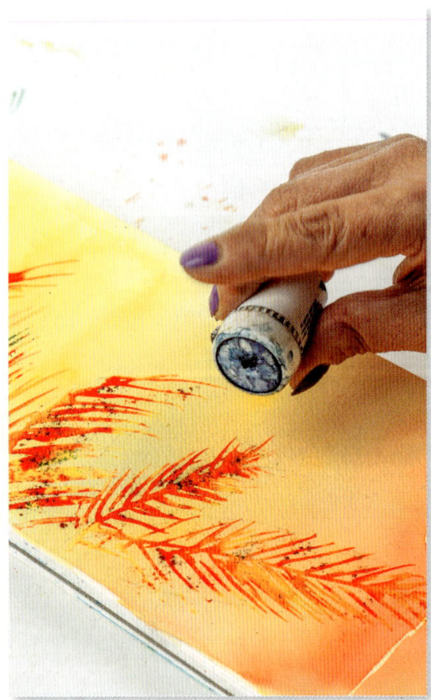

11 Finally, sprinkle the ultramarine blue to give you a combination of the three colours.

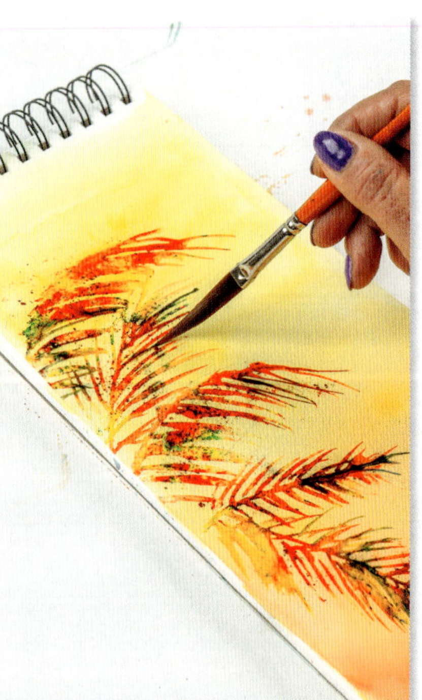

12 Use your clean brush and water to accentuate the fronds.

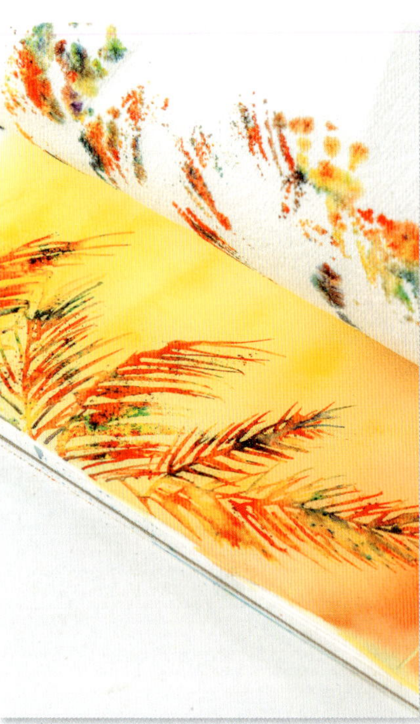

13 If you find that your colours are a little strong, place a piece of kitchen paper over the top and press down into the wet area, then lift off carefully.

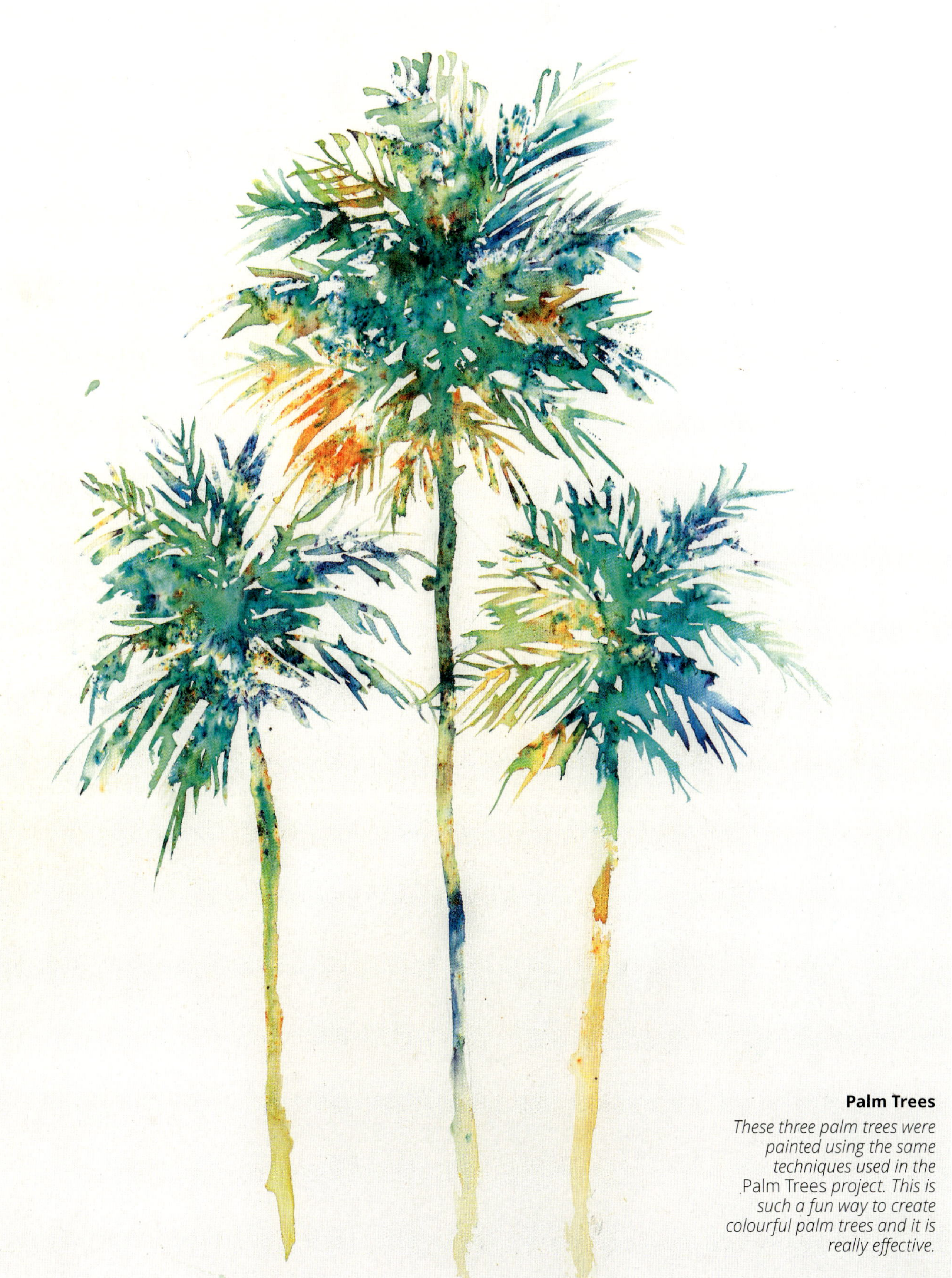

Palm Trees

These three palm trees were painted using the same techniques used in the Palm Trees project. This is such a fun way to create colourful palm trees and it is really effective.

Elephant

In this project we will paint a magnificent elephant using just three Brusho colours, a black waterproof pen and some wax resist to create highlights. Your painting requires very little detail as we will create an explosion of colour over the top of the ink drawing, with soft washes of darker Brusho bringing this majestic animal to life. No two elephant paintings will look the same, so you are guaranteed to produce a painting that is unique to you.

YOU WILL NEED

- Bockingford watercolour paper 300gsm (140lb) Not surface, half imperial (38 x 56cm/15 x 22in)
- 3B pencil
- Eraser
- Black waterproof pen
- Brusho paint: cobalt blue, alizarin crimson, sunburst lemon
- Size 8 brush
- White ink or acrylic
- Jug of clean water
- Spray bottle with water
- Palette
- Wax crayon or candle wax
- Bleach solution – 50% bleach: 50% water
- Old brush for bleach
- Kitchen paper

Tip

I am using three primary colours for this project. You can experiment with any red, any blue and any yellow to give a different effect.

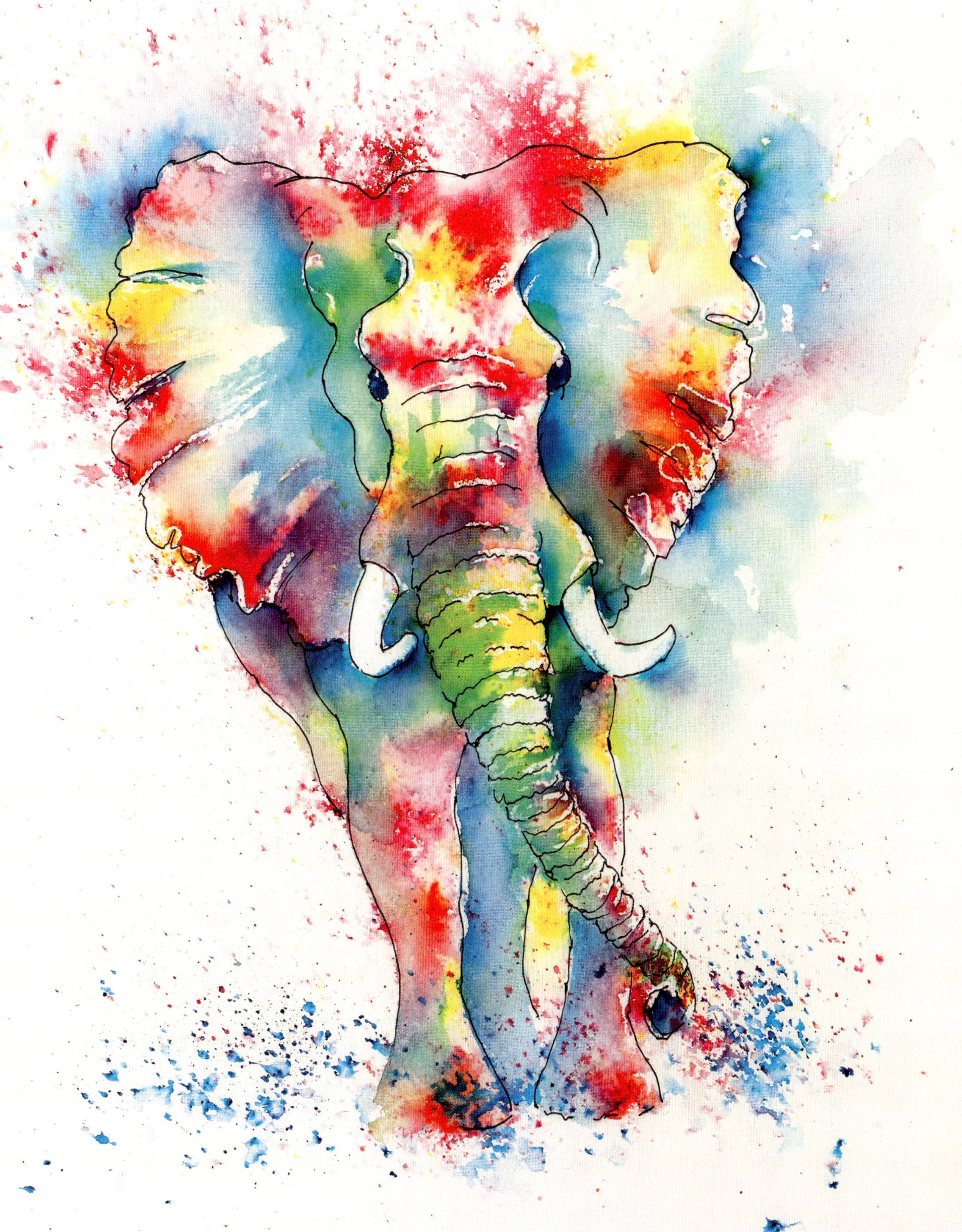

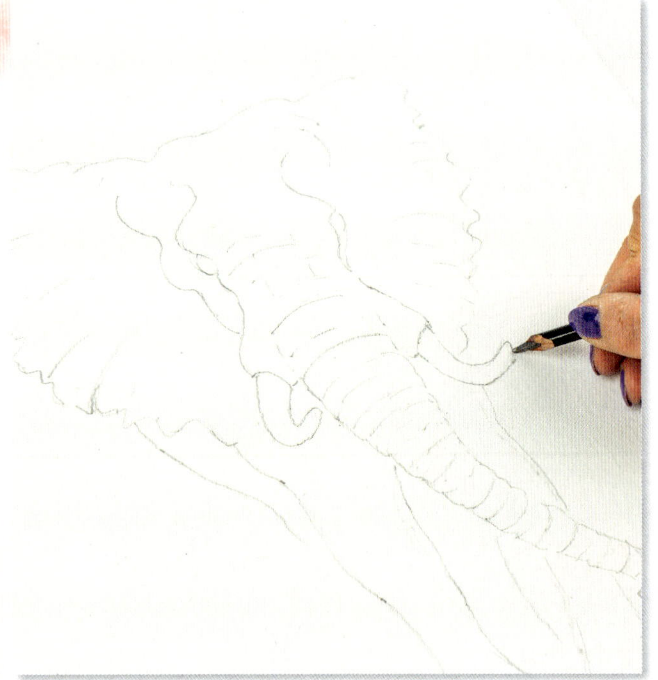

1 Create a very loose pencil drawing without any details.

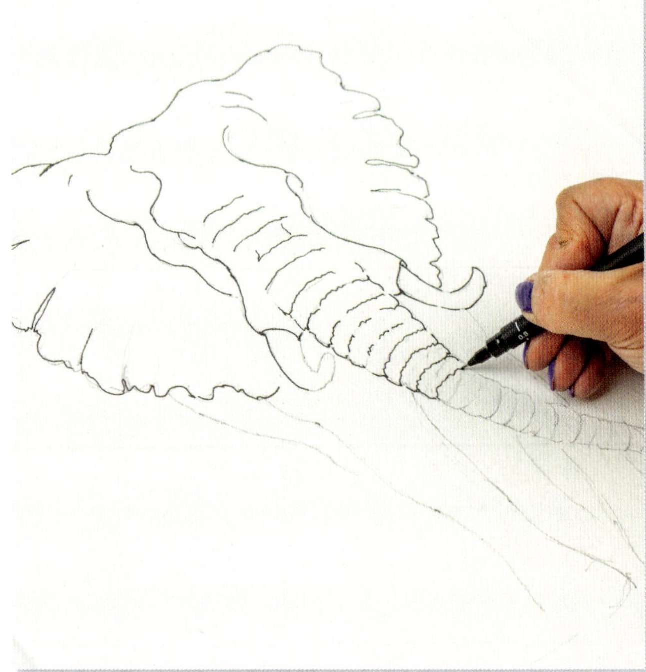

2 Using a black waterproof pen, go over your pencil drawing. Try to make bold, confident marks to suggest the shape of the elephant. Once the ink is dry, use an eraser to remove the pencil lines underneath.

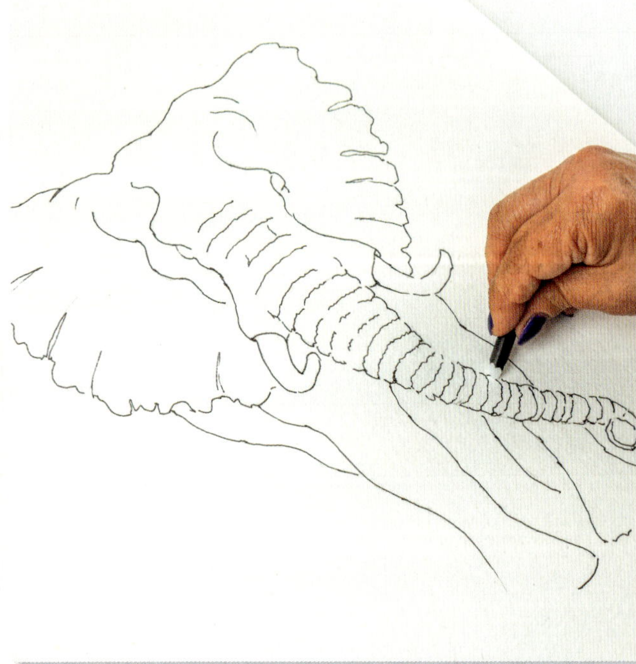

3 Apply wax to the areas of your painting where you would like to introduce a bit of sparkle, especially those lovely, curved lights on the long trunk.

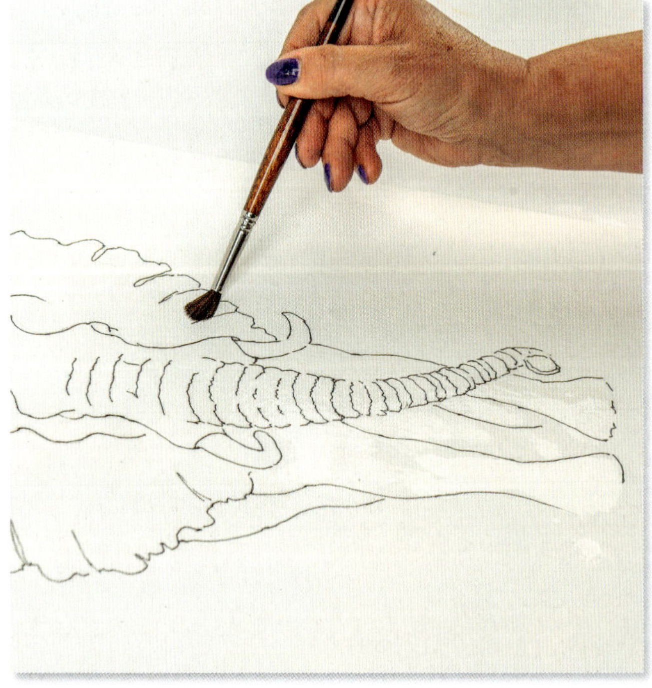

4 Wet the elephant all over using your brush.

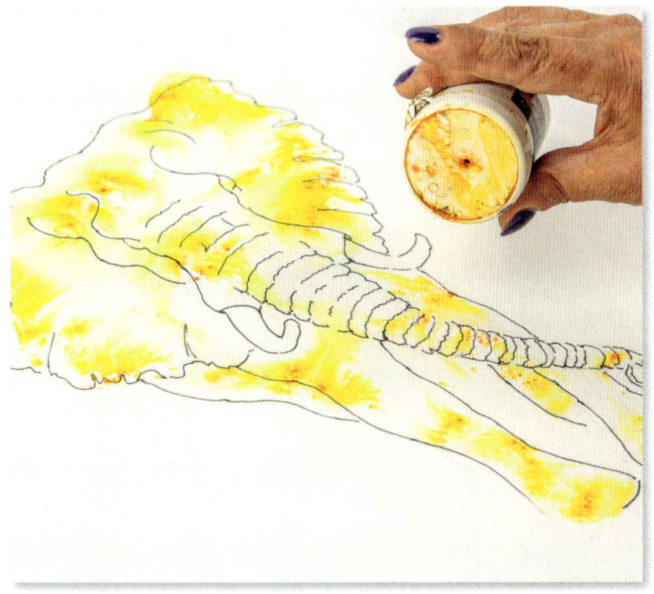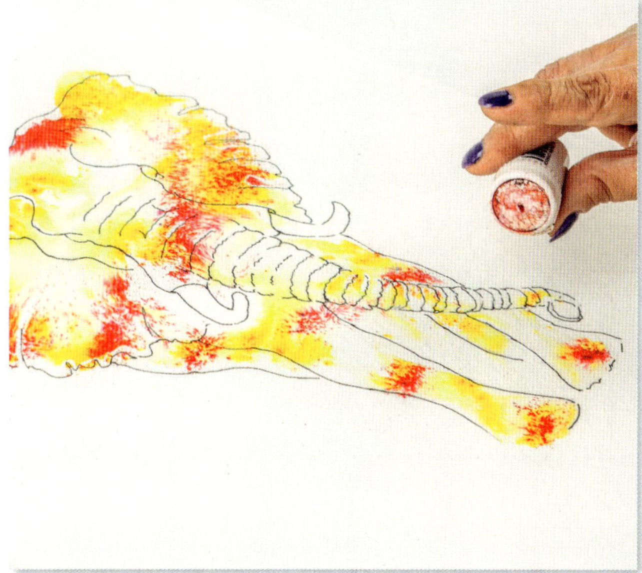

5 Sprinkle the sunburst lemon randomly onto the wet paper. You don't need to be precise; in fact I would encourage you to let your colour explode outside the lines and not to confine it within the elephant outline. Don't worry about painting neatly around the tusks as a little bleach will lift the colour away later.

6 Repeat with the alizarin crimson.

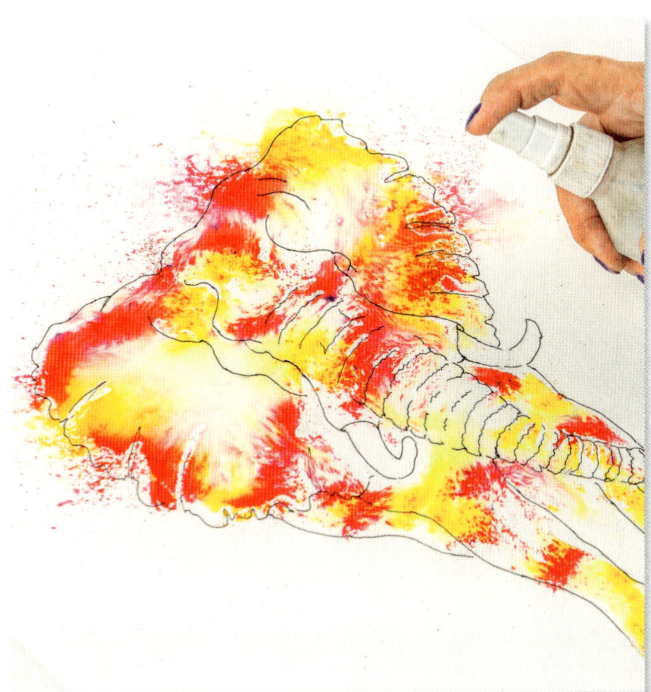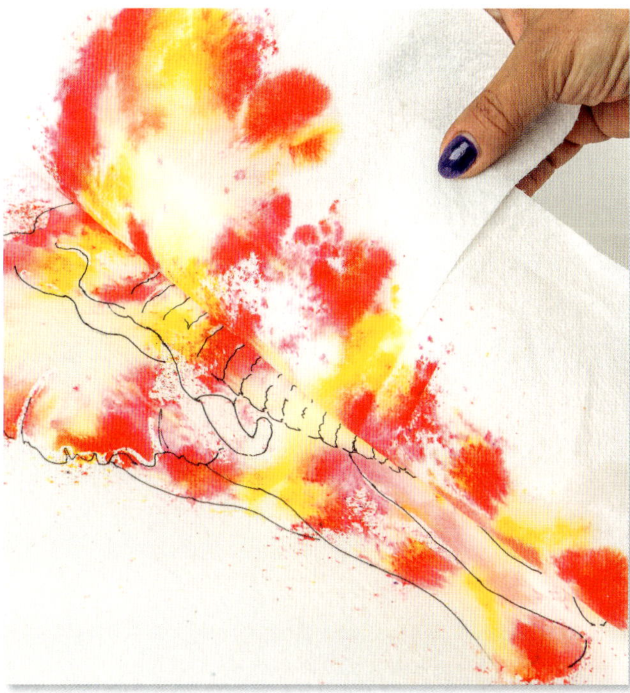

7 Spray clean water over the powder paint to encourage the colour to spread.

8 Pat with kitchen paper to mop up any excess paint, then leave the paper to dry.

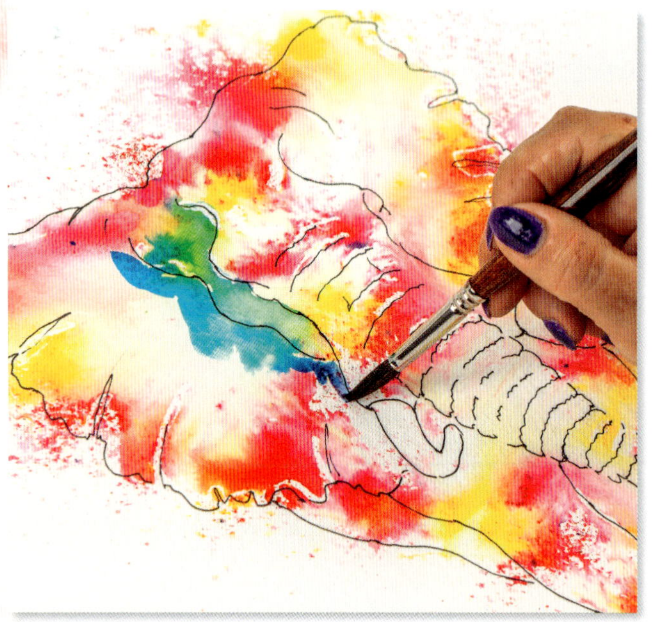

9 Using the cobalt blue, mix a stronger wash in your palette and start to define the darker areas of the elephant, especially around the ears and trunk. When you apply your wet brush to the dry pigment on your paper, the water on your brush will reactivate the dry colour, so you will see secondary colours appear: for example the blue and the yellow will create areas of green.

10 Use your brush to soften the colours radiating out from the trunk on the left-hand side. Avoid rubbing the colours together otherwise they will go muddy. Let the colours blend themselves on the paper.

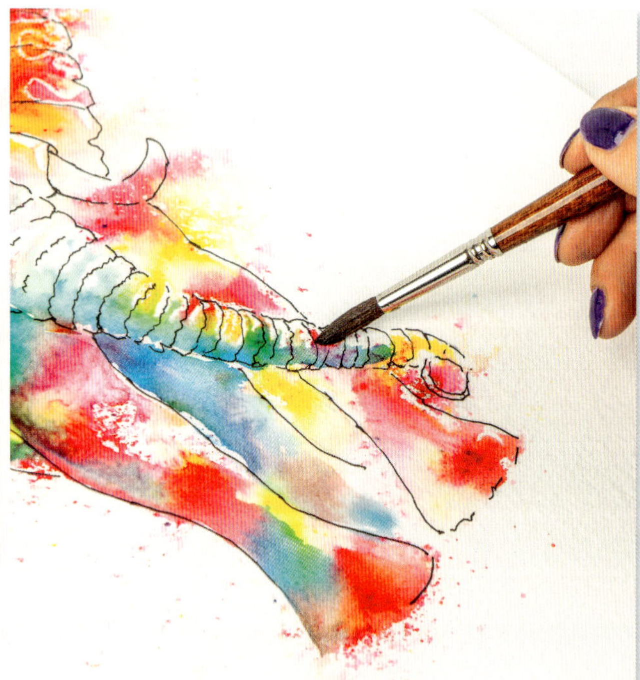

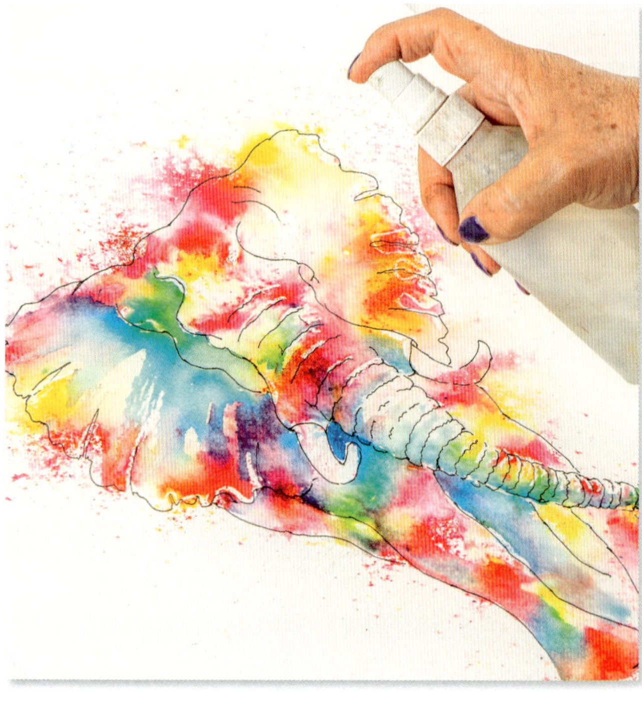

11 Continue with the cobalt blue down the trunk, adding value to the trunk itself.

12 Spray with water over the area you have just painted.

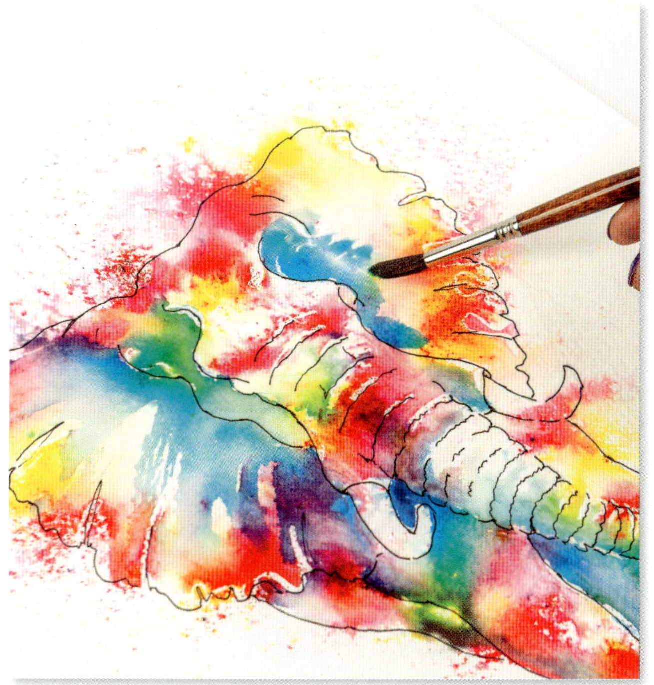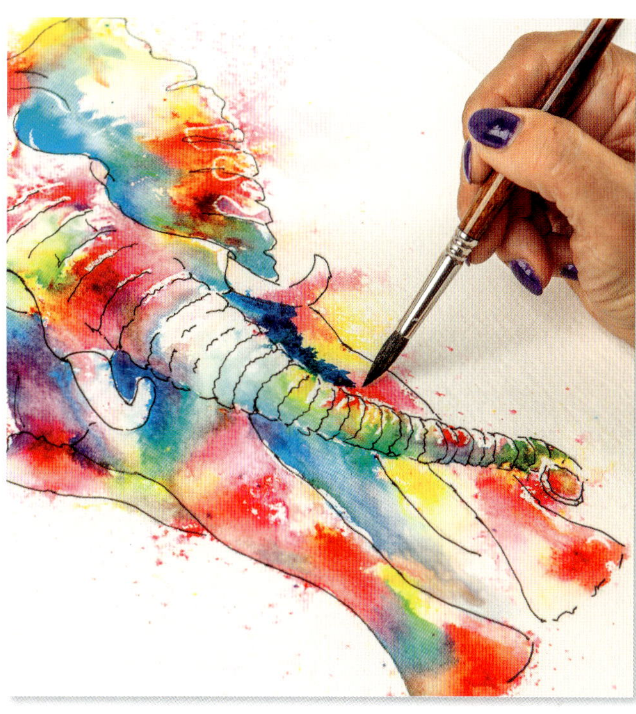

13 Continue adding cobalt blue to the other ear and around the head.

14 Using a darker wash of cobalt blue, paint the other side of the trunk.

15 Spray the right-hand side as you did for the left side.

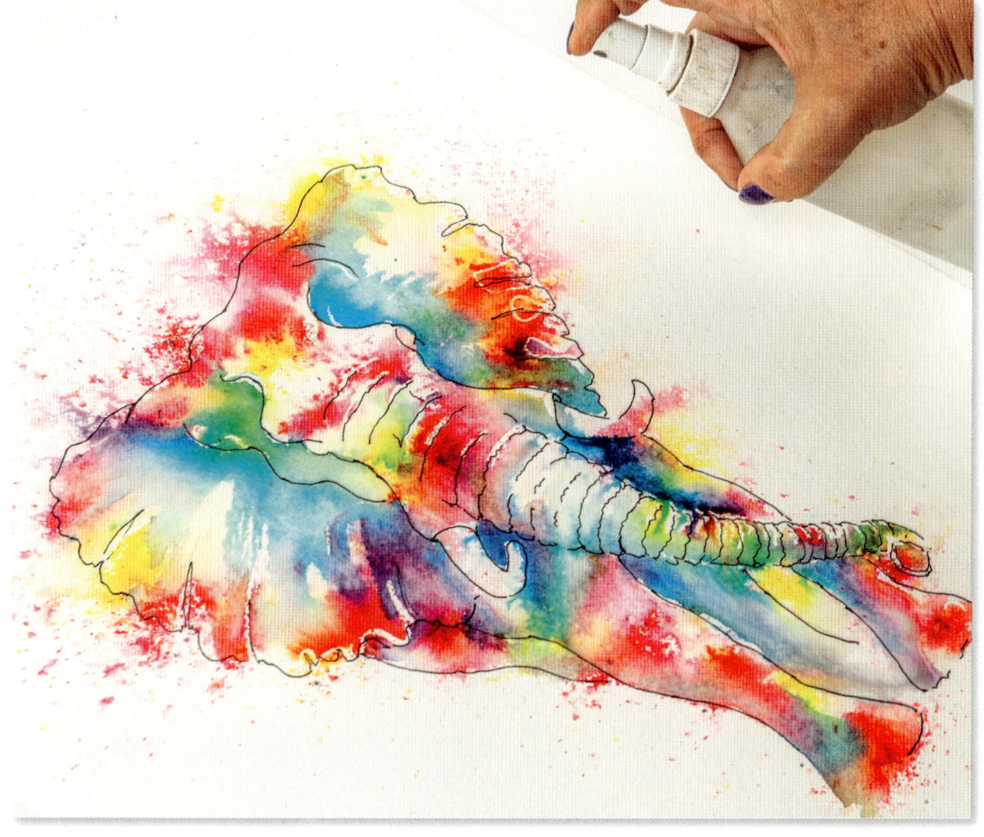

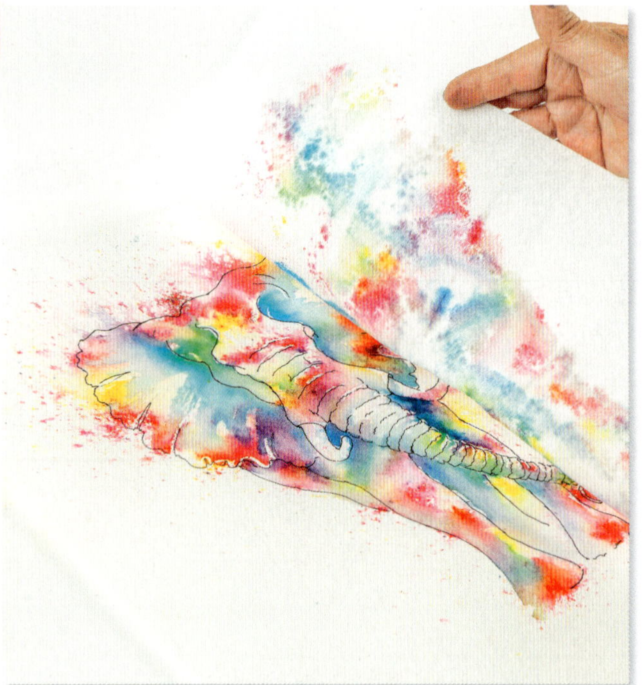

16 Blot the page with kitchen paper.

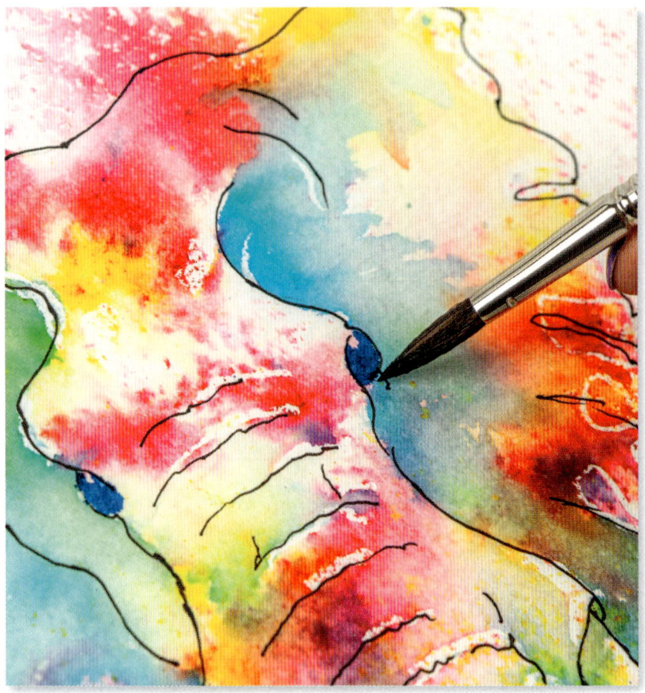

17 Add stronger darks for the eyes using the same cobalt blue.

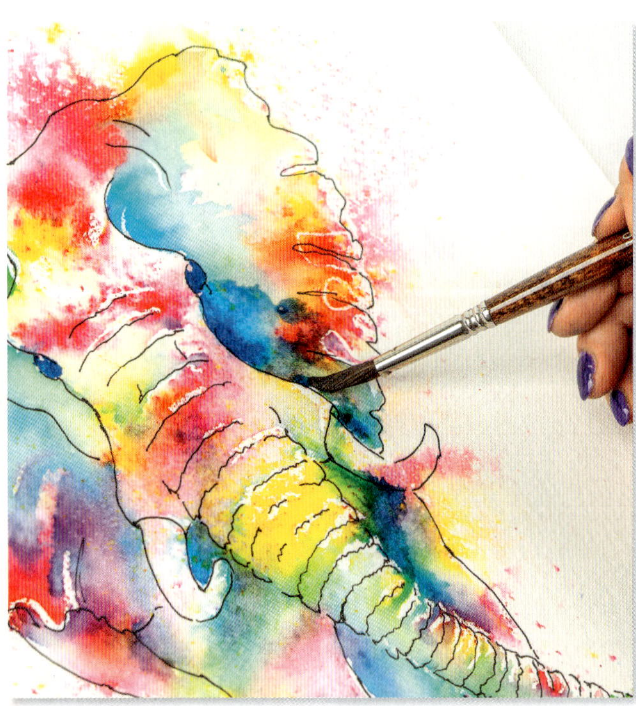

18 Also add this stronger wash underneath the eye to emphasize the trunk.

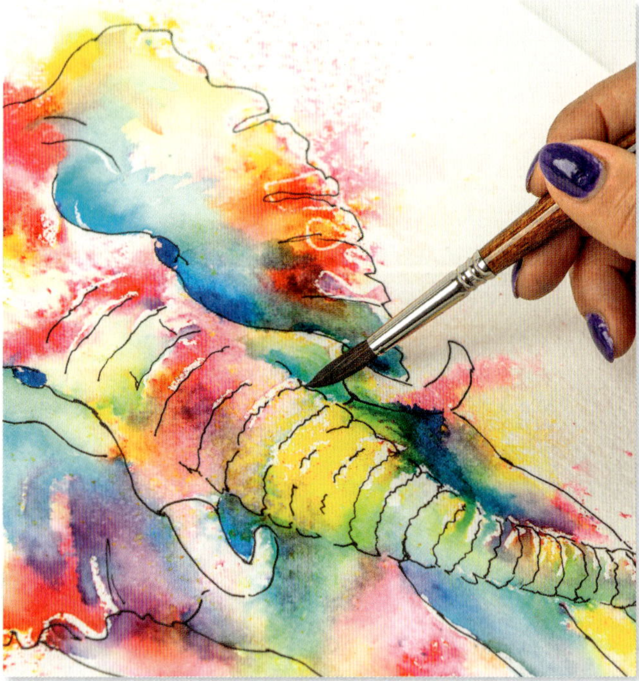

19 Add a dark value on the inside of the trunk to make it stand out.

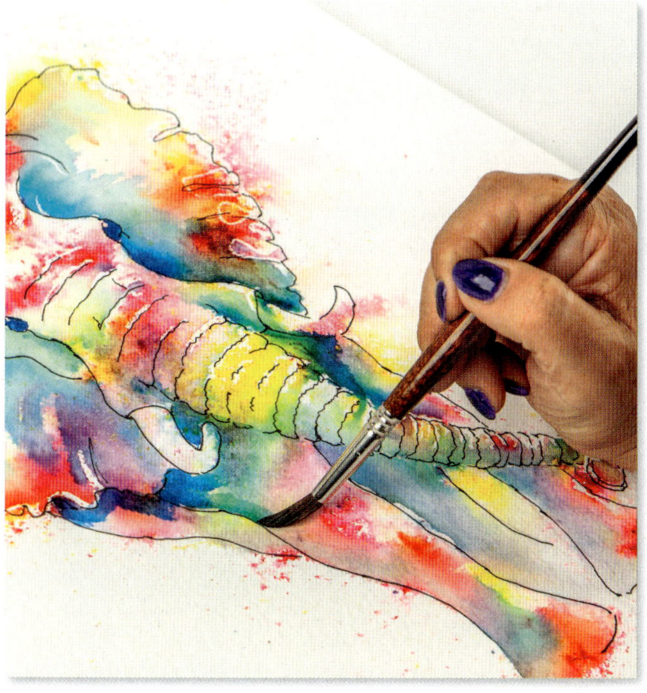

20 Add a little dark pigment underneath the left ear too.

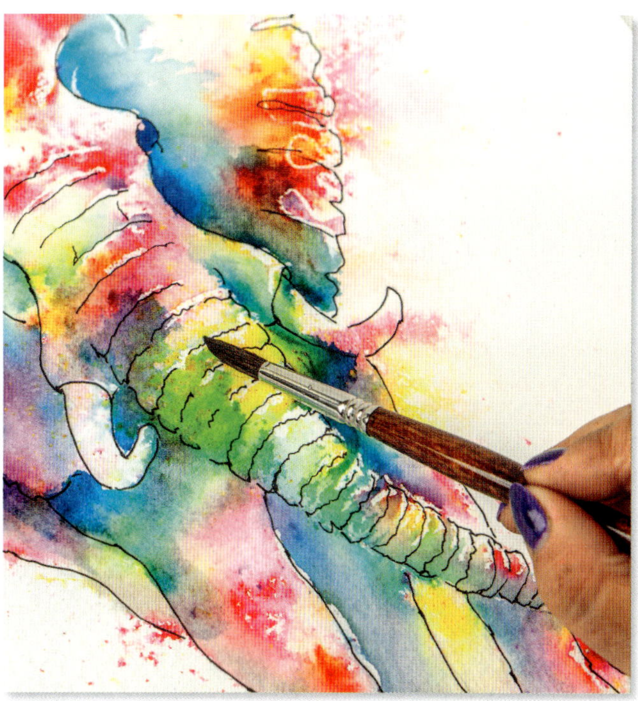

21 Add a bit more depth of colour across the middle of the trunk.

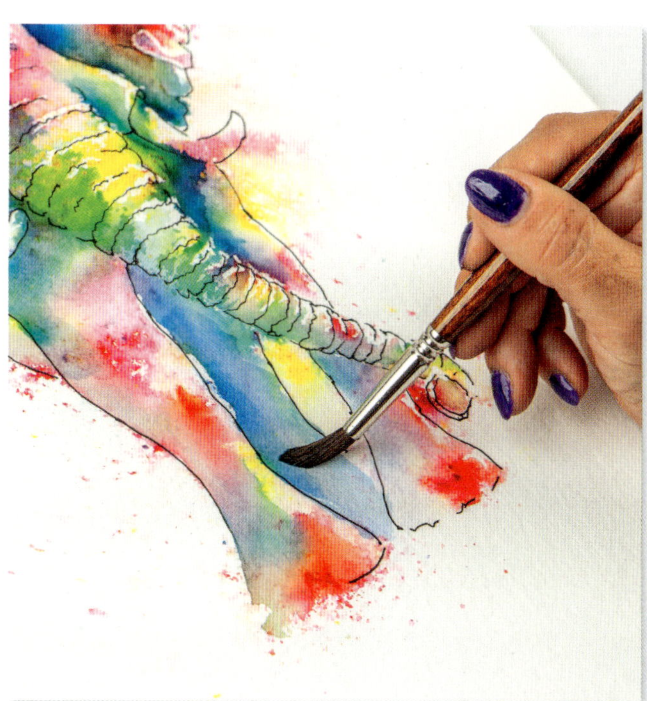

22 Add a darker value behind the elephant's front leg. The addition of this darker colour behind makes the paler colour of the left leg in front stand out.

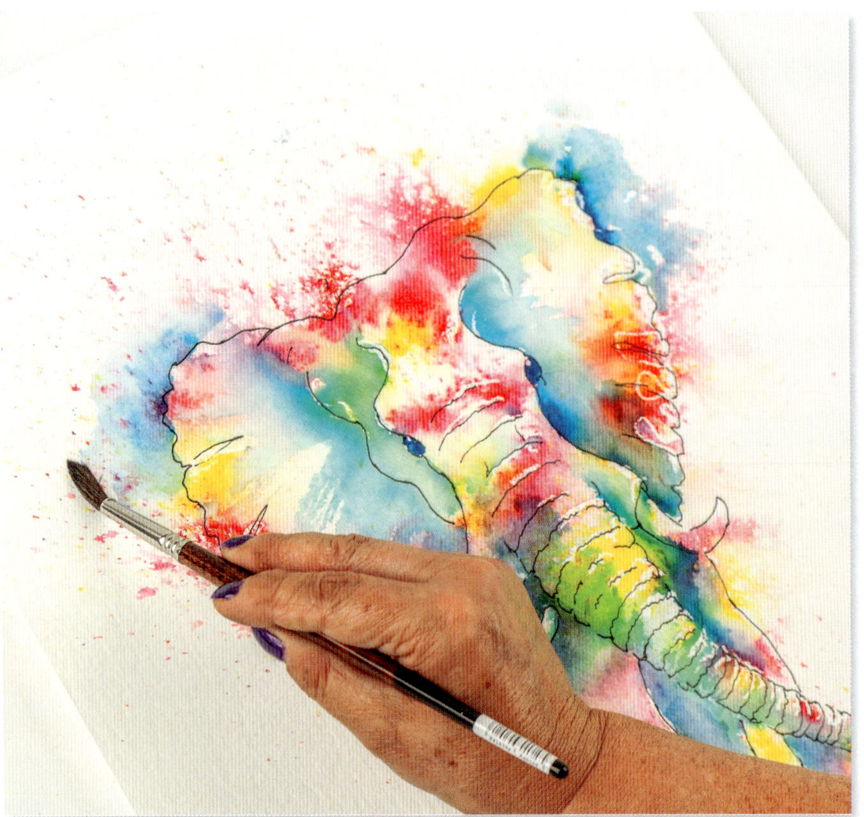

23 Use the cobalt blue to add some negative painting around the elephant's shape. I add mine on the right ear and the same on the left. Soften away with the water. The water reactivates the sprinkled colours you added earlier. Allow to dry.

Tip

Even a finished painting can be reactivated with a spritz of water.

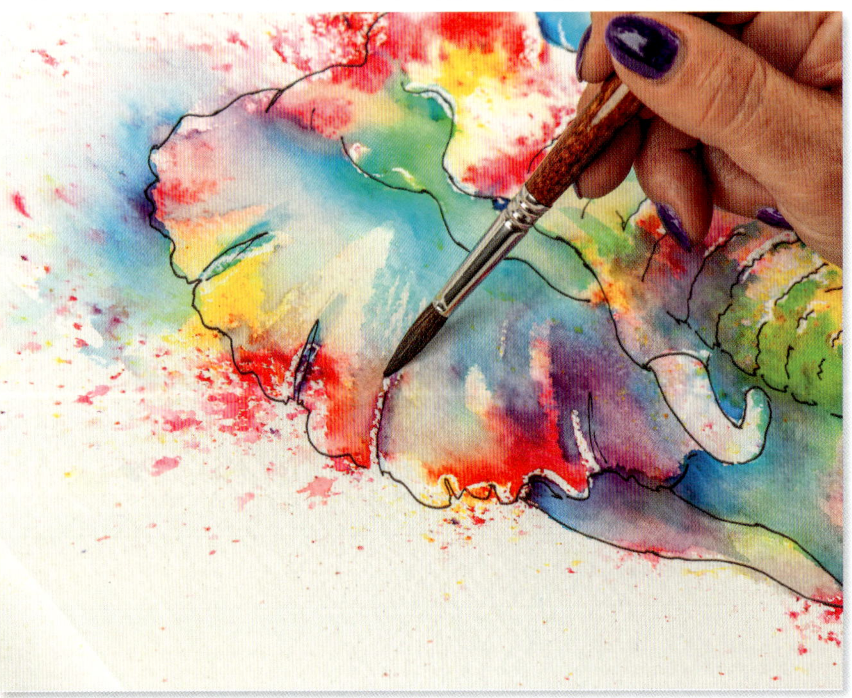

24 To emphasize the appearance of the creases in the elephant's ears, use the cobalt blue to add thin, linear marks.

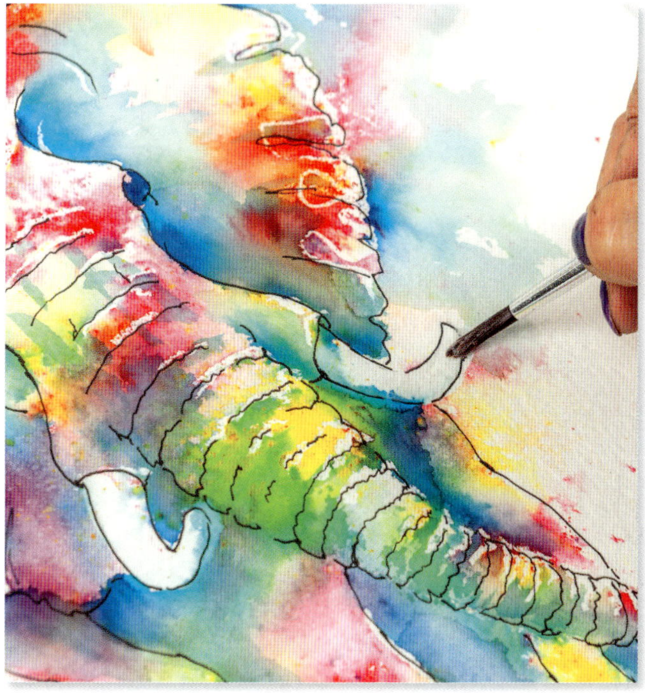

25 Using a diluted mixture of bleach and an old brush, lift out the white of the tusks.

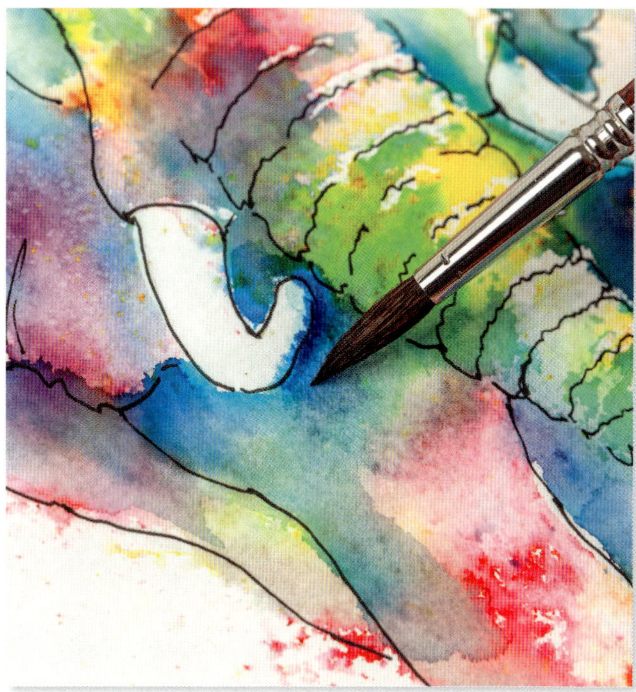

26 When dry, go back to your cobalt blue, placing it around the tusk area to further make the white pop.

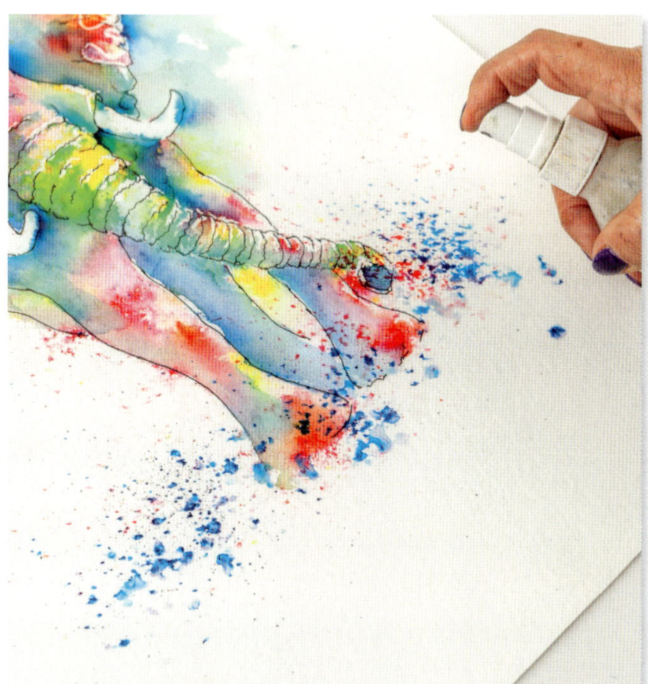

27 Sprinkle the alizarin crimson and the cobalt blue around the elephant's feet to ground him and give the impression of dust around his feet.

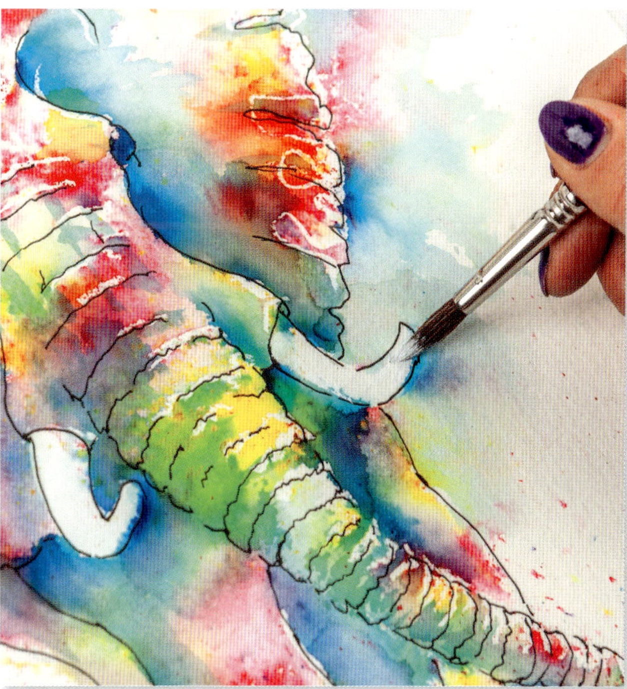

28 Use white ink or acrylic if there are areas you need to get back. I am using it to whiten the trunk where the cobalt blue has bled into the bleached section.

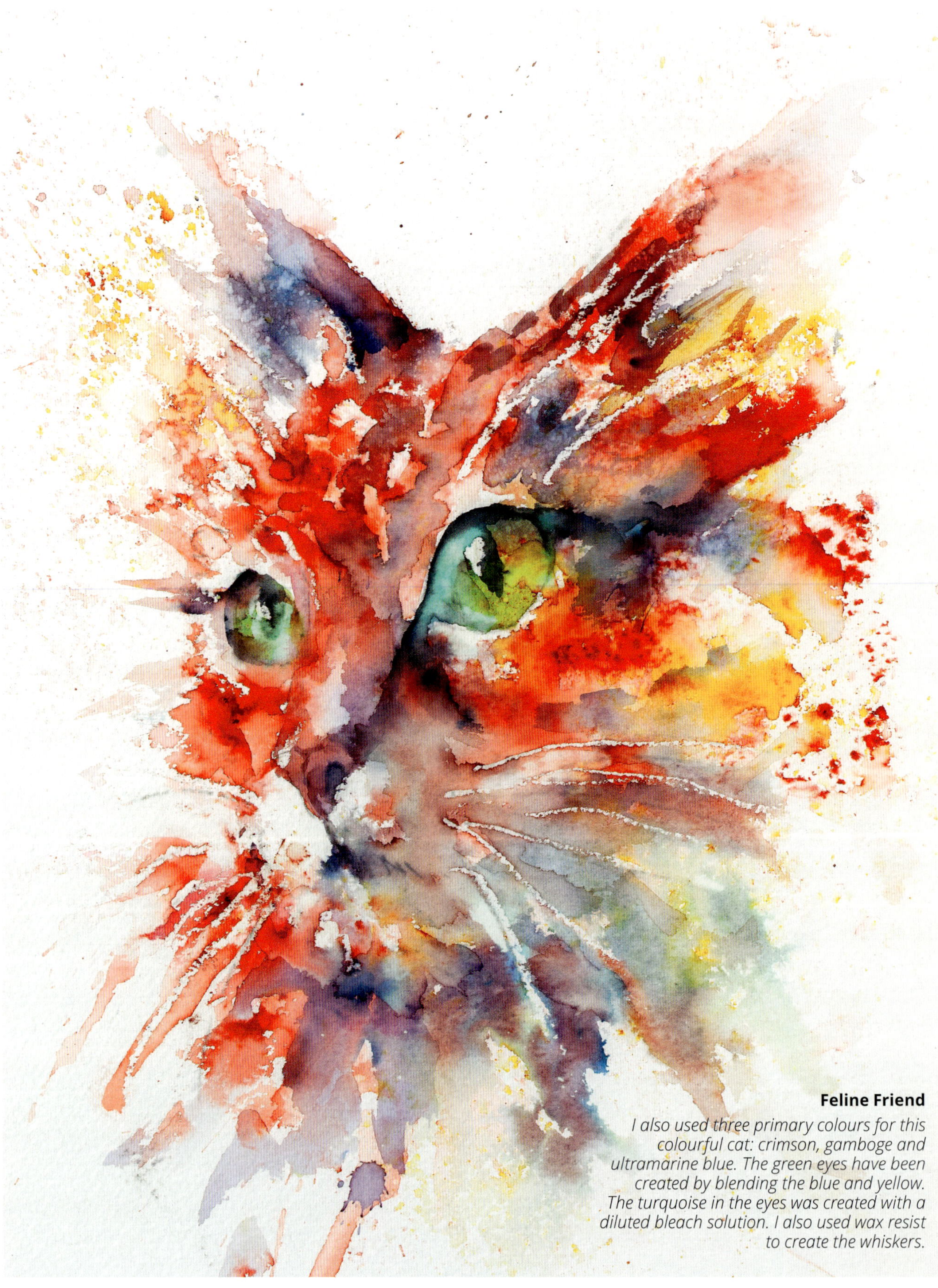

Feline Friend
I also used three primary colours for this colourful cat: crimson, gamboge and ultramarine blue. The green eyes have been created by blending the blue and yellow. The turquoise in the eyes was created with a diluted bleach solution. I also used wax resist to create the whiskers.

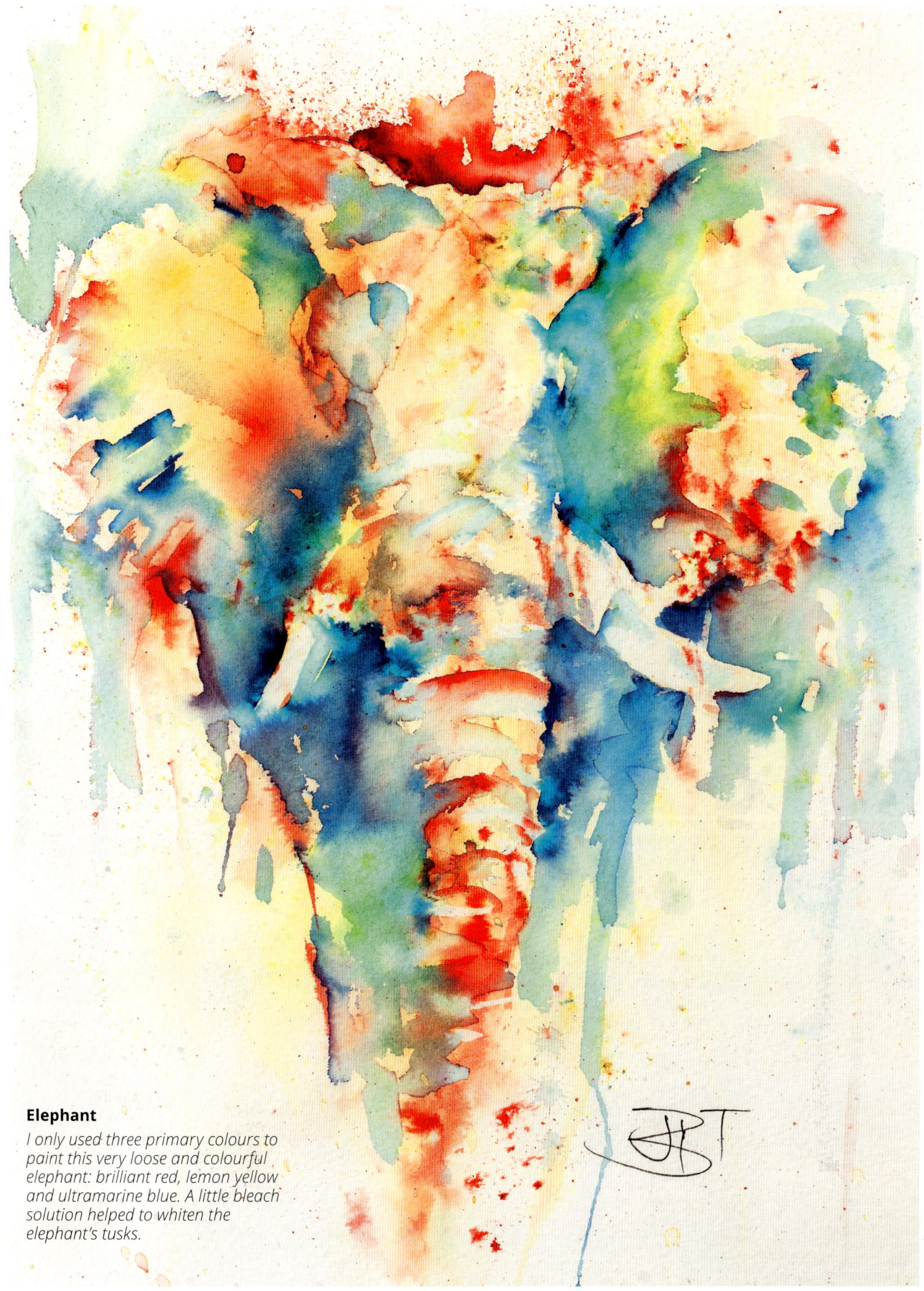

Elephant

I only used three primary colours to paint this very loose and colourful elephant: brilliant red, lemon yellow and ultramarine blue. A little bleach solution helped to whiten the elephant's tusks.

Lavender & Butterfly

This delightful project is a joy to paint and gives you the opportunity to practise the sprinkle and spray method as well as the wax resist technique. You can also apply a little bleach if you think your painting would benefit from it. The violet Brusho is the perfect choice for this summer subject, and look how well the little butterfly connects with the lavender flower with the aid of a little sprinkle of Brusho.

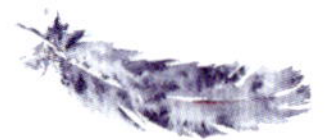

YOU WILL NEED

- Bockingford watercolour paper
  300gsm (140lb) Not surface,
  half imperial (38 x 56cm/15 x 22in)
- 3B pencil
- Eraser
- Brusho paint: violet, sunburst lemon, turquoise
- Size 10 brush
- Spray bottle with water
- Wax crayon or candle wax
- Palette
- Kitchen paper
- Bleach solution – 50% bleach: 50% water (optional)
- Old brush for bleach (optional)

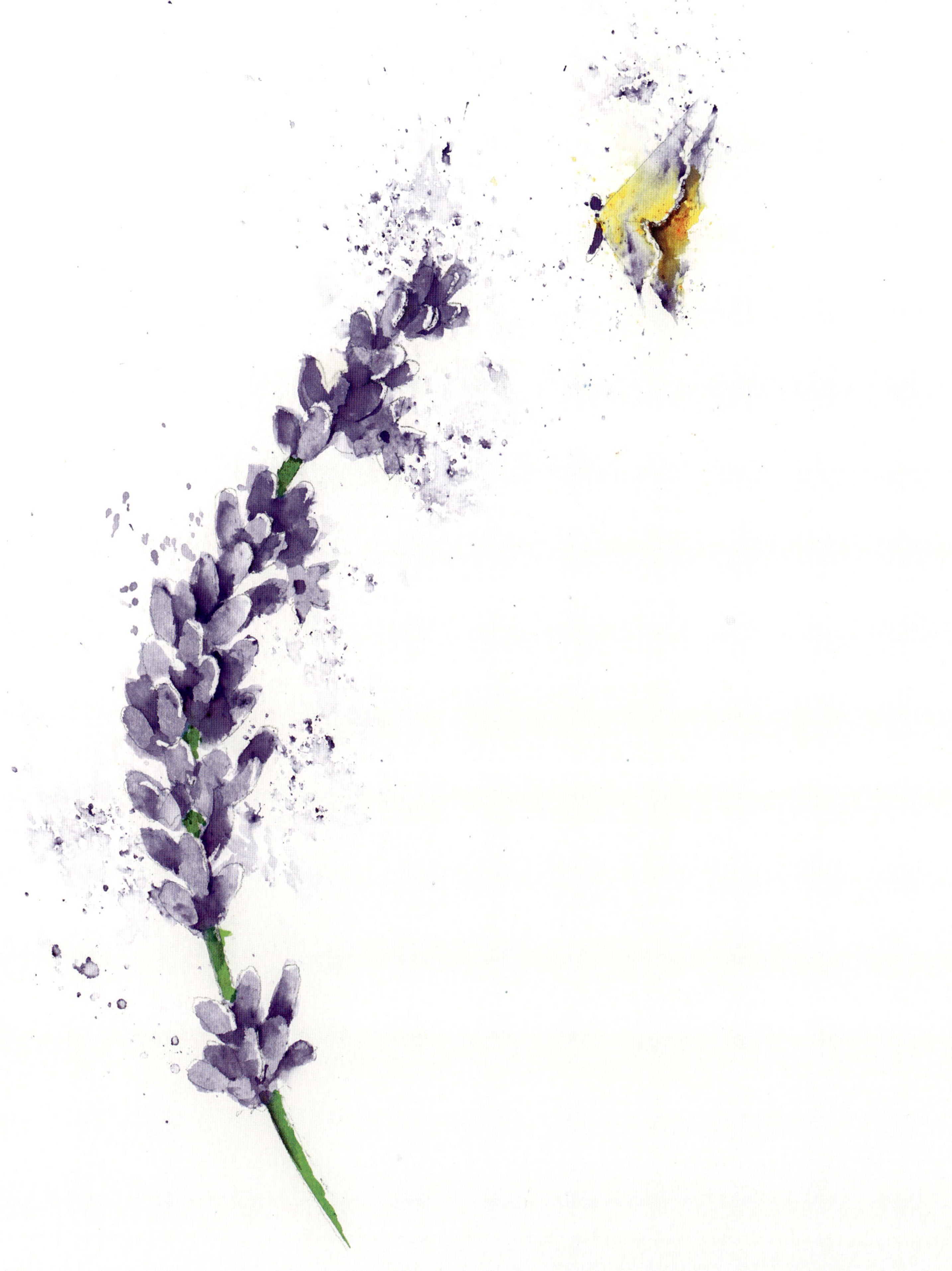

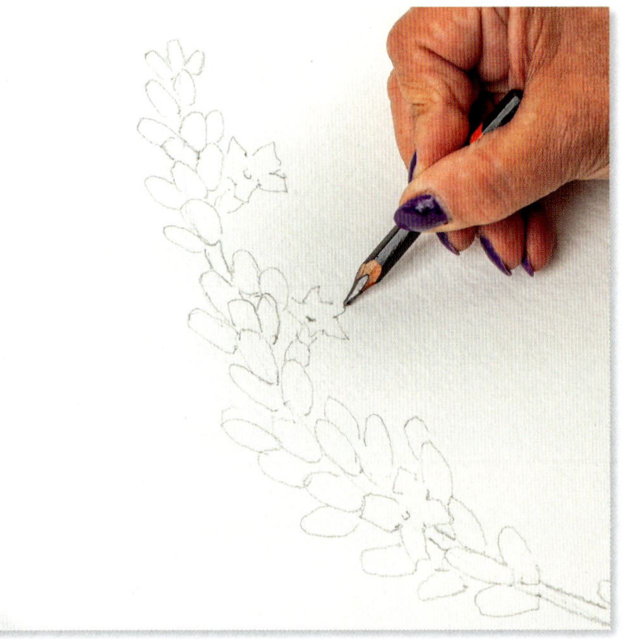

1 With your pencil, loosely draw out your lavender shape and butterfly. There is no need for lots of detail, just sketch in a few little buds of the flower.

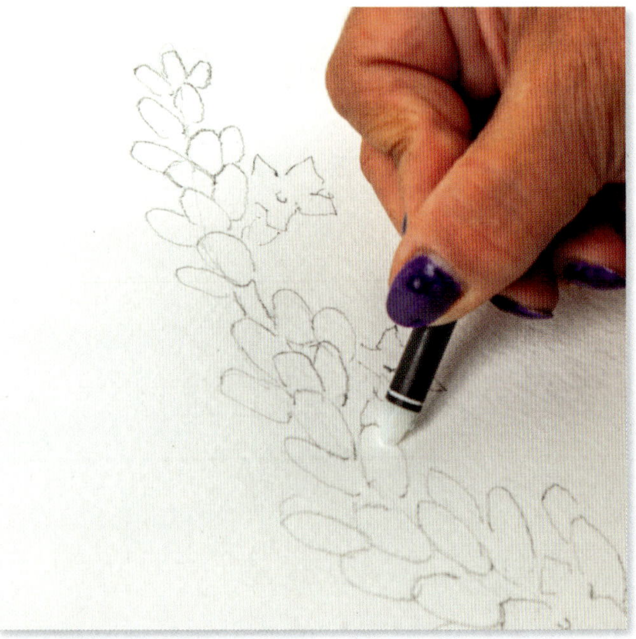

2 Apply wax to the small shapes you wish to highlight, especially around the tops of the buds. I am applying most of the wax resist on the right-hand side of the outline to give a hint of light catching the small buds.

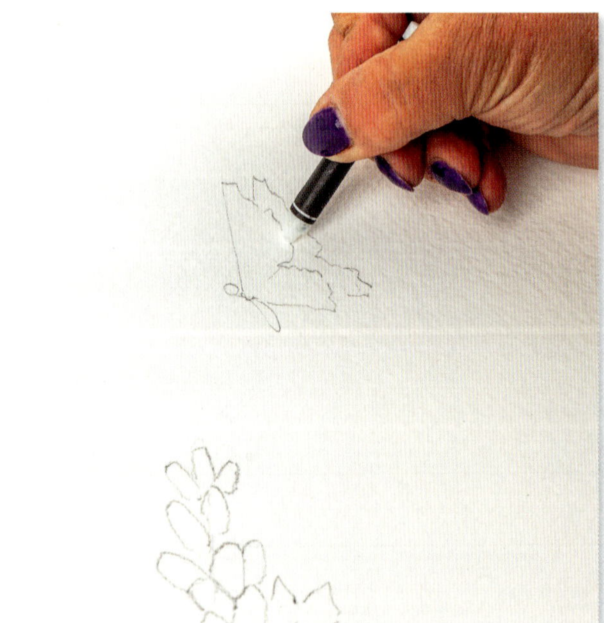

3 Add wax to the outside edge of the inner wing of the butterfly.

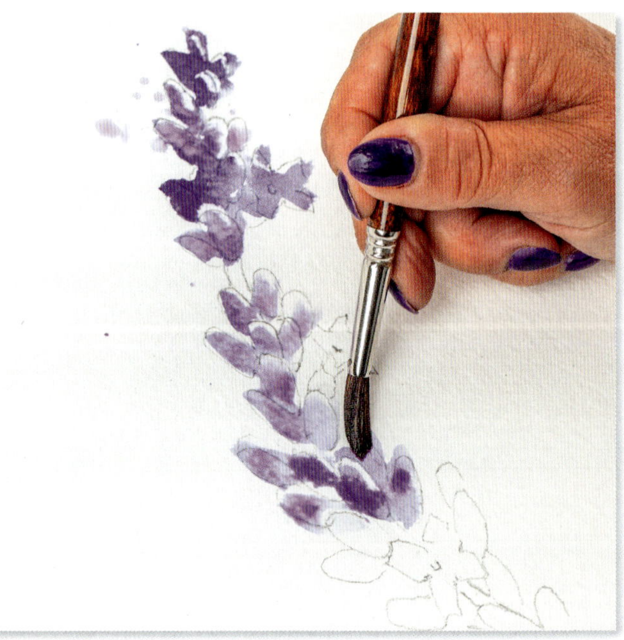

4 In a palette mix a very light wash of the violet and cover all the flower shapes. Don't forget to leave little gaps between the flower shapes for where the stem will later be added. Push your brush into the paper to create the shape. Don't worry about not keeping within the lines. In fact, I'd encourage you to break the lines.

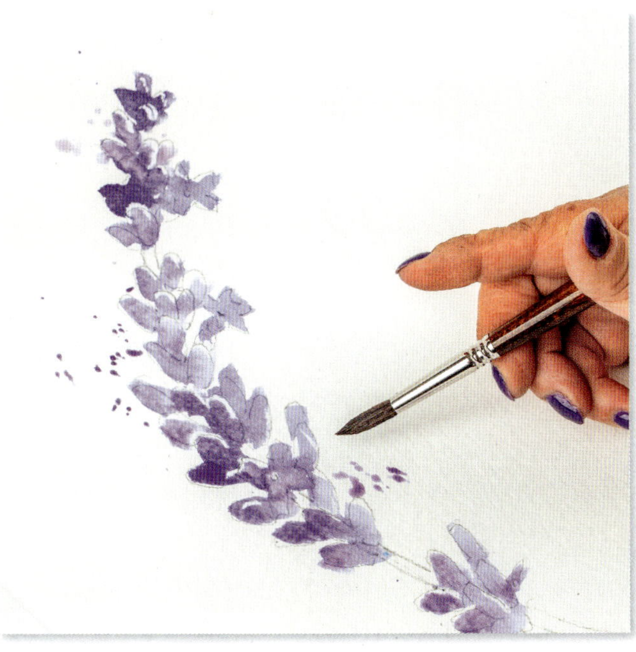

5 Add light spattering around the outside of your flower.

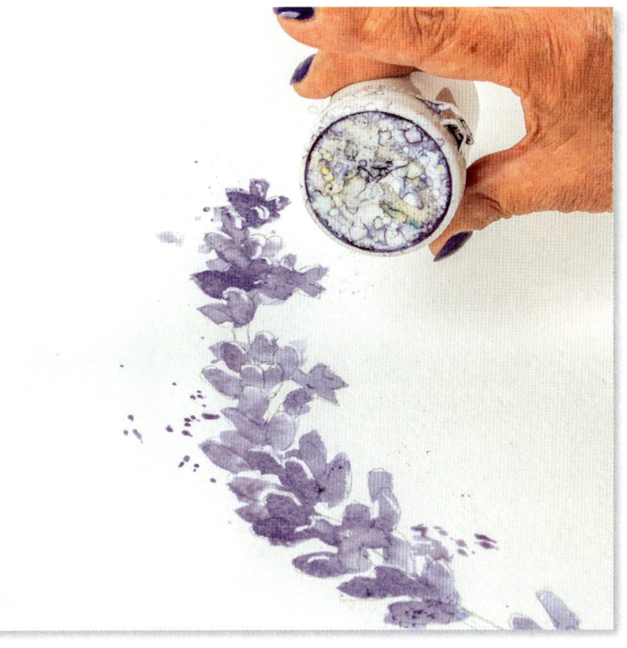

6 Carefully sprinkle violet Brusho around the flower shape.

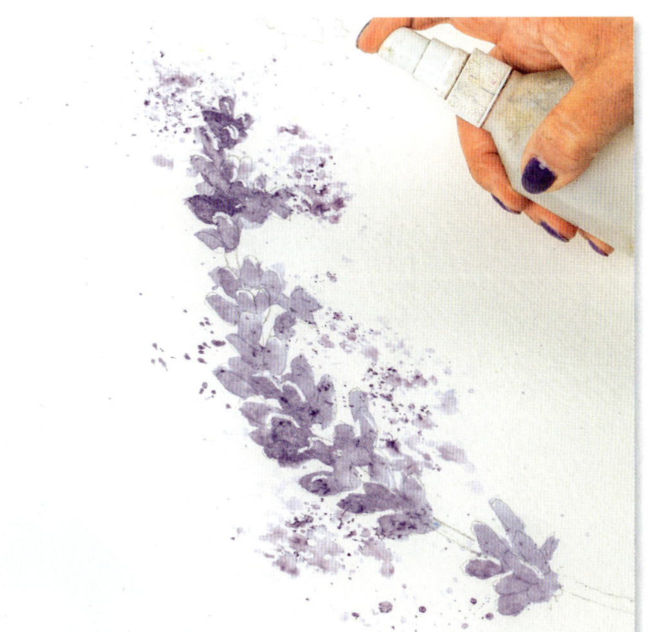

7 Give this a little spray of water to bring the flower to life.

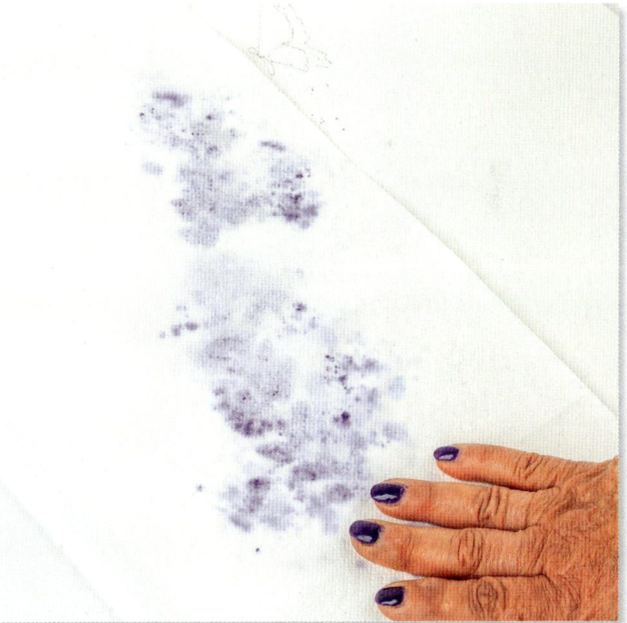

8 Pat with kitchen paper and keep the paper in place to mask the flower while you paint the butterfly.

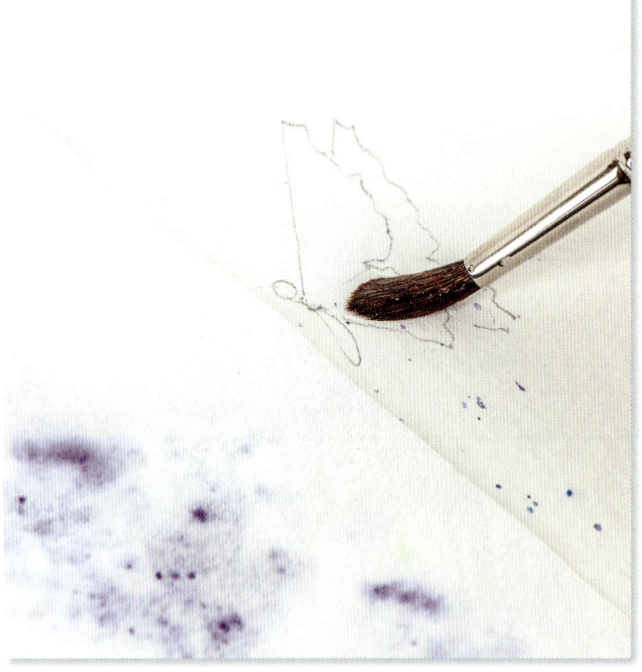

9 While you are waiting for this to dry, wet the butterfly area.

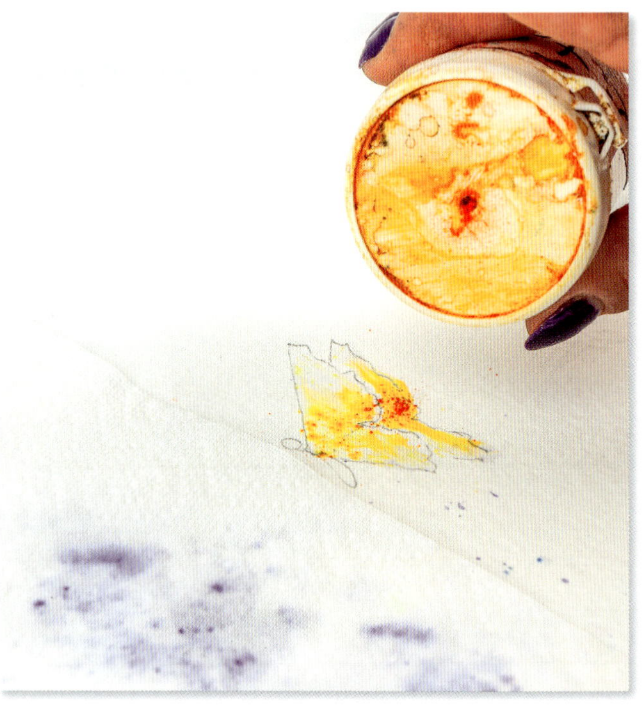

10 Sprinkle a little sunburst lemon powder into the bottom half of the wet area.

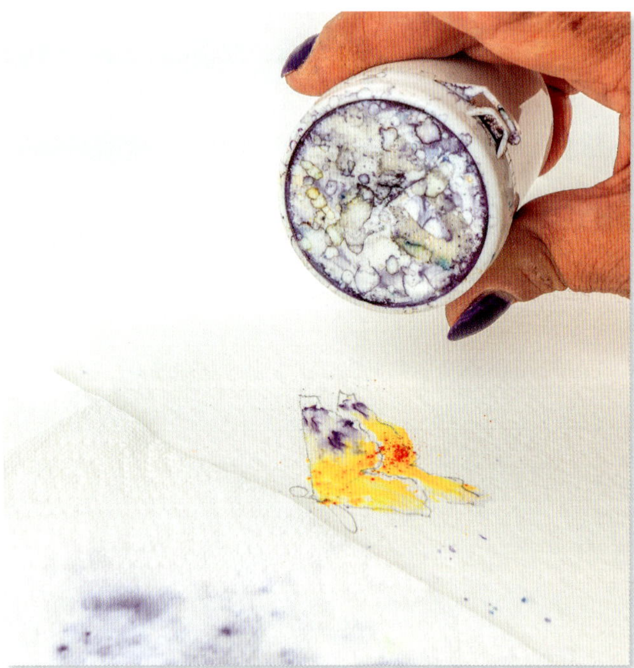

11 Sprinkle a little violet into the top half of the butterfly area.

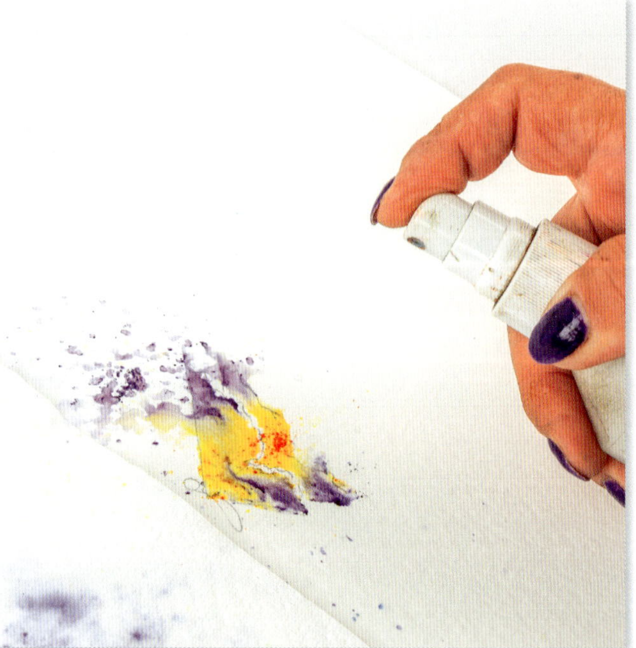

12 Bring your butterfly to life by activating the colours further with a spritz of clean water.

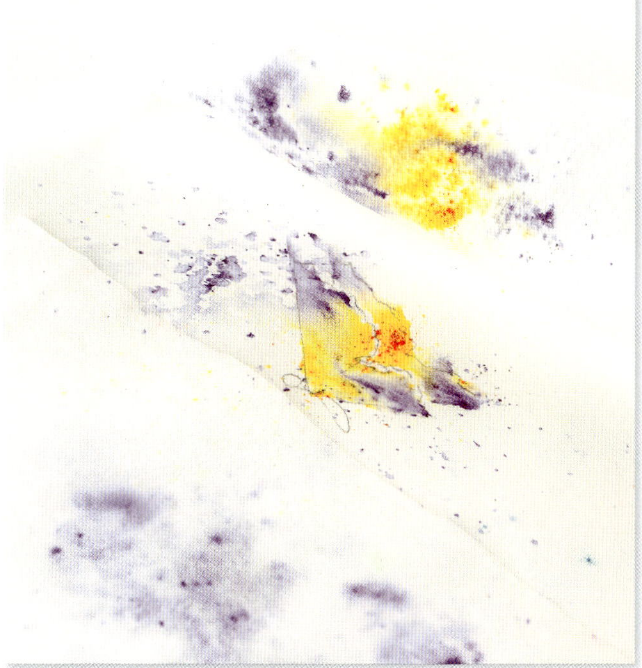

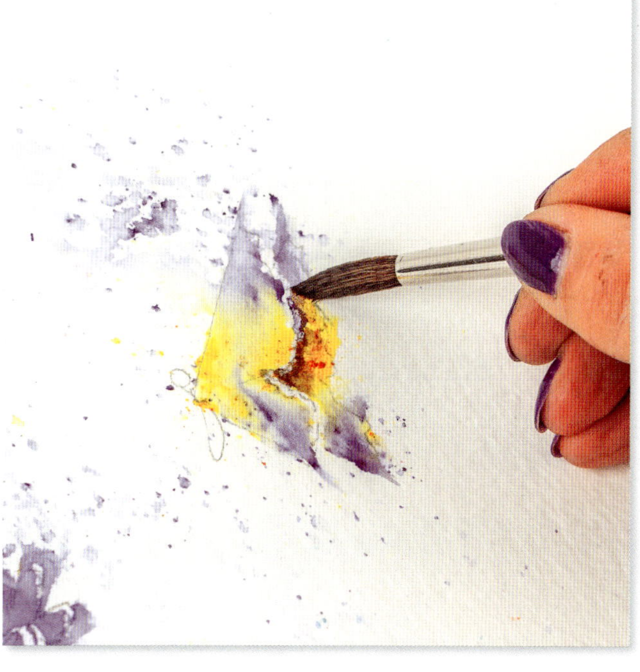

13 Dab with kitchen paper. Remove both pieces of kitchen paper from the painting to reveal the lavender and the butterfly.

14 Once the butterfly is dry, use a darker wash of the violet to separate the wings.

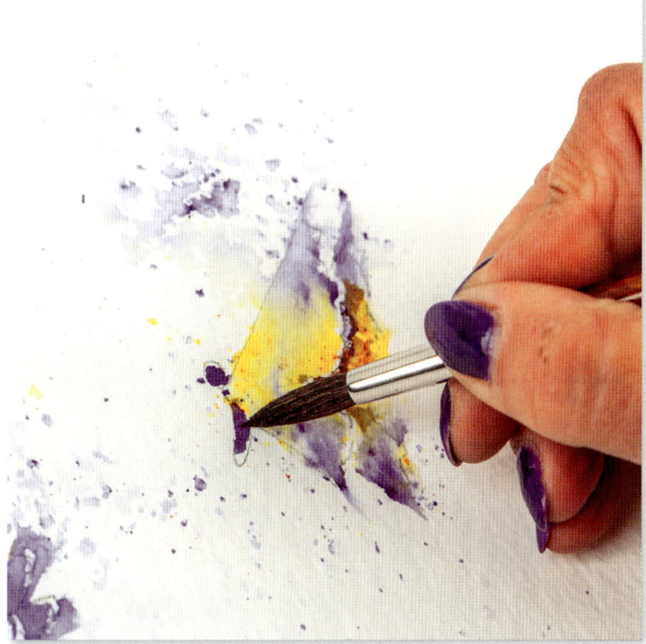

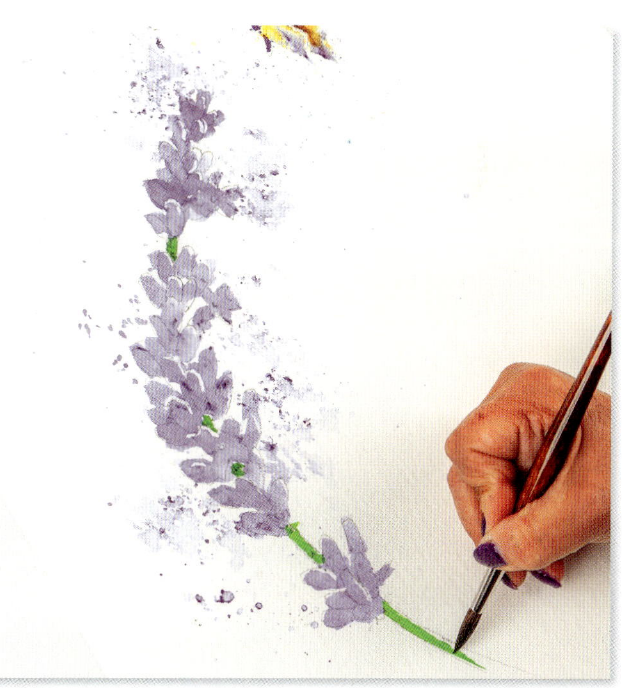

15 Using the same wash, add in the body of the butterfly.

16 Make a green wash for the stem by mixing sunburst lemon and turquoise in your palette. Where you left gaps for the stem in step 4, now apply your mix to small areas to indicate the stem peeping through the buds.

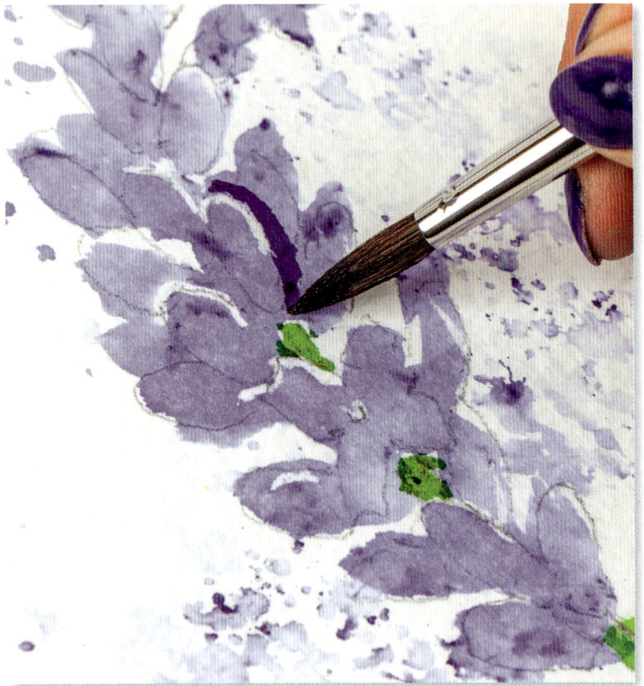

17 Using a darker wash of violet mixed in the palette, negatively paint around some of the little flower shapes. The wax you applied earlier will now start to show.

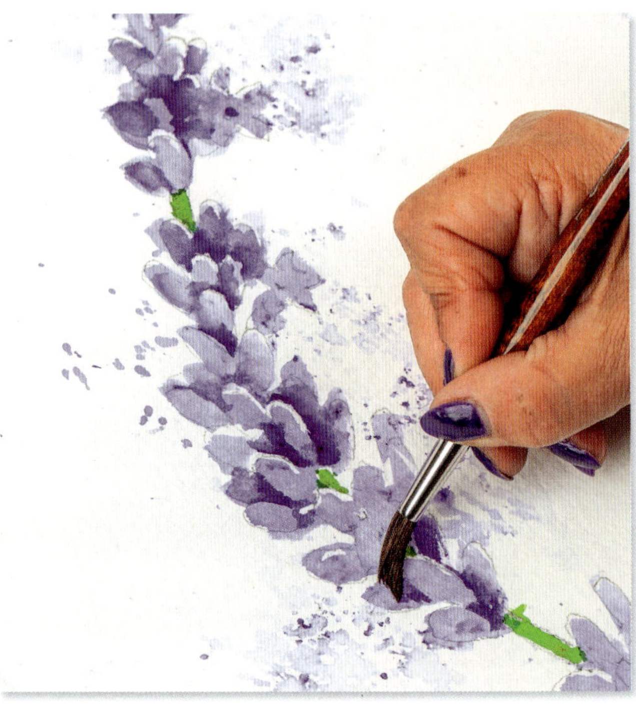

18 Soften away the hard lines with your brush, pulling the paint away.

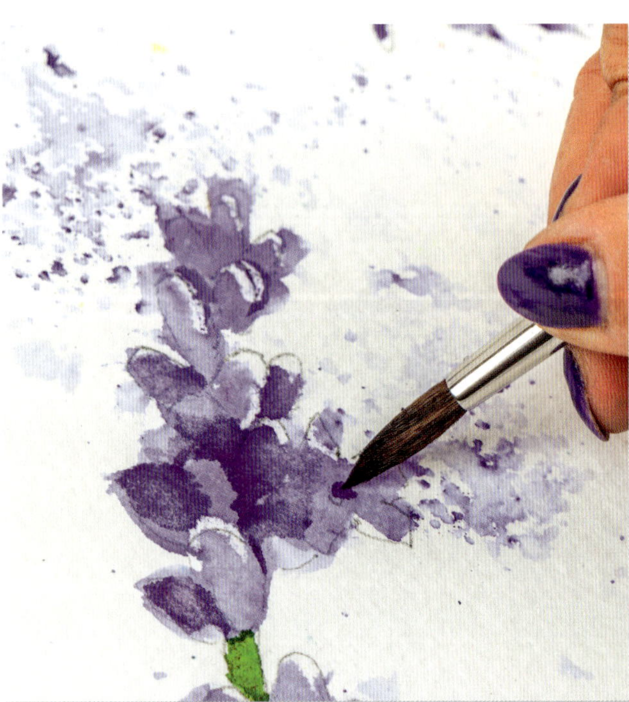

19 Add a darker mixture of the violet to really show off the light shapes of the little flowers.

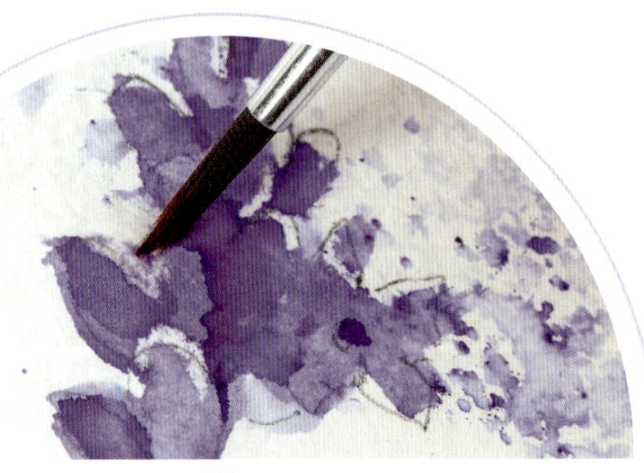

Tip

If you want to do any tidying, you can always use bleach to do so. Don't forget to swap to your old brush. Here I am defining the shape of the petal by lifting out some colour with the bleach.

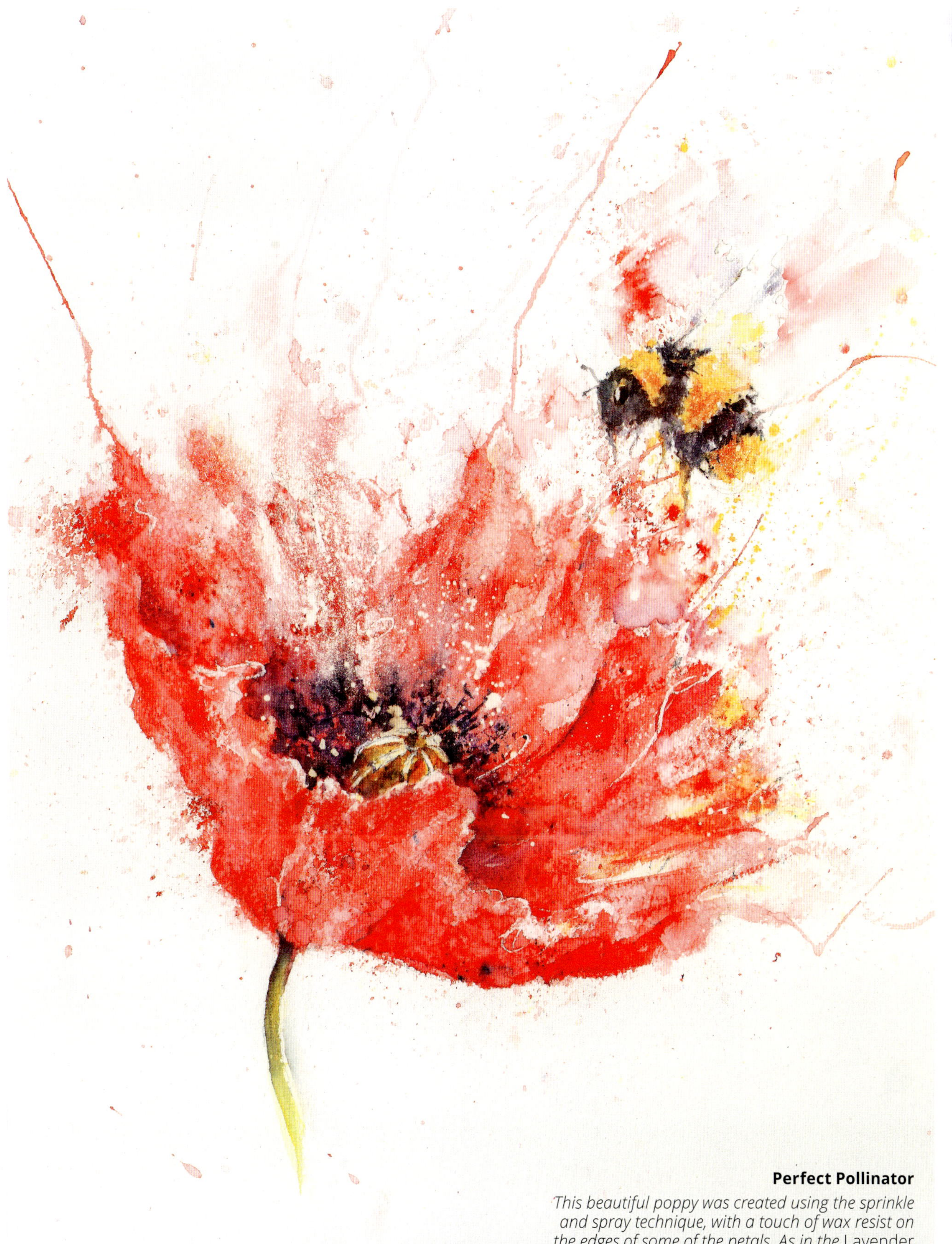

Perfect Pollinator

This beautiful poppy was created using the sprinkle and spray technique, with a touch of wax resist on the edges of some of the petals. As in the Lavender & Butterfly project, I added an insect to bring the painting to life – this time a cheeky bumblebee.

Cottage in the Snow

If you are excited about using the bleach technique, then this is the project for you. All you need to create this atmospheric winter house is black Brusho and some bleach. You will love watching the snow slowly falling onto your paper, and the billow of smoke coming from the chimney.

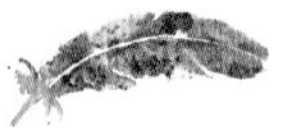

YOU WILL NEED

- Bockingford watercolour paper 300gsm (140lb) Not surface, half imperial (38 x 56cm/15 x 22in)
- 3B pencil
- Eraser
- Brusho paint: black
- Size 8 and 12 brushes
- Spray bottle
- Bleach solution – 50% bleach: 50% water
- Old brush for bleach
- Old toothbrush for bleach
- Palette
- Scrap paper
- Kitchen paper

Tip

I recommend testing out your bleach solution against a dark wash of the black on your chosen paper. This vital preparation will give you confidence that you know how the bleach, paper and Brusho will react to each other and how your finished painting will look.

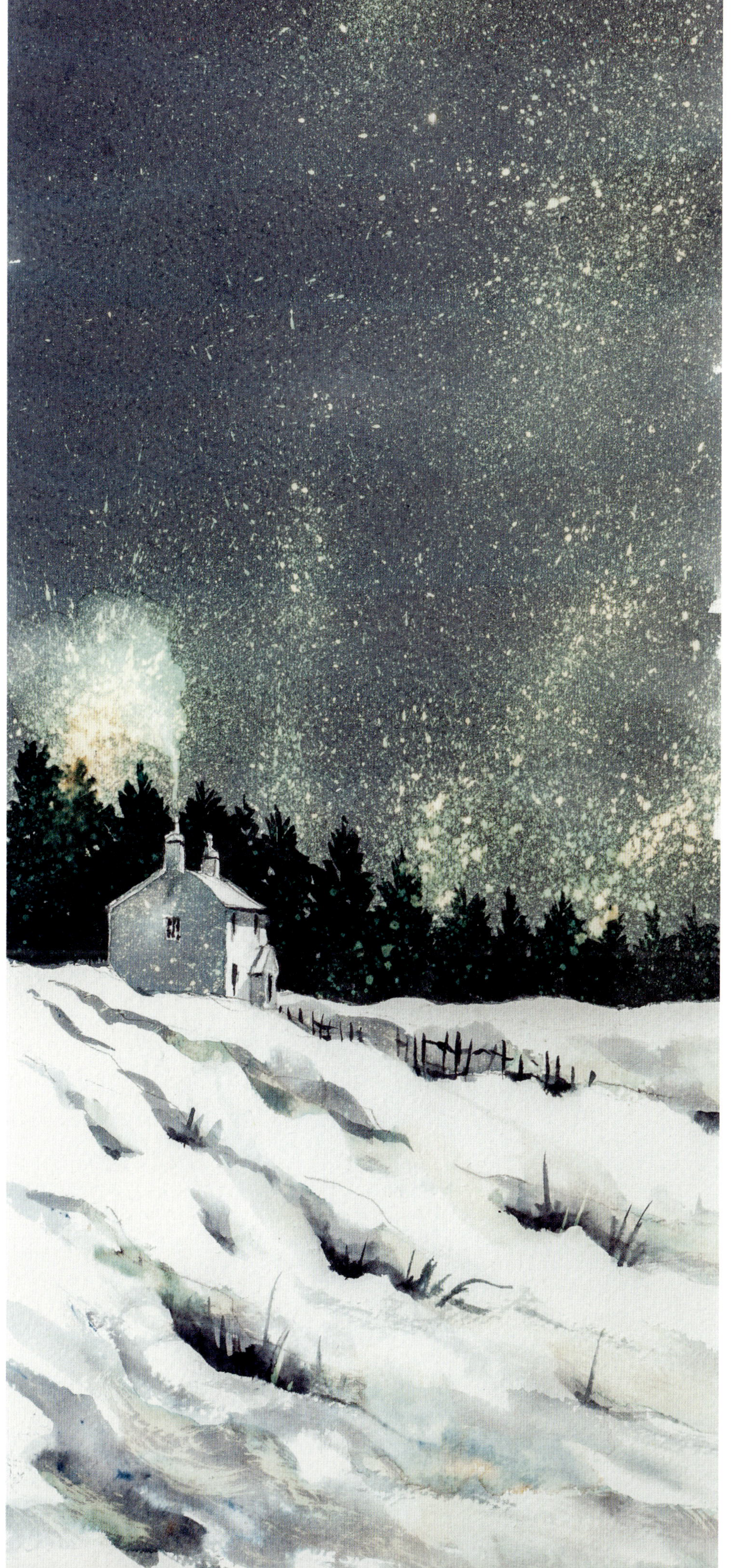

Cottage in the Snow

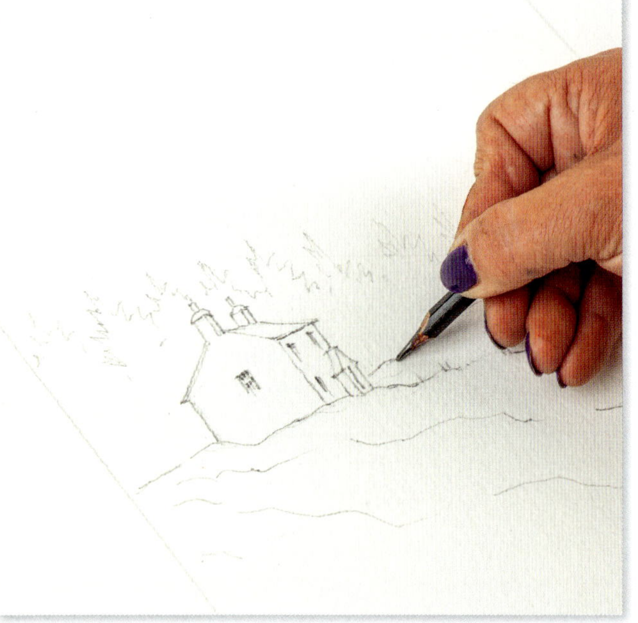

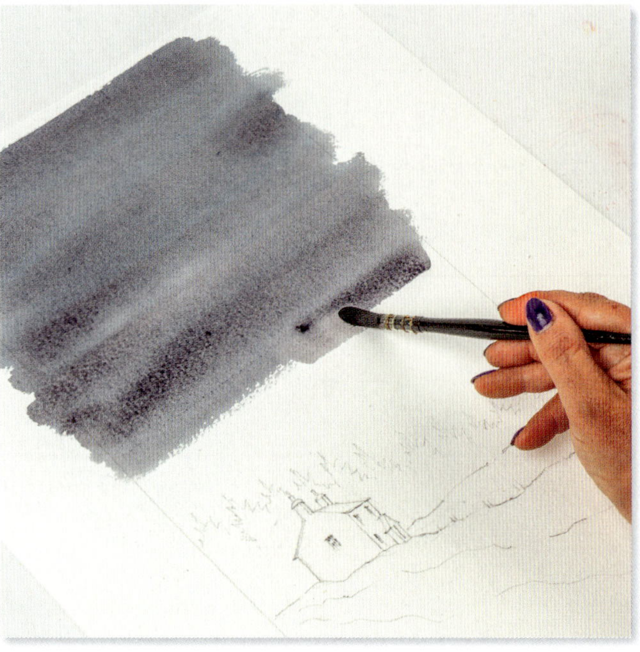

1 Using a soft pencil, sketch out the little cottage on the hill.

2 Mix a black wash in the palette. Using a size 12 brush, apply a flat wash into the sky area using broad horizontal strokes and working your way down the page.

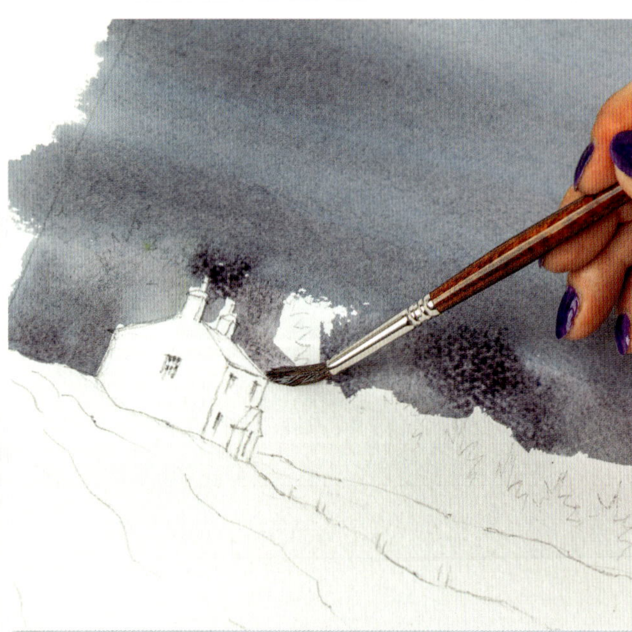

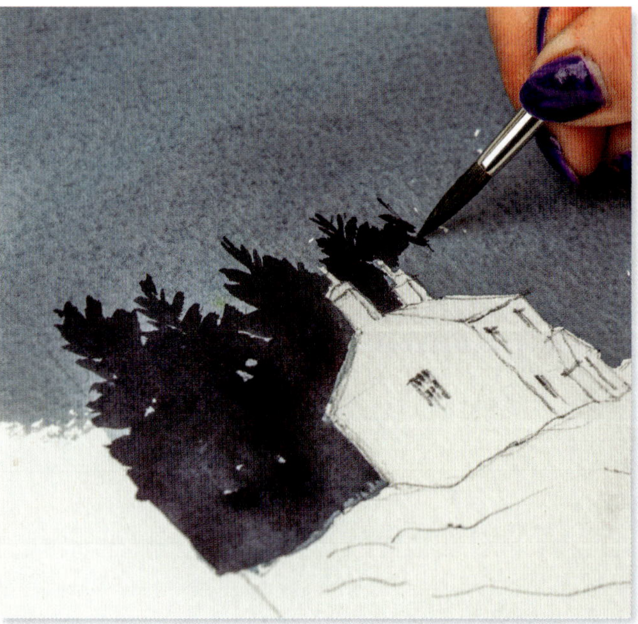

3 Change to your size 8 brush. Work upside down if you find it easier to paint around the cottage shape and down to the horizon. Let the sky area dry.

4 Mix a darker wash of the black for the distant trees and stay with your size 8 brush to paint in the trees. Carefully paint around the chimney pots.

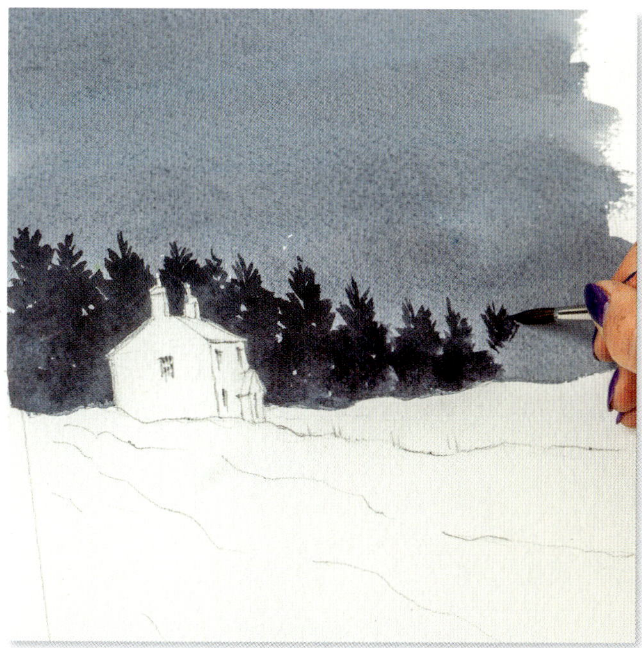

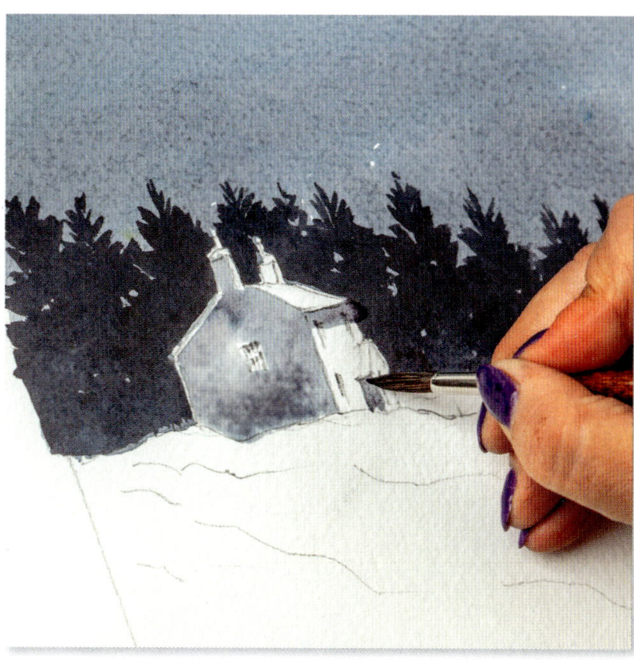

5 Be patient – the trees will take a while to put in, but they will look great once they are finished. Allow the trees to dry.

6 In a palette, mix a weak wash of the black and paint the shadows on the house and chimneys. Remember to test the wash on a scrap of paper before applying it to your painting. Let this stage dry.

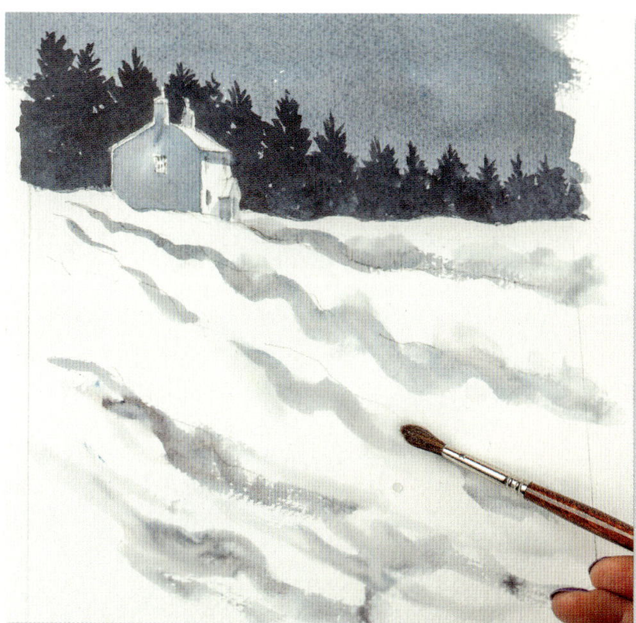

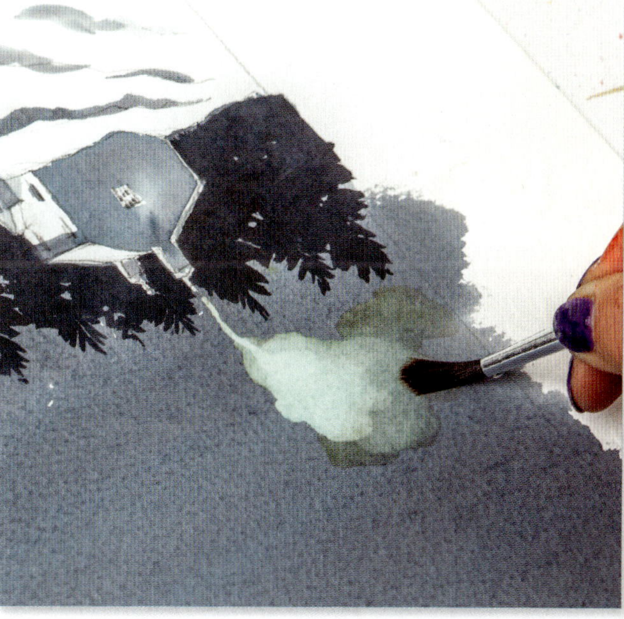

7 Take your brush and indicate slightly darker snowy areas. Use small brushstrokes for the distance and use wider marks in the foreground. Add water in the foreground to soften the marks away. Don't worry if you overdo this section as we will use the bleach later to lift away. Allow to dry.

8 Turn your painting upside down. Spray the bleach solution onto a scrap of paper. With your old brush, dip into your bleach and, starting at the chimney, create the smoke coming from the cottage chimney. Be patient and don't overdo it as the bleach takes a few minutes to work.

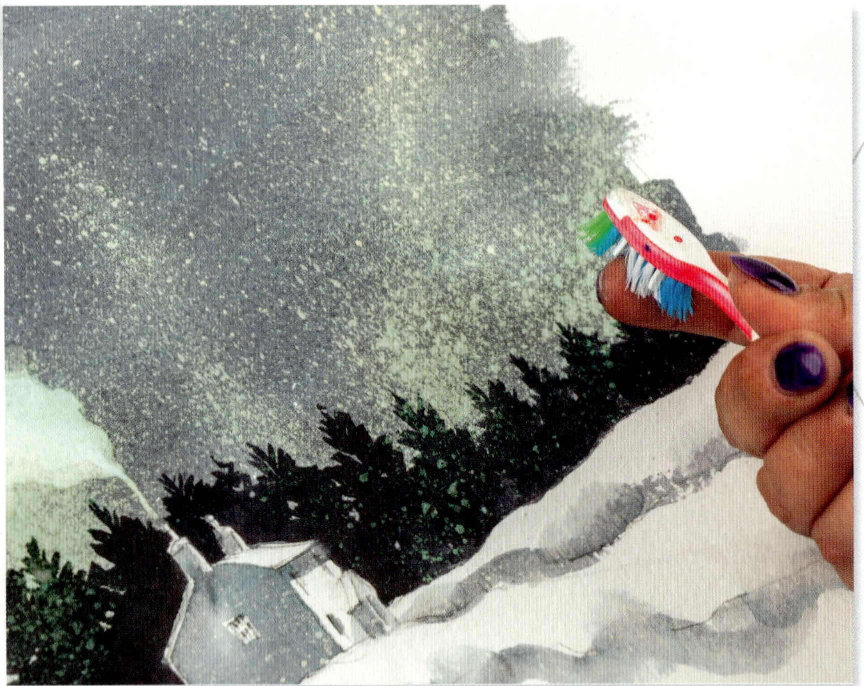

9 Turn your painting the right way round and let's paint some snow! Press your toothbrush into the bleach solution on your scrap paper. Starting at the top right of the page, spatter the solution into the sky, trees and cottage. In a few minutes, you will have wonderful snowfall.

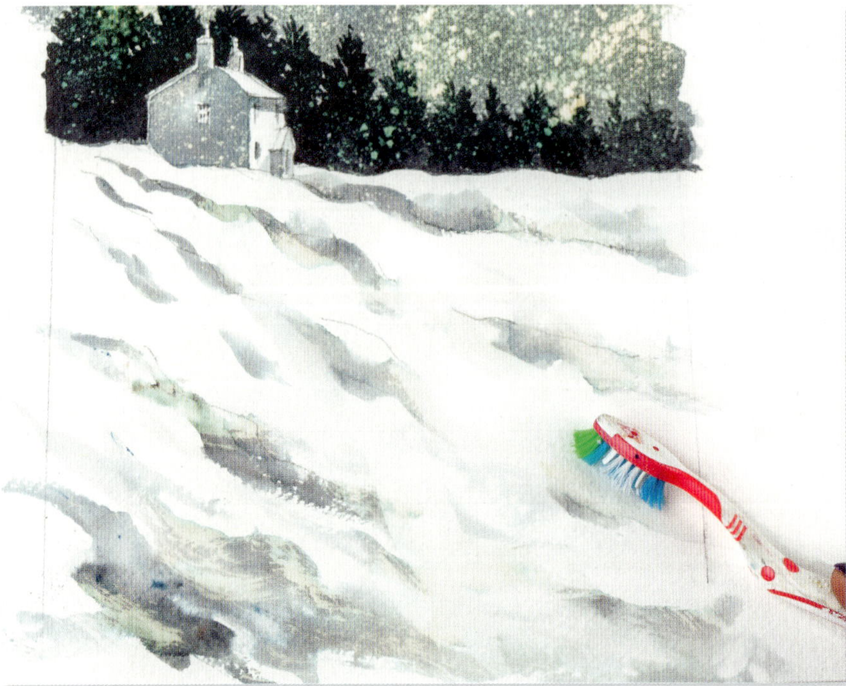

10 Spray more bleach solution on your scrap paper and press your toothbrush into it. Drag your toothbrush over the ridges of snow in the foreground. Dragging it through the wash will lift some of the wash away and lighten areas. Allow to dry.

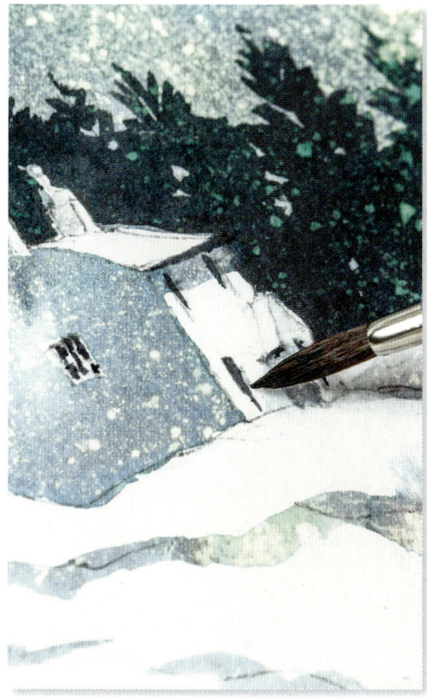

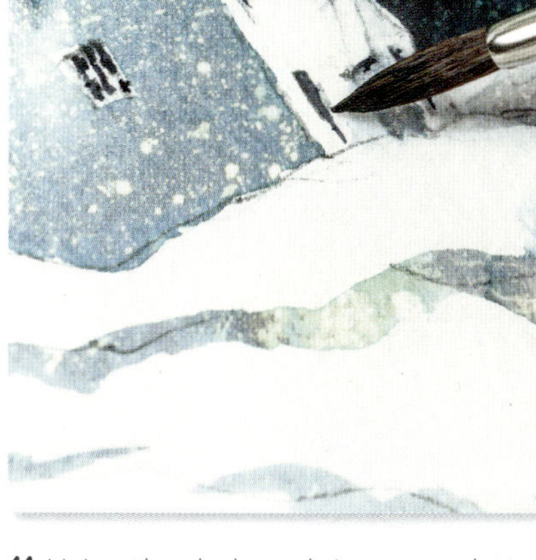

11 Using the dark wash in your palette, add more darks to the windows.

12 Using the same wash, add some darks in the foreground. I have added posts and fences.

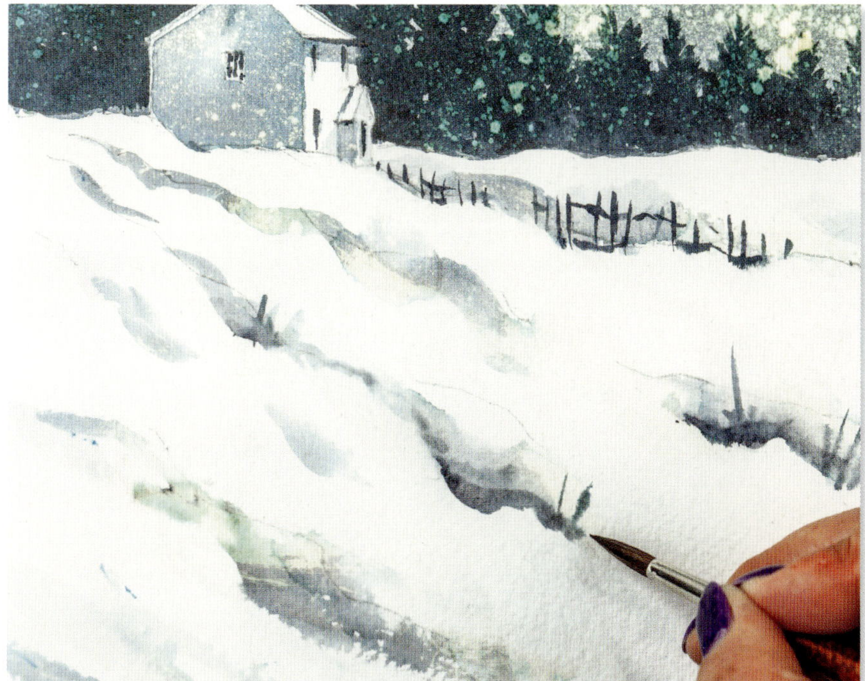

13 Add a darker section into a dip in the snow to suggest some wintry grasses showing through. Smooth out the dark wash with your brush and follow the contours of the hill.

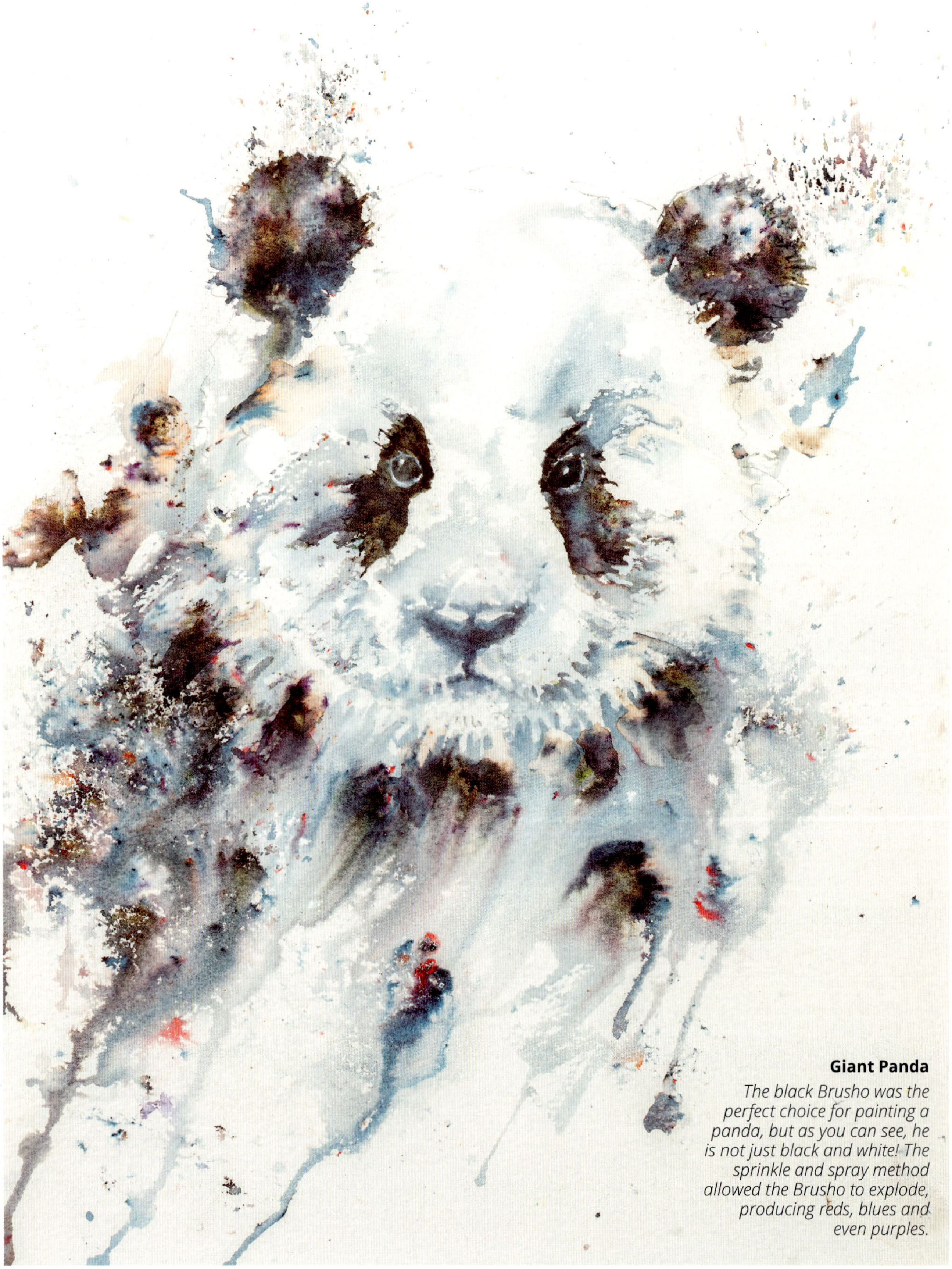

Giant Panda

The black Brusho was the perfect choice for painting a panda, but as you can see, he is not just black and white! The sprinkle and spray method allowed the Brusho to explode, producing reds, blues and even purples.

Black Cat

The explosion of 'colourful' black Brusho creates the shape and form of the cat. It's hard to believe that just one Brusho colour can produce so much colour! I used a little bleach solution to lift out the whiskers.

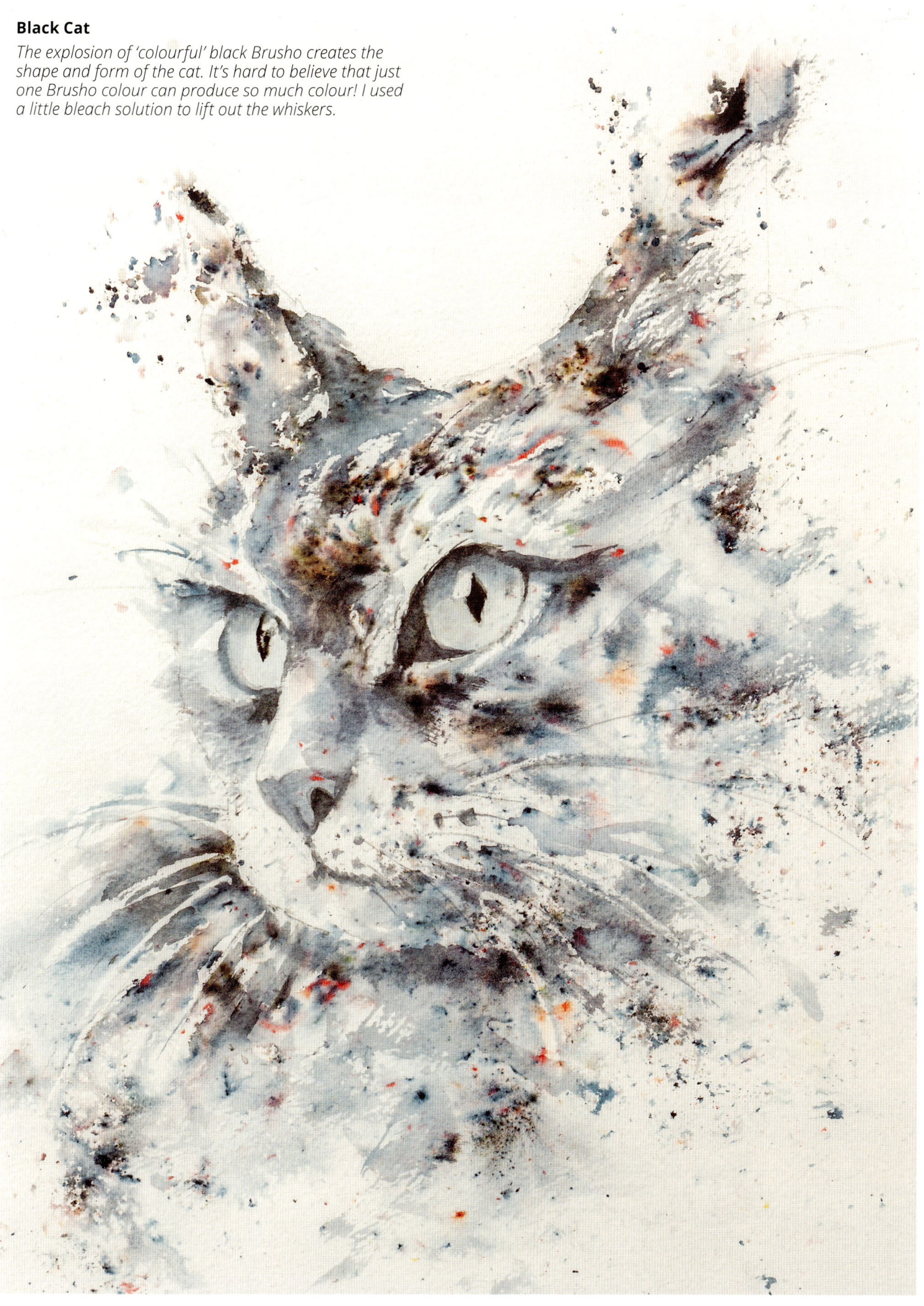

Allium

Let's paint a beautiful Brusho allium. I love these tall-stemmed beauties with their globe-like flowers that just explode from the centre. The allium represents patience, good fortune and prosperity. As you can see, this painting has just three complementary colours: red, yellow and green. Why not play around with three other colours to produce a different coloured allium?

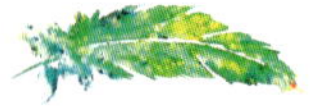

YOU WILL NEED

- Bockingford watercolour paper 300gsm (140lb) Not surface, half imperial (38 x 56cm/15 x 22in)
- 3B pencil
- Eraser
- Brusho paint: crimson, purple, sunburst lemon, leaf green
- Size 10 brush
- Spray bottle with water
- Palette
- Wax crayon or candle wax
- Kitchen paper

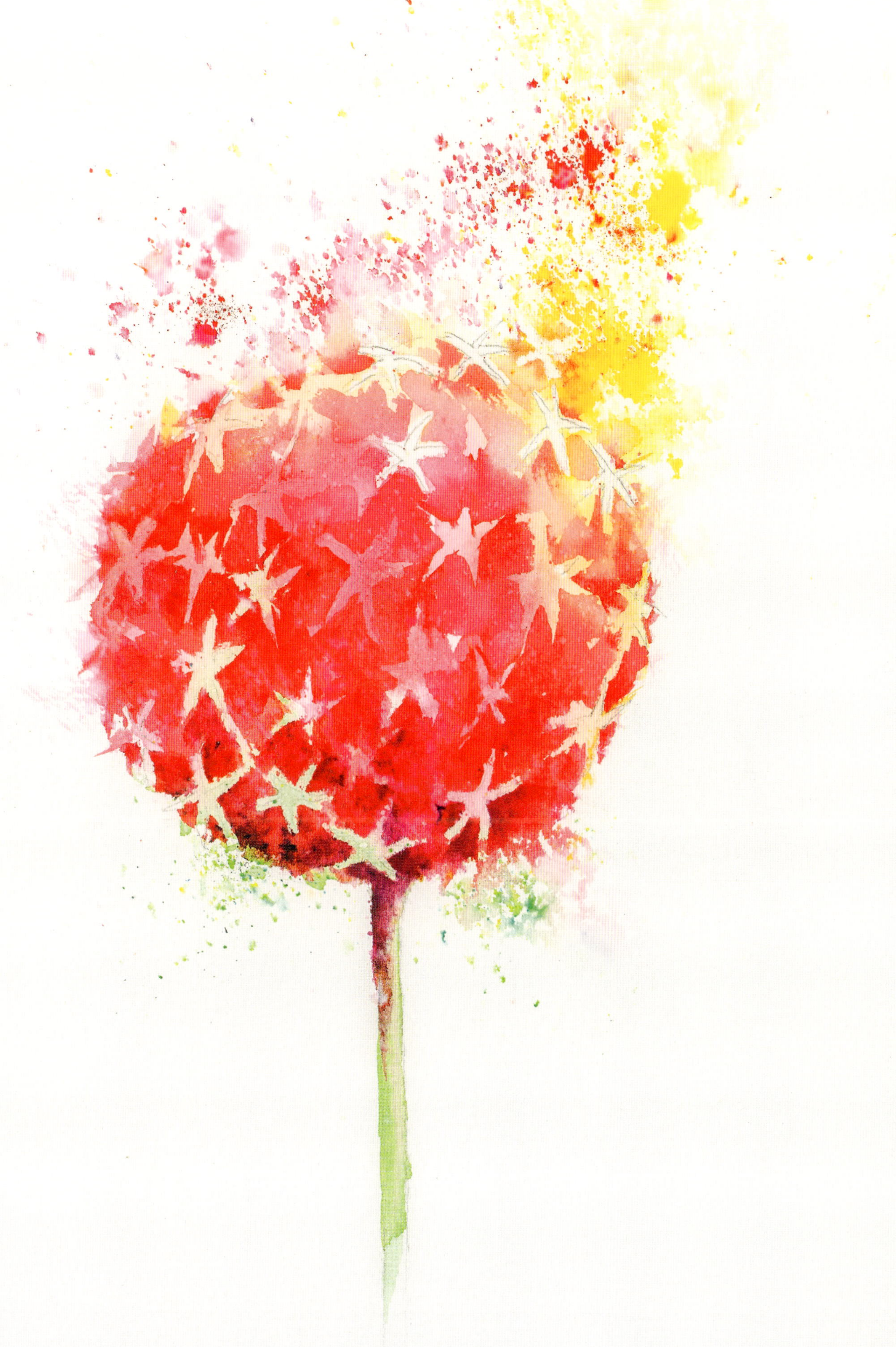

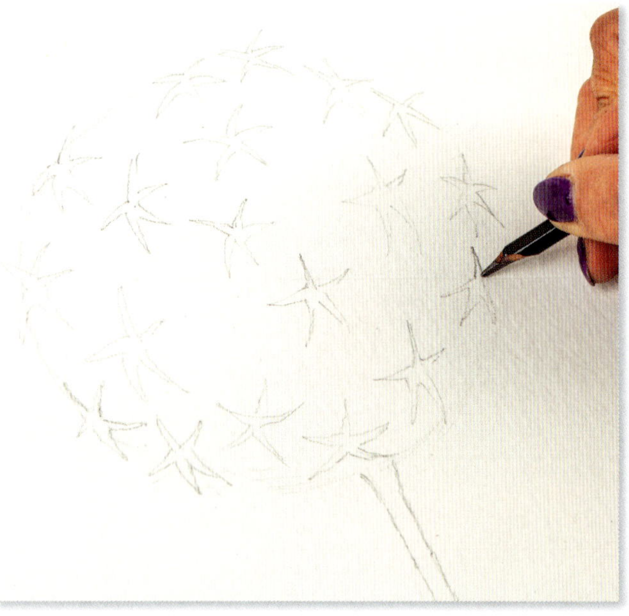

1 Using pencil, make an initial drawing of the flower. Suggest the shape and form of the whole flower including the small star-shaped flowers that make up the sphere of the flower head and follow its curve. You don't have to draw every small flower, just a few that are face-on and some side-on as they follow the curve of the flower.

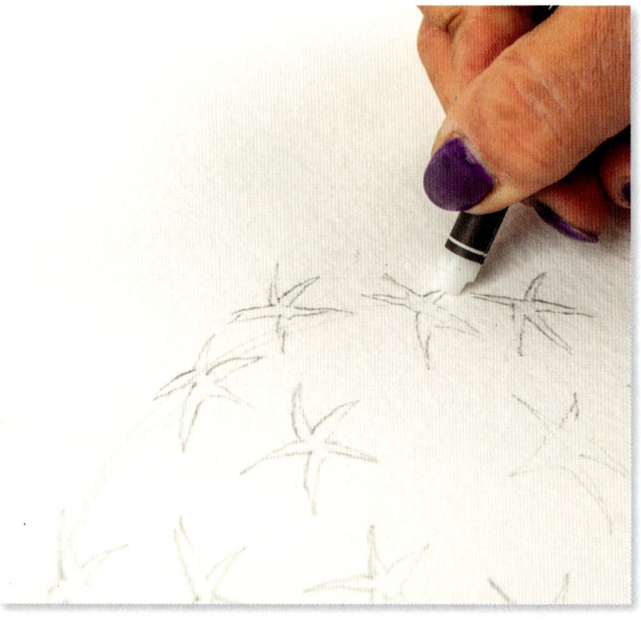

2 Use wax to highlight the small star-shaped flowers at the top right-hand of the flower head.

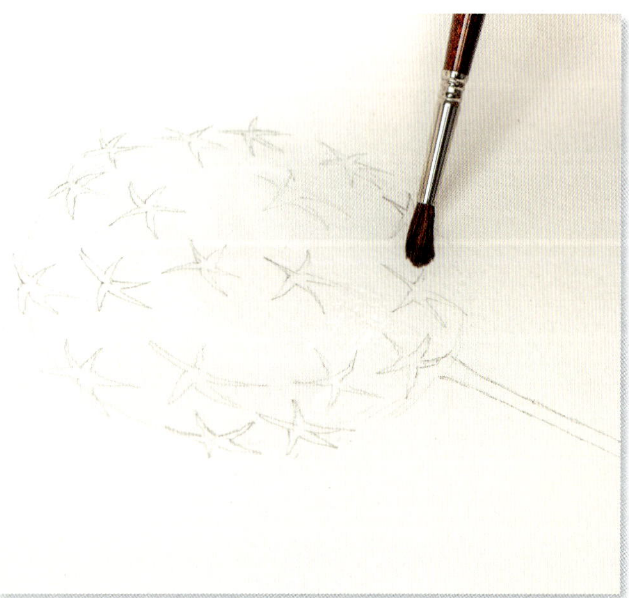

3 In a palette, prepare three separate washes of crimson, sunburst lemon and leaf green. Make these washes weak as we will work light to dark. Wet the whole flower head with the brush, ready to receive the Brusho wash.

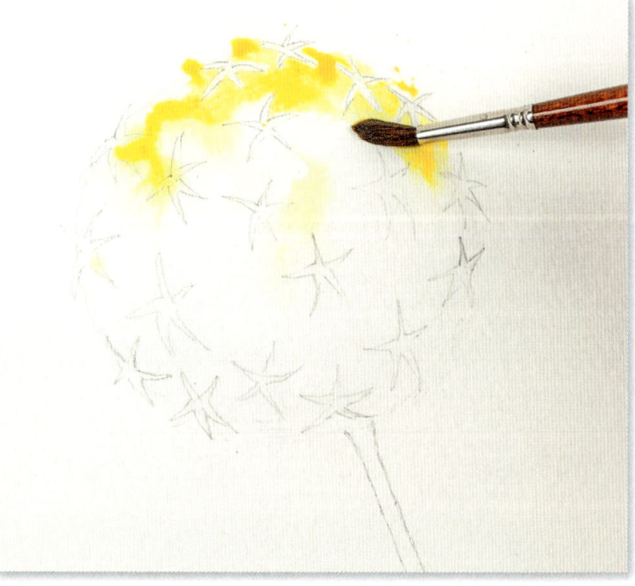

4 Using the wet brush, pick up some sunburst lemon wash and add it to the top right-hand side of the flower head.

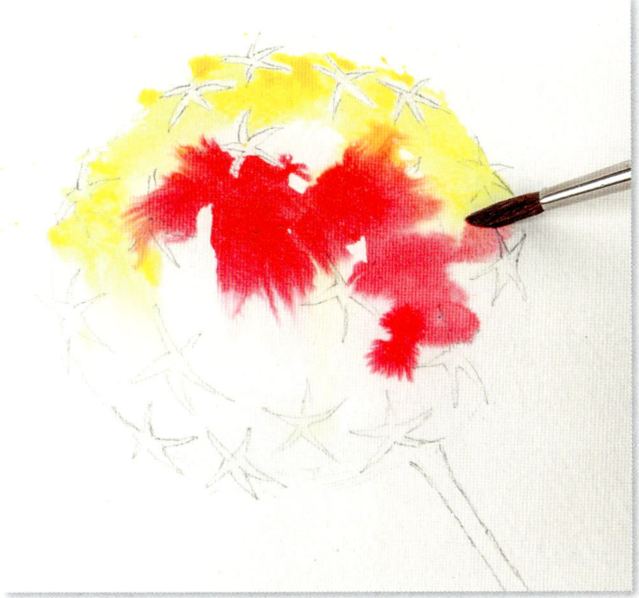 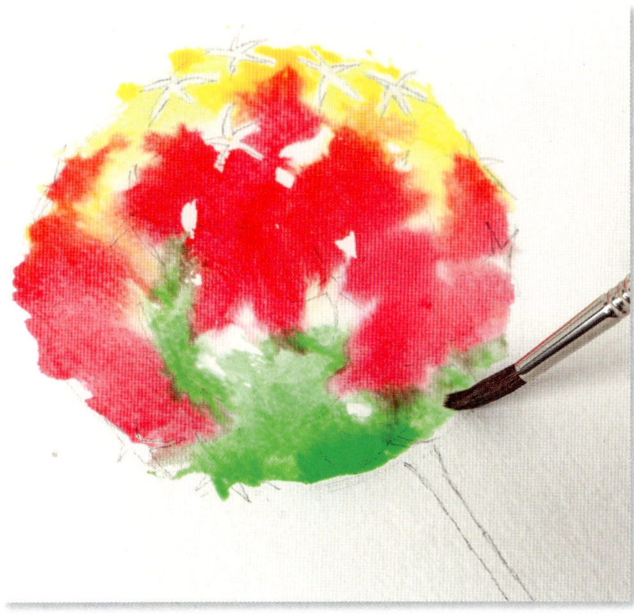

5 Add the crimson wash directly underneath the sunburst lemon, while the yellow is still wet.

6 Add the leaf green wash to the base of the flower head. Allow it to run into the crimson above and use your brush to pull it down into the green stem.

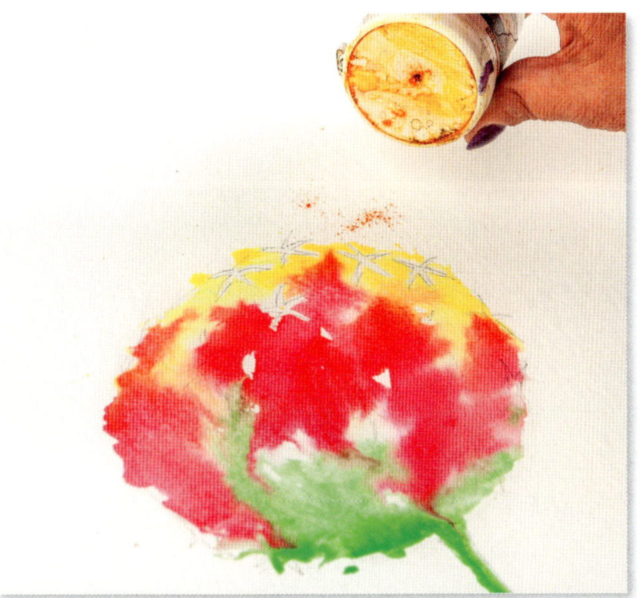 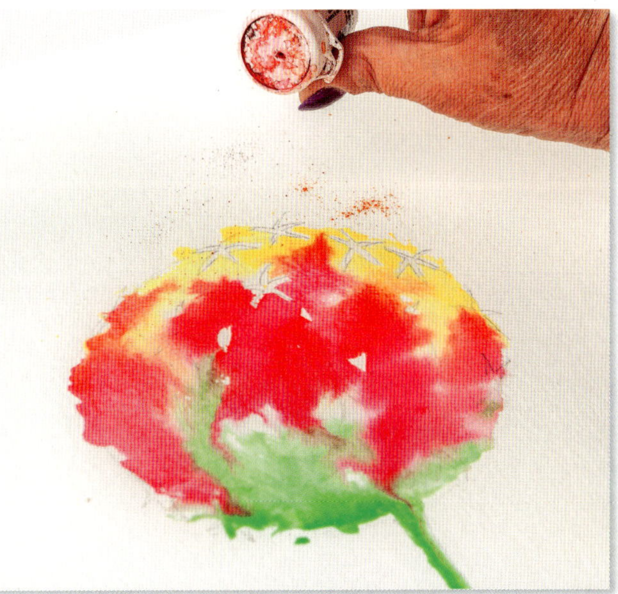

7 Add a sprinkle of sunburst lemon Brusho powder into the top right-hand corner, to break the regular shape of the flower head.

8 Repeat with the crimson Brusho crystals.

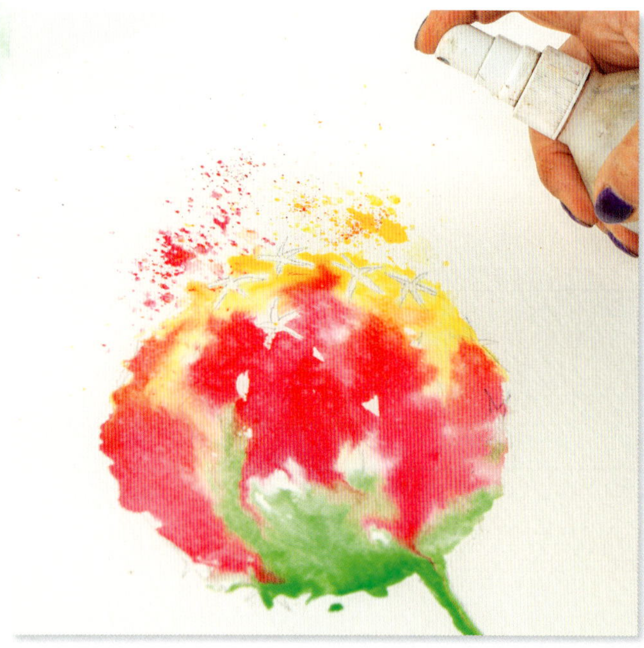

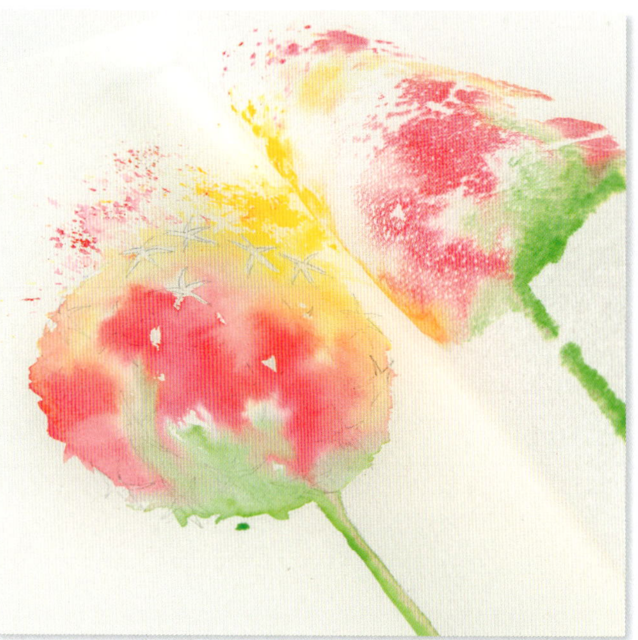

9 Add a spray of water to activate the powder above the flower head.

10 Use kitchen paper to blot the page. Allow to dry completely.

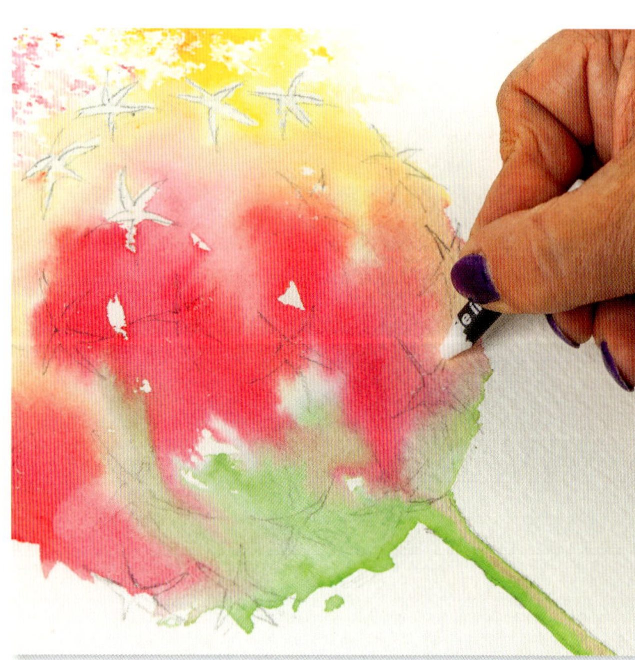

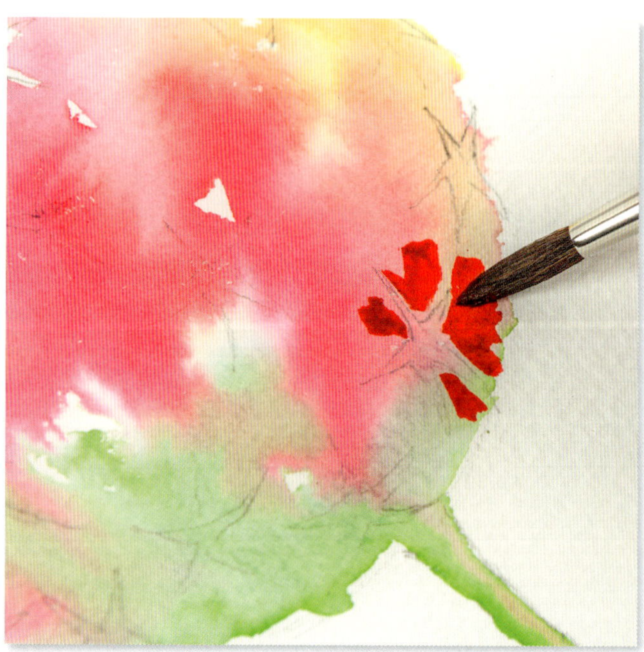

11 Cover the remaining star-shaped pencil lines with wax. (There is no need to apply more wax to the star shapes you already applied wax to in step 2.) This will preserve the coloured wash of the star shapes when we add further washes later and the lighter colour will shine through!

12 Mix a stronger wash of the crimson. Starting at the base of the flower, negatively paint around the existing wax star shapes. Using this darker colour around the star shapes helps to define them.

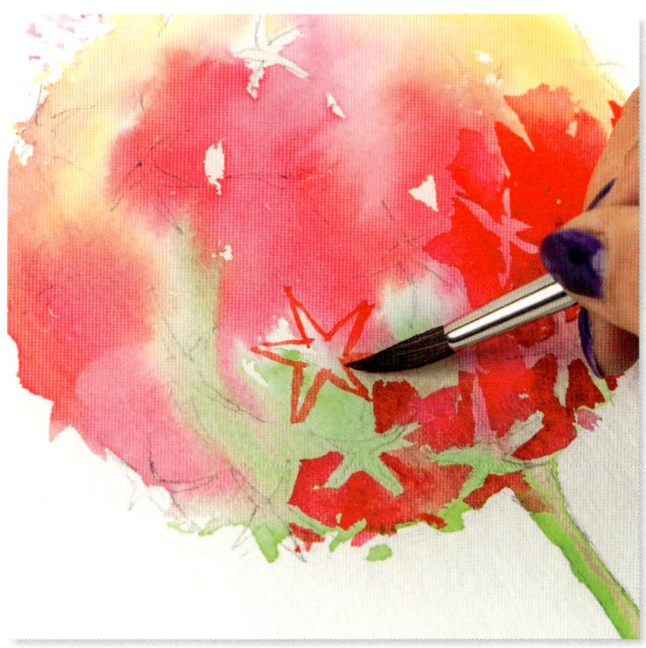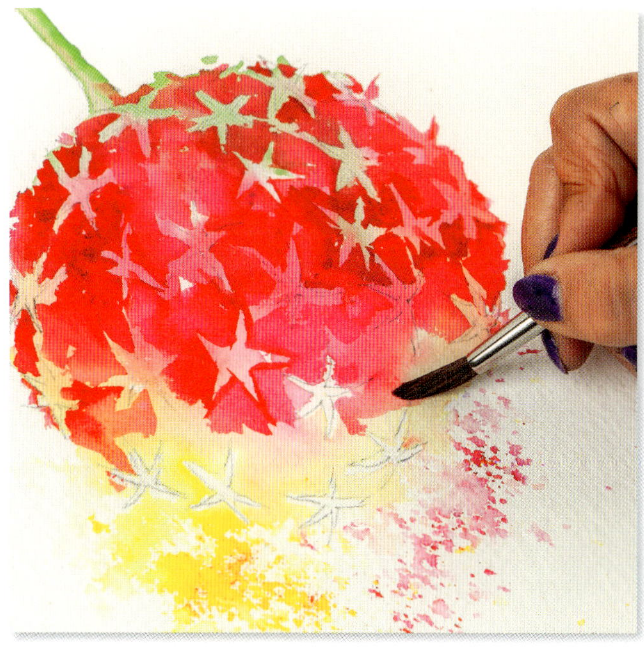

13 Also paint in new star shapes with your brush. Don't worry if they are not perfectly shaped.

14 Make sure your strong wash becomes weaker as it travels to the top of the flower, by adding more water to the wash as you go. Turn your paper if that makes it easier for you to work.

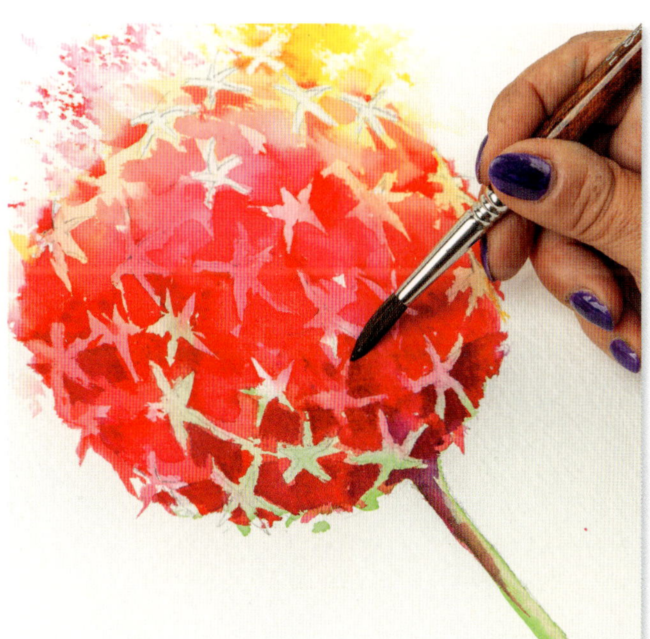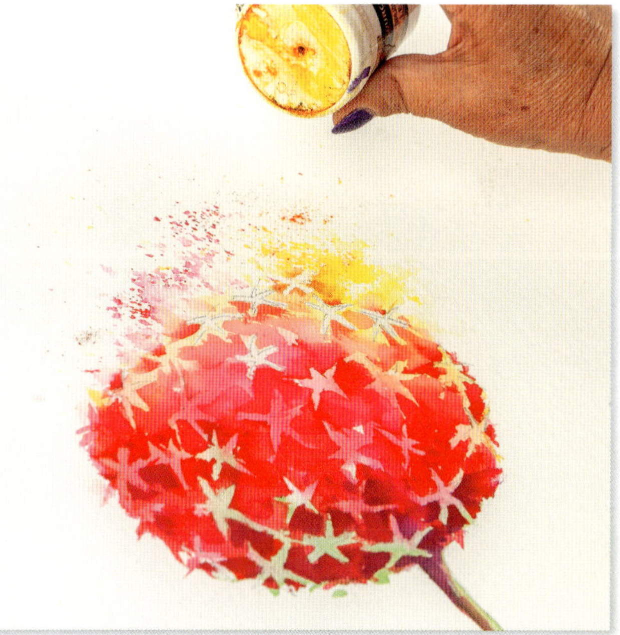

15 Let this wash dry. Mix crimson and purple together to create a stronger wash. Use this to paint around the star-shaped flowers at the base of the flower head to make them more prominent.

16 Add an extra bit of crimson sprinkle in the top right-hand corner above the flower head. Repeat with the sunburst lemon.

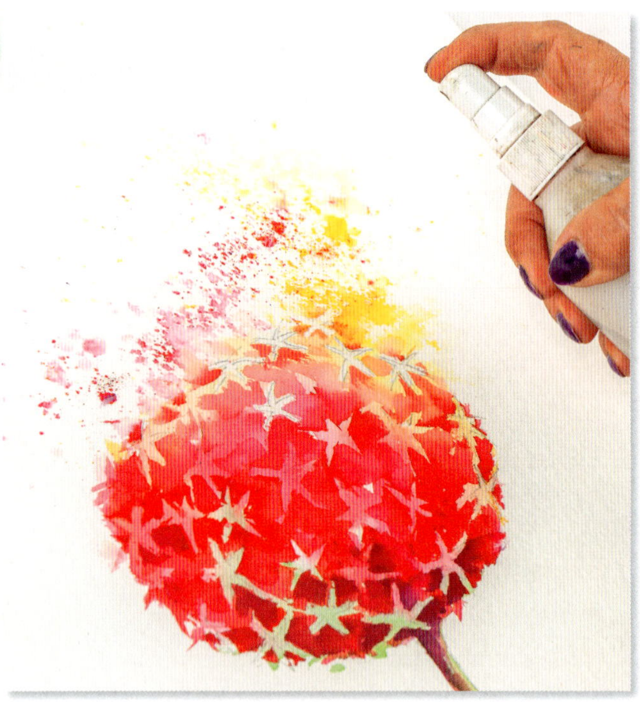

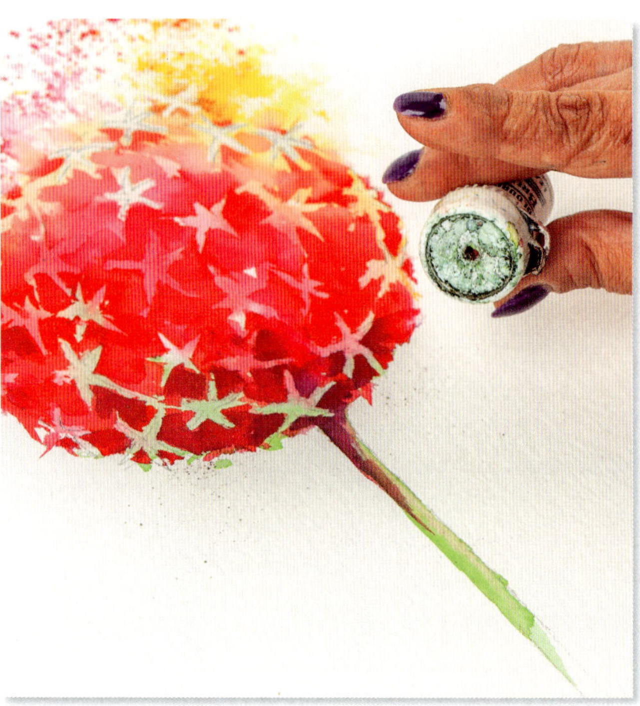

17 Carefully spritz with clean water and watch the colours explode. Allow to dry.

18 Sprinkle leaf green Brusho to the right of the stem.

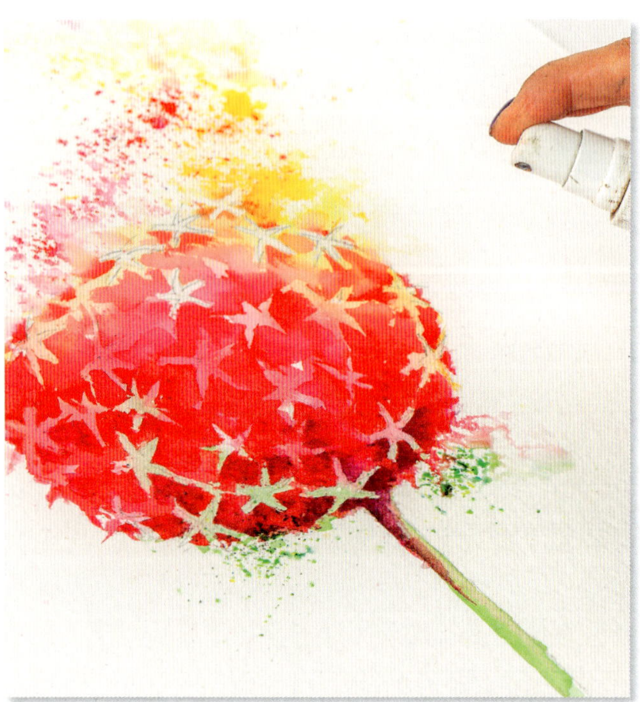

19 Again, carefully spray and watch the water do its magic. Allow to dry.

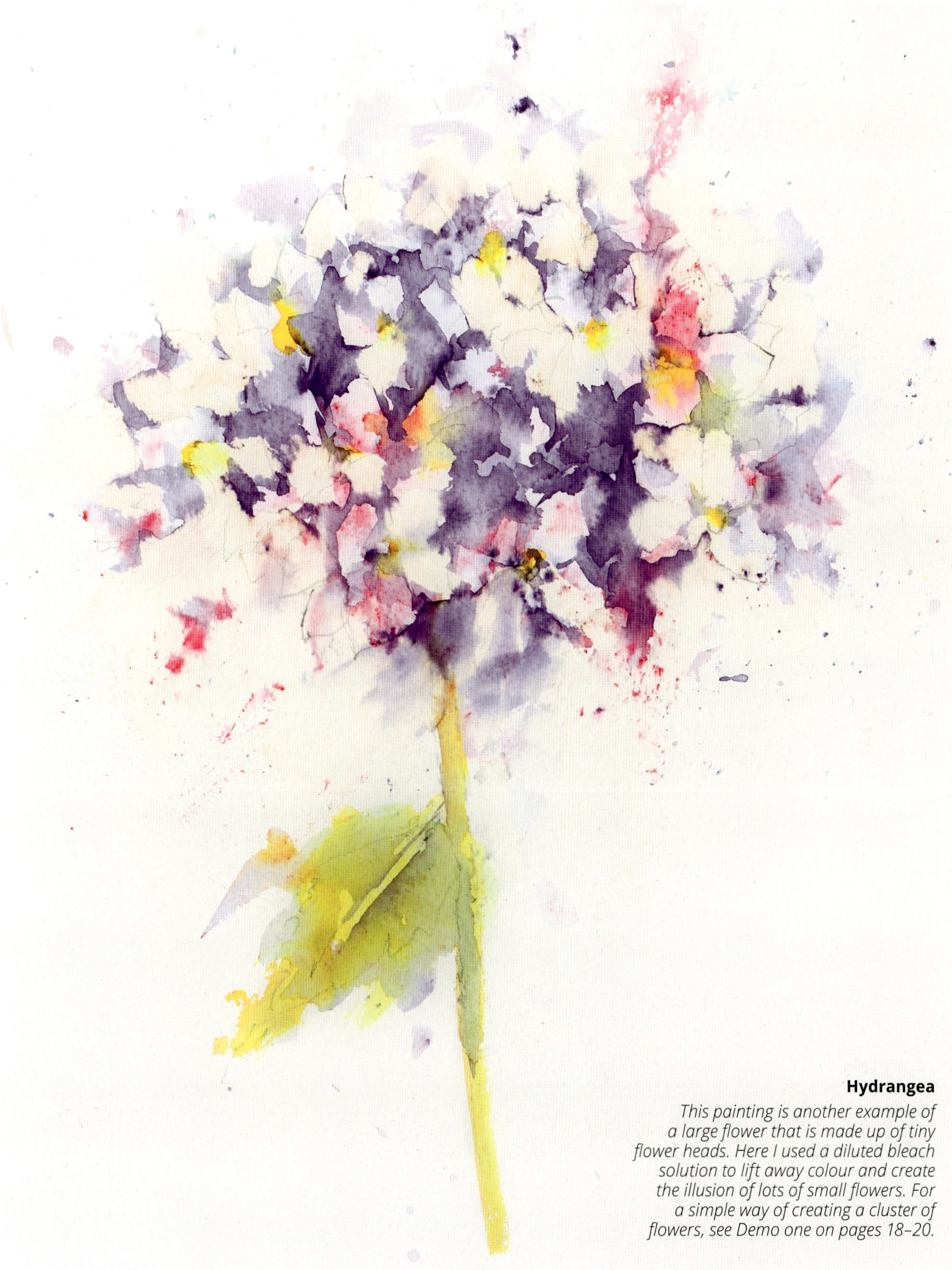

Hydrangea

This painting is another example of a large flower that is made up of tiny flower heads. Here I used a diluted bleach solution to lift away colour and create the illusion of lots of small flowers. For a simple way of creating a cluster of flowers, see Demo one on pages 18–20.

Crashing Waves

This wave crashing against the rocks is a perfect way to explore the bleach technique. If we were painting this subject with watercolour we would have to carefully mask out or paint around a white section such as the wave. It is very liberating knowing that you can create a beautiful white crashing wave using a simple technique.

Experiment with the paper and colours you wish to use to give you confidence that your bleach solution will lift colour away. Try to be patient as bleach doesn't react instantly; it takes a few minutes to view the results.

This subject is such fun to paint and very exciting to see the crashing wave start to appear.

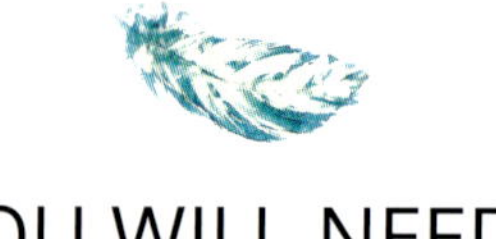

YOU WILL NEED

- Bockingford watercolour paper
  300gsm (140lb) Not surface,
  half imperial (38 x 56cm/15 x 22in)
- 3B pencil
- Eraser
- Brusho paint: gamboge, turquoise, brilliant red
- Size 8 and 12 brushes
- Spray bottle with water
- Spray bottle with bleach solution – 50% bleach: 50% water
- Palette
- Old brush for bleach
- Scrap of paper
- Ramekin with clean water
- Jug of clean water
- Kitchen paper

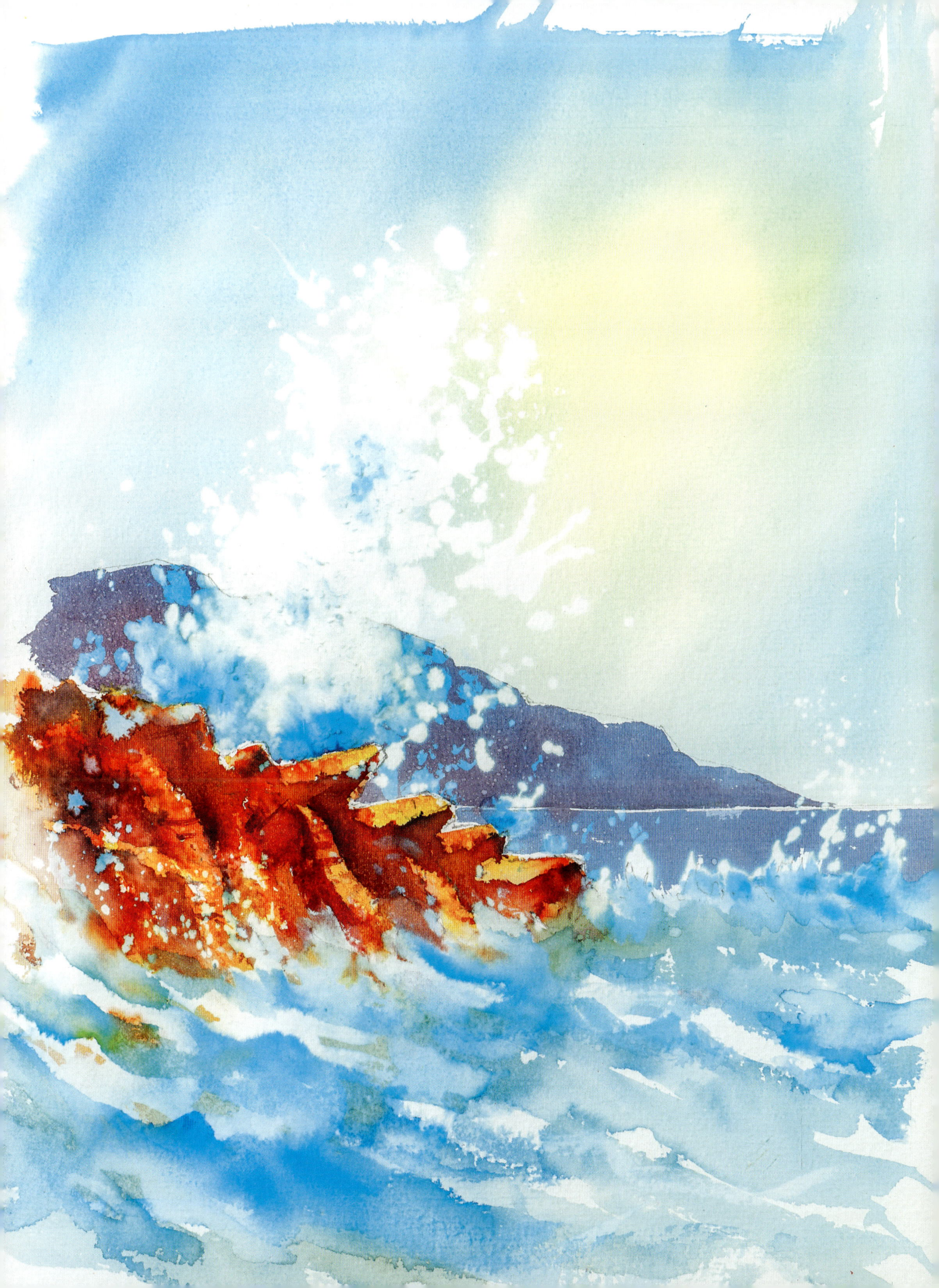

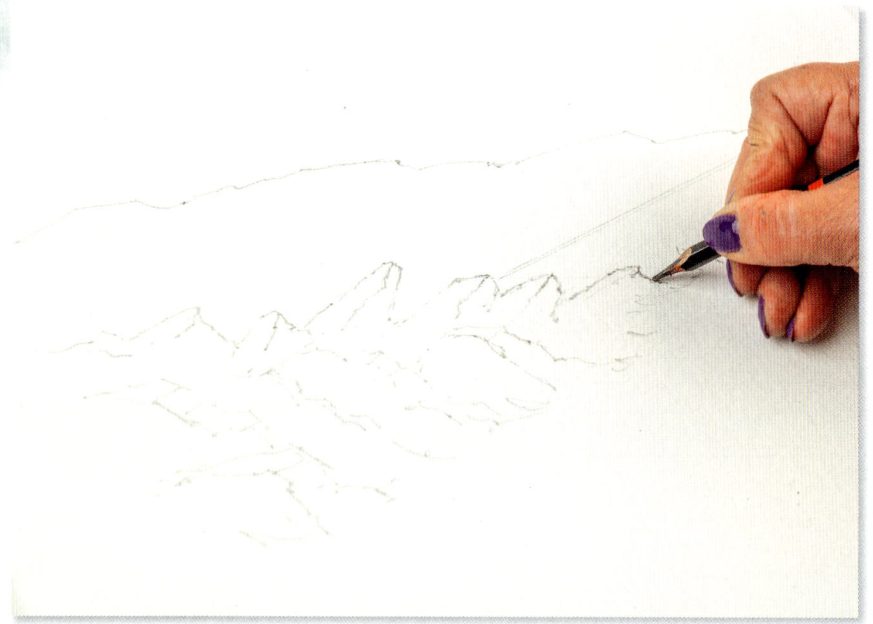

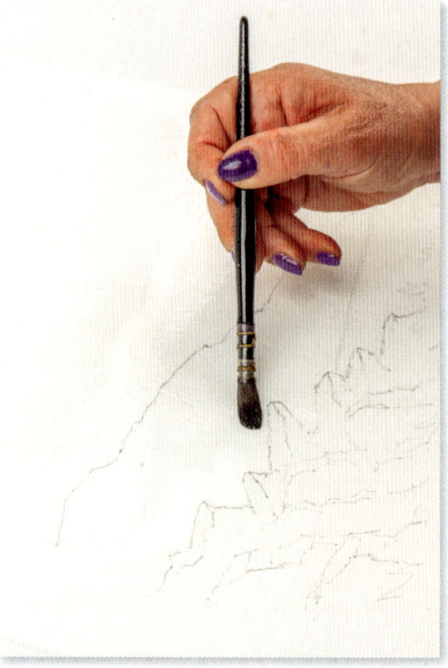

1 Using a soft pencil, sketch out the shapes of the rocks, horizon line and distant hill.

2 Using a brush, wet the page all the way down to the rocks.

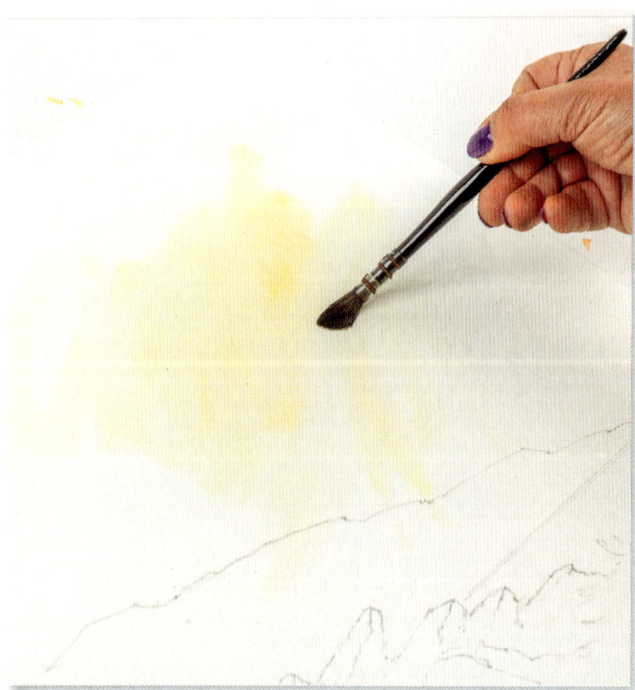

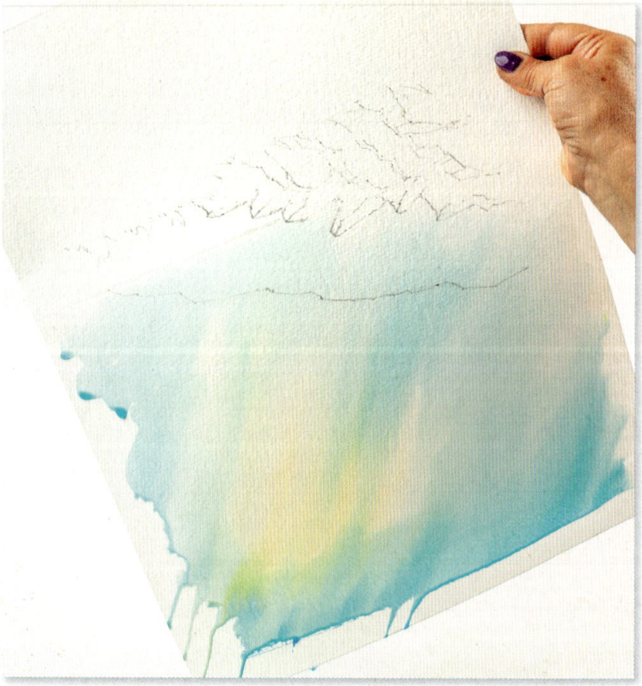

3 In your palette, mix a wash of gamboge and a separate wash of turquoise. Place a little of the gamboge in the sky area with your size 12 brush.

4 Add a slightly stronger turquoise wash, tipping your paper sky down to ensure a flow of sky wash. Let this dry.

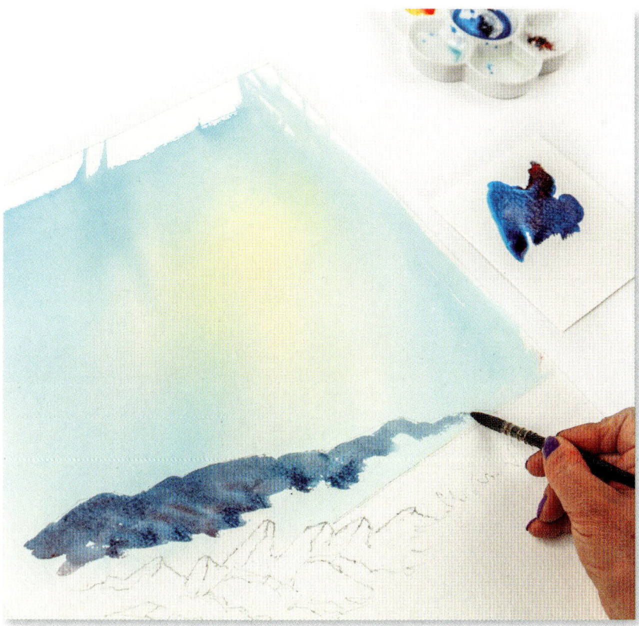

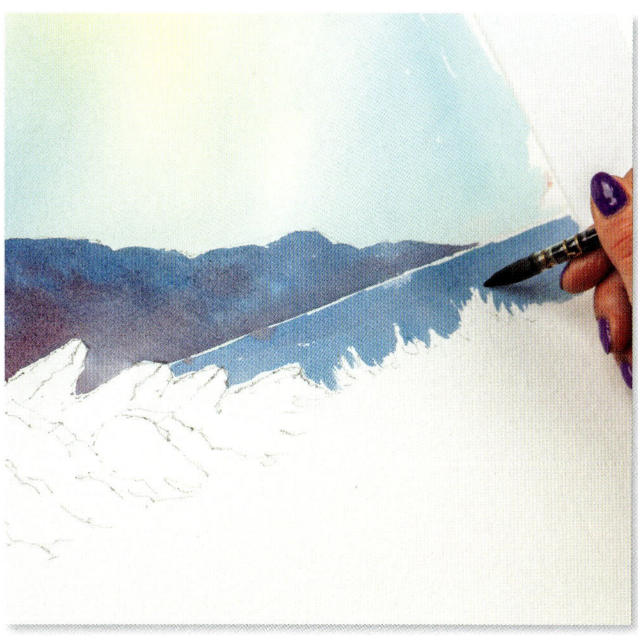

5 Using the turquoise and a little brilliant red, make a wash in your palette. Block in the distant hill with your size 12 brush. This wash should be much stronger than your sky wash. Let this dry. Rotate your paper if you need to.

6 Using a wash of the turquoise, paint the distant sea starting at the horizon line, working your way down to where the blue sea meets the smaller waves. Paint around the splashes with your size 12 brush. Don't worry if your small waves disappear – we will be using our bleach solution later to make them magically appear again. Let this dry.

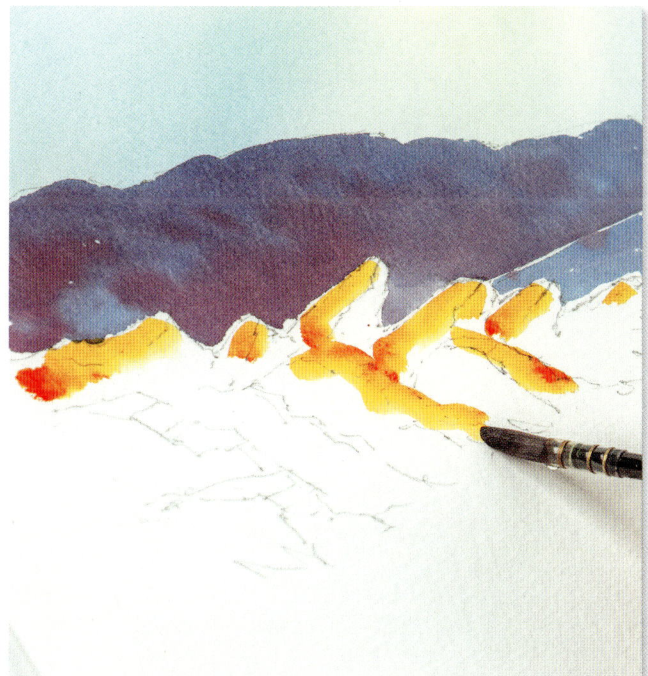

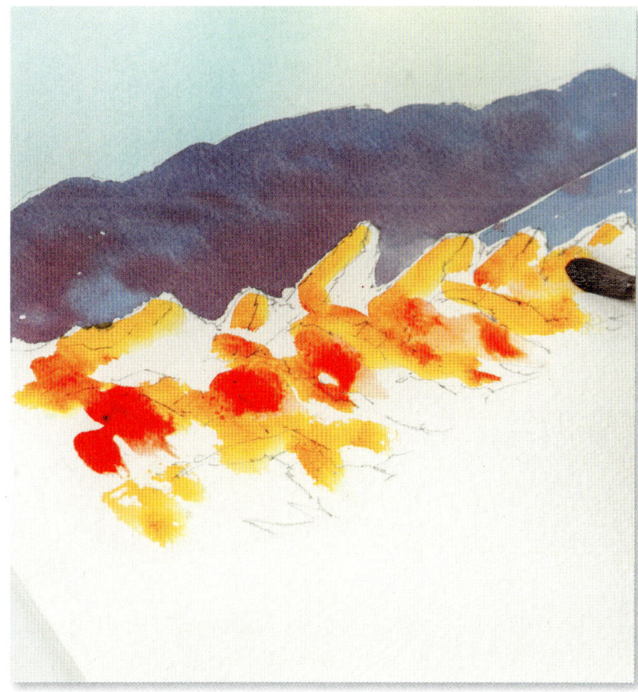

7 Using a wash of the gamboge, paint over the rock shapes.

8 Add a little of the brilliant red, but make sure that the gamboge is prominent. Allow to dry.

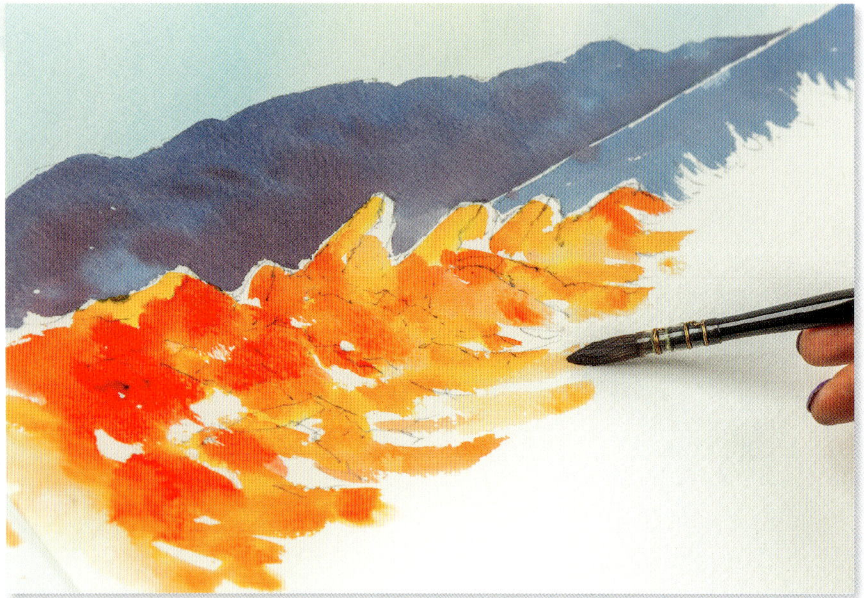

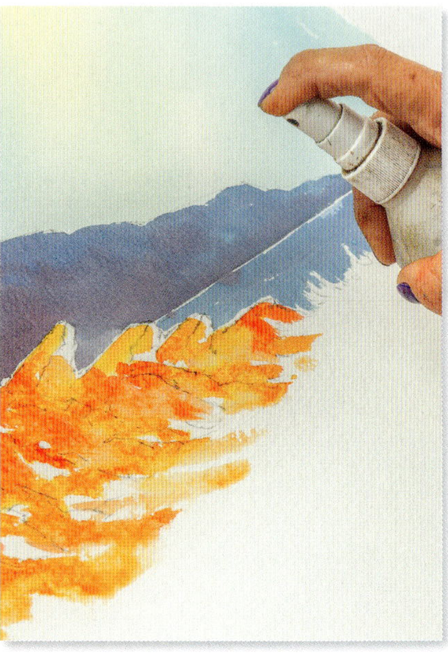

9 Blend the wash into where the rocks will meet the water. Use your brush to soften this wash into the water area, following the flow of the water.

10 You can spray this area to activate the colours and create a slight texture on the rocks. Let this dry.

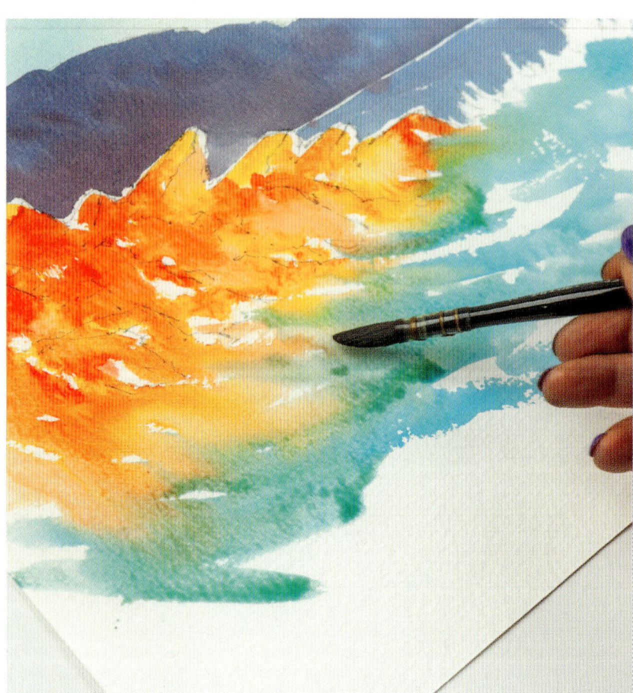

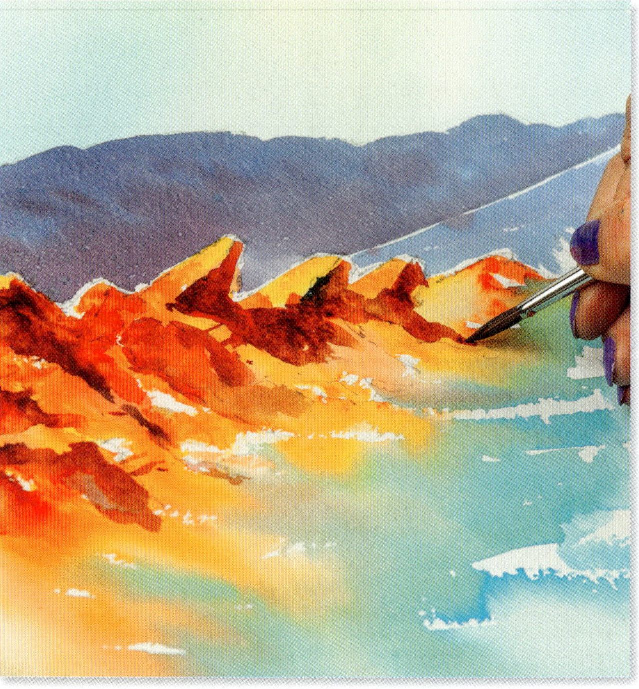

11 Pull the waves down and across using your size 12 brush.

12 Using a stronger wash of the turquoise and brilliant red, paint in stronger values on the rocks with your size 8 brush, remembering to leave sections of gamboge to create light on the rocks.

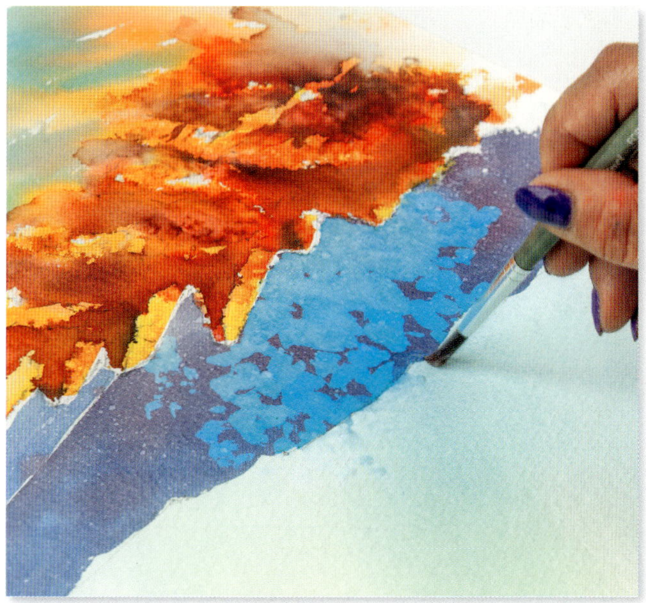

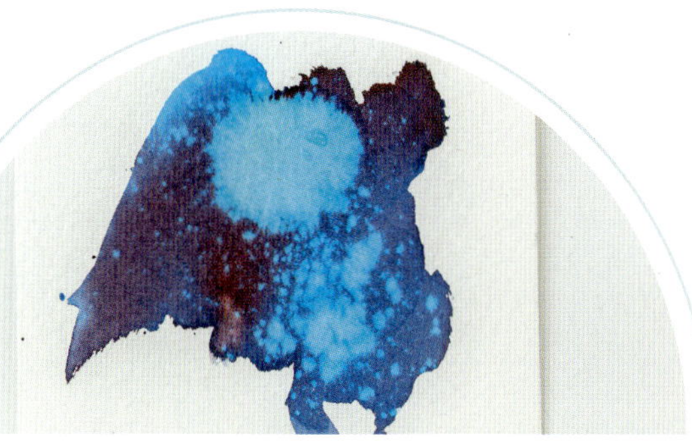

Test out your bleach solution on a piece of scrap paper using the same wash as on your painting. I can see that my distant hill won't lift as much as I want, so I make my bleach solution stronger.

13 Now for the big crashing wave! Spray the bleach solution onto a piece of scrap paper or a palette. Turn your picture upside down if you find it easier. Start to apply the bleach to the hill with your old brush to give the impression of the froth on the waves.

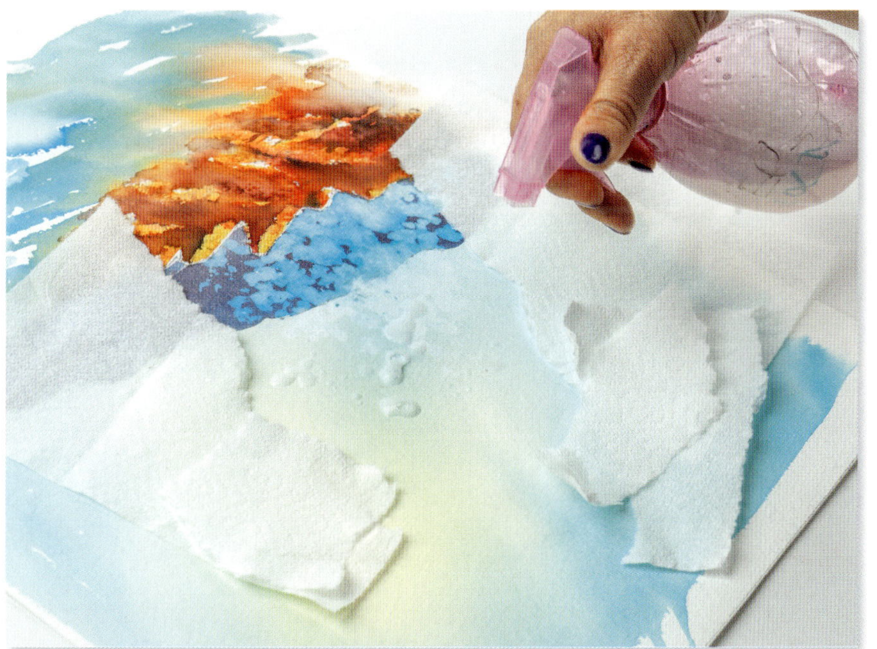

Tip

Remember that the bleach solution may take a minute to lift away colour, so try to be patient and soon your big crashing wave will start to appear.

14 If you are feeling brave you can spatter the bleach solution to suggest smaller drops of water. Mask off the edges of the hill with kitchen paper to avoid the bleach spray reaching it. Take care and always spatter the solution away from you to avoid any accidents.

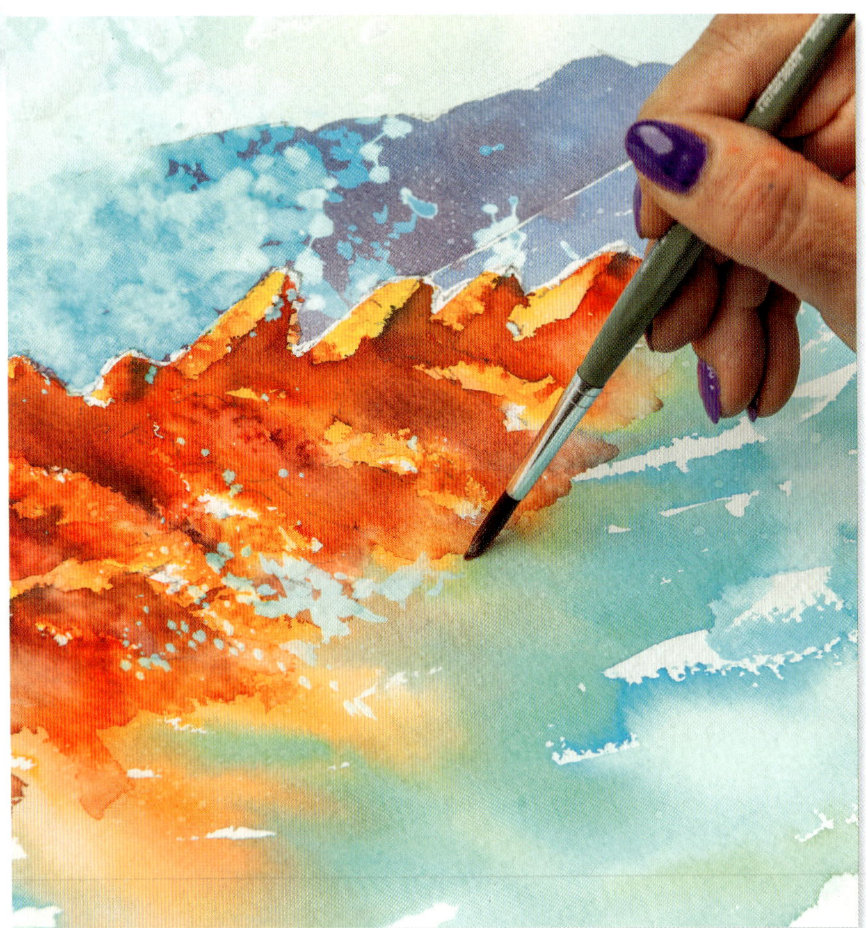

15 Use your bleach solution to lift away some colour at the base of the rocks to suggest the water crashing against them. Do the same with the smaller wave at the edge of the water. Let this dry.

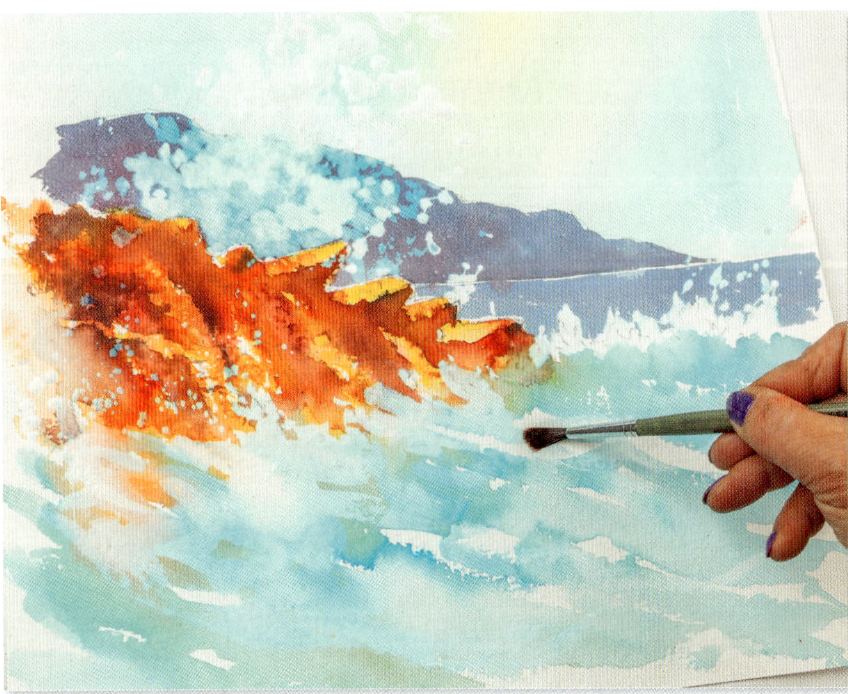

16 Still using your bleach solution, pull your brush down into the wave area. You can spatter the bleach solution by tapping it off the end of the brush. You want the distant hill to almost disappear under the choppy sea. Allow to dry.

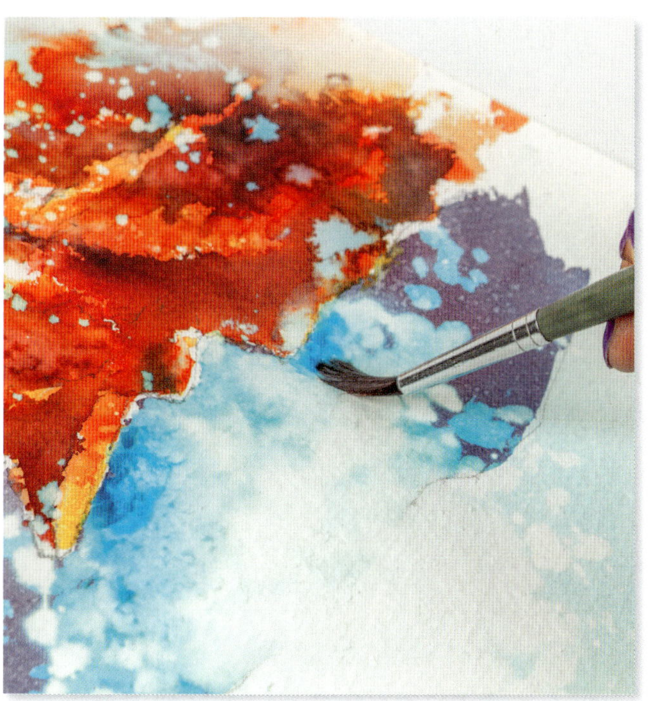

17 Using a weak solution of turquoise and your old brush, add some value to the large wave and where the wave meets the rocks. Again, turn your picture upside down if you find it easier. Try not to cover all of the white area, just add subtle blues especially at the top of the rocks. You can use this blue wash to soften down any of the bleach waves you have created if you think it is needed. By adding darks, you highlight the lights.

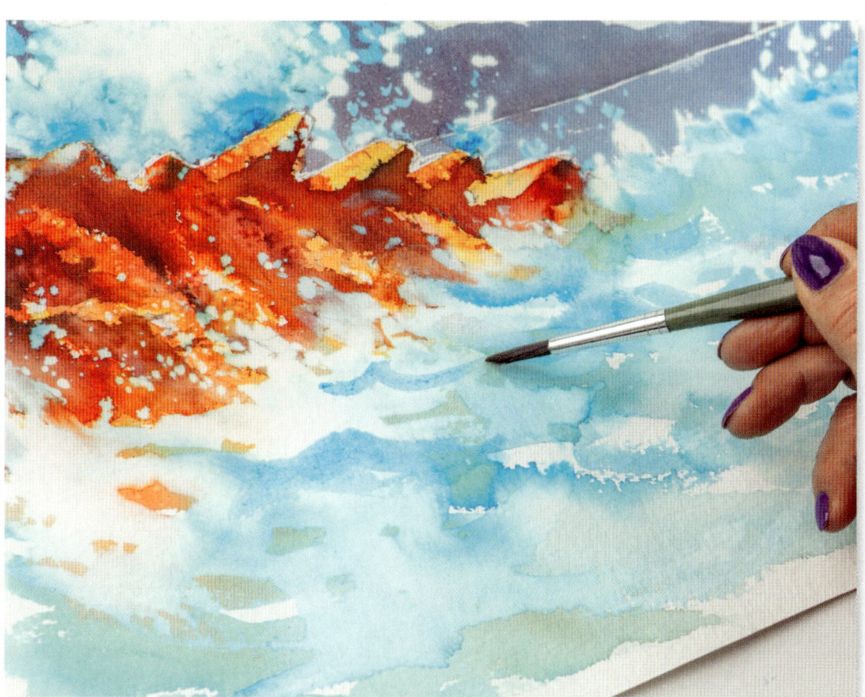

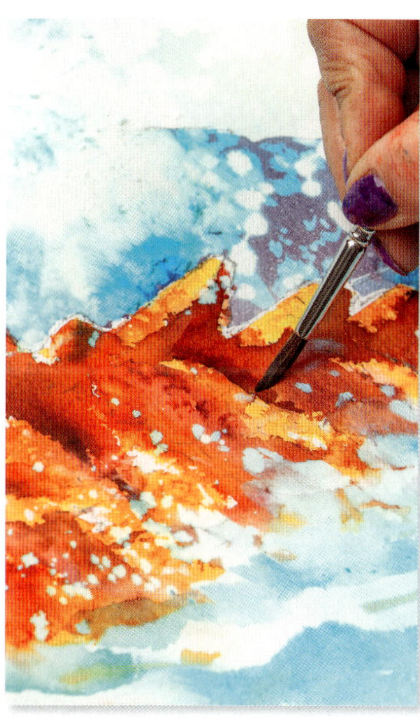

18 Bring this darker wash down into the water area at the base of the rocks, softening the whites and following the flow of the water. This knocks back the bleach. If you would like more texture on the rocks you can give this area a spritz or shake out a few crystals of Brusho into the wet wash. Allow to dry.

19 Using a dark wash of turquoise and brilliant red, paint in the darkest values on the rocks, placing them next to the yellow lights so the rocks have lovely light highlights.

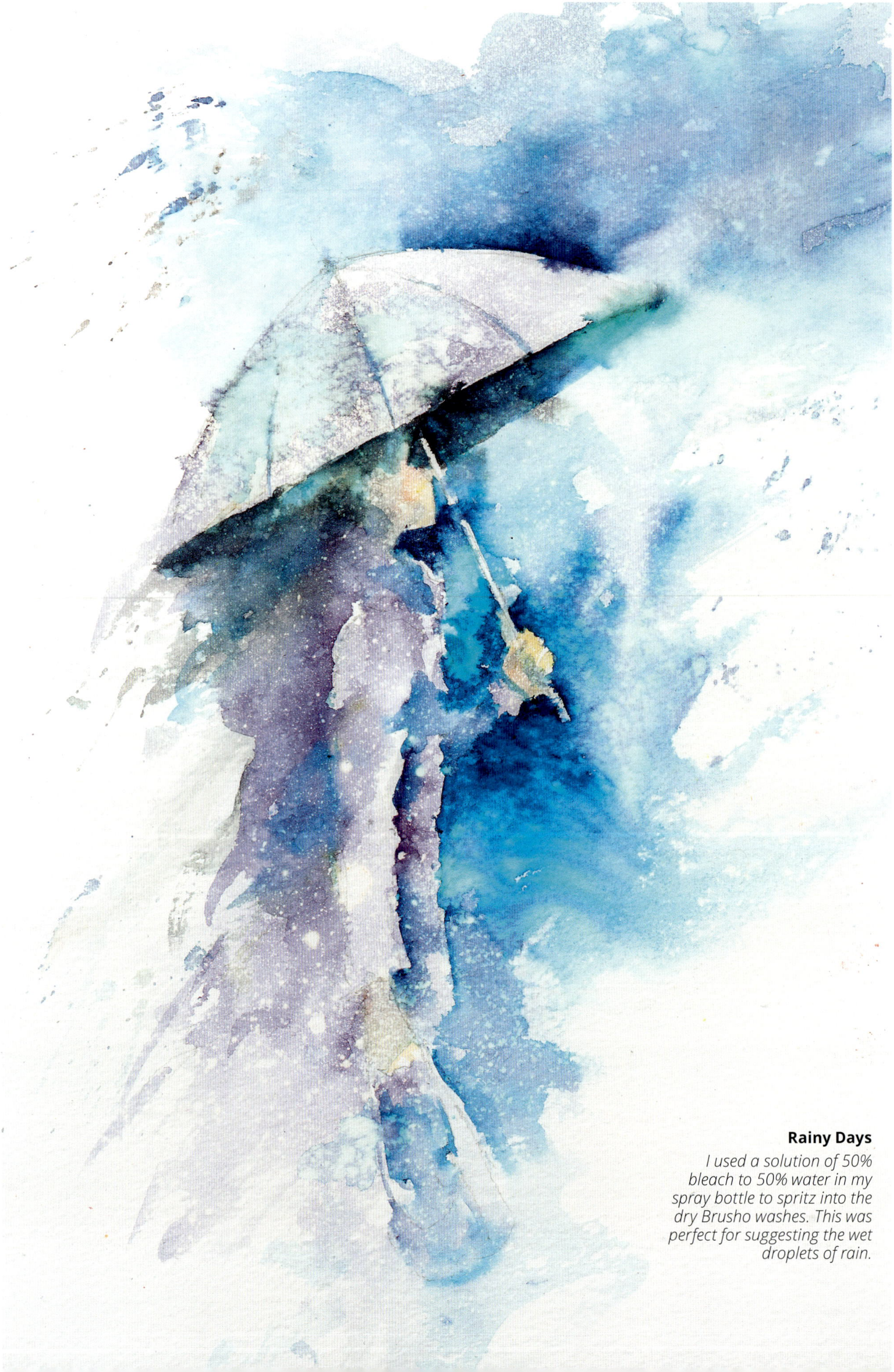

Rainy Days

I used a solution of 50% bleach to 50% water in my spray bottle to spritz into the dry Brusho washes. This was perfect for suggesting the wet droplets of rain.

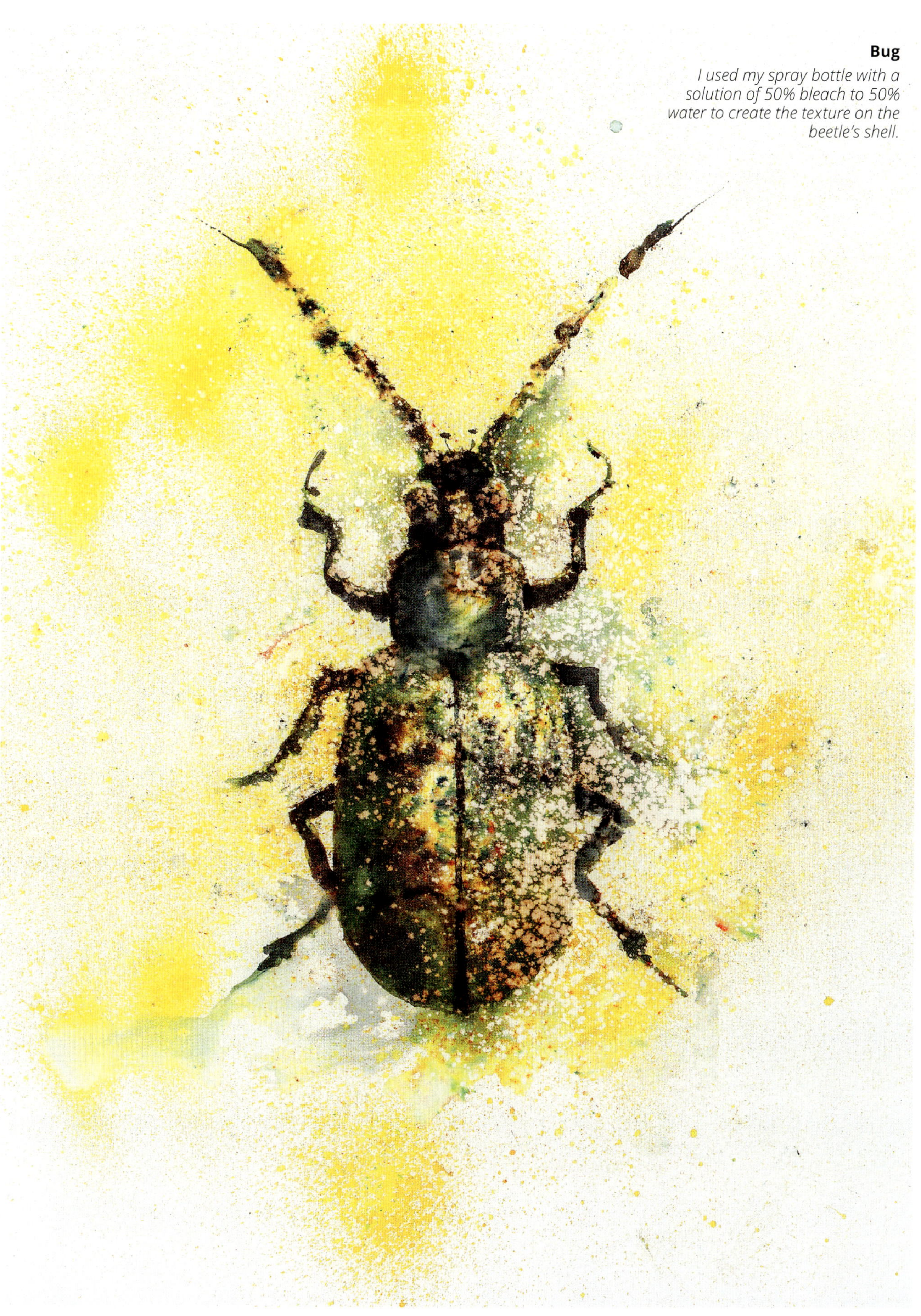

Bug

I used my spray bottle with a solution of 50% bleach to 50% water to create the texture on the beetle's shell.

Taking it further

I frequently tell anyone who wants to paint with Brusho that it is important to experiment and play in order to understand the properties of the medium. I often still have my own 'play days', where my aim is not to create a finished painting, but to have fun experimenting, pushing the boundaries and trying new ideas. My experimenting days have certainly played a huge part when it comes to my more advanced Brusho artwork such as that featured here and on the following pages.

Bridge on the Canal
For this painting I used Brusho in a similar way to how I use watercolours. The soft variegated washes blend together harmoniously on the page to suggest the foliage, water and reflections.

There were also some surprises in this painting, such as the red Brusho crystals that jumped into areas I did not intend them to jump into! However, on balance I feel that they add to the overall charm of the painting.

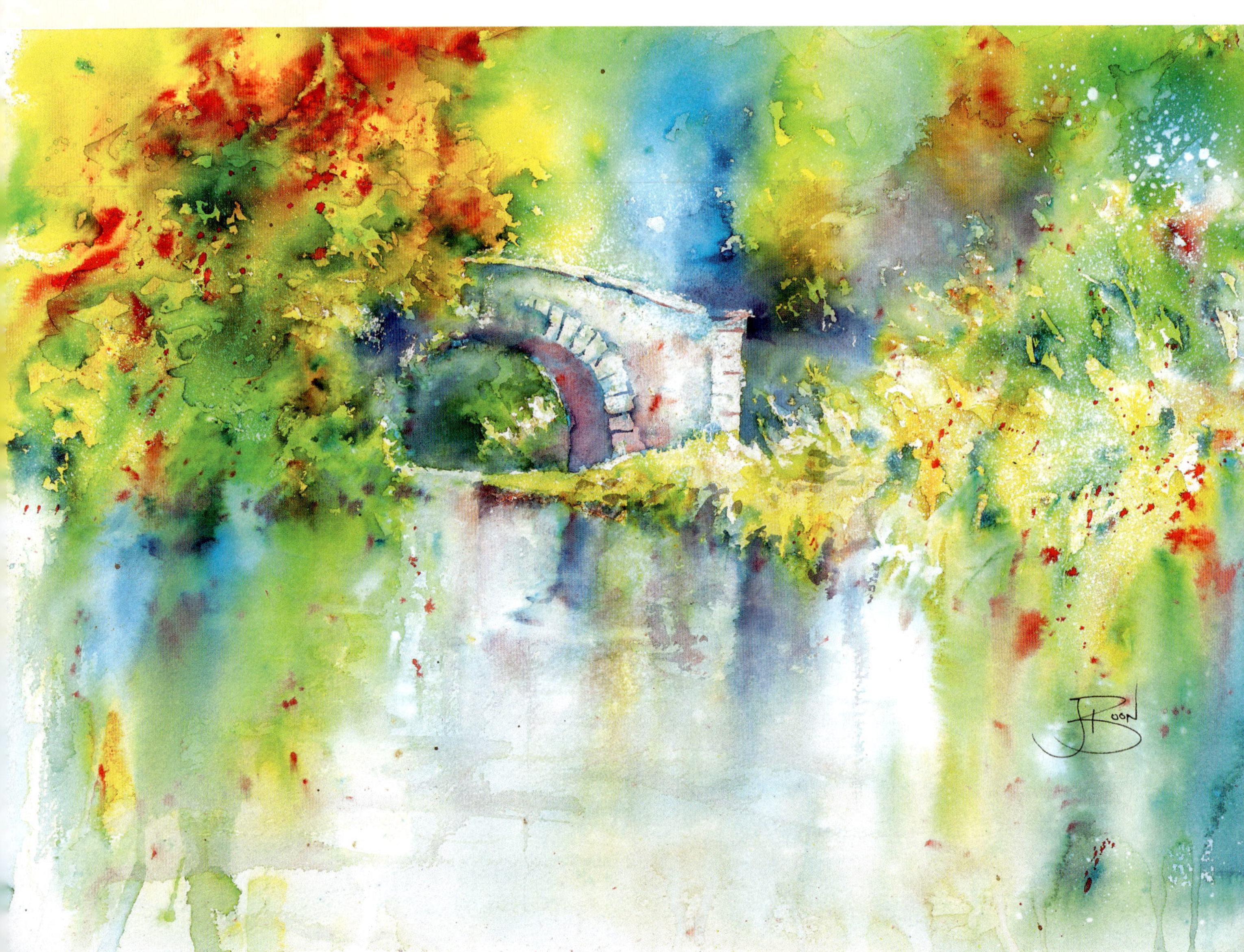

Autumn Landscape
In this landscape, you can see how my sprinkle and spray technique created the tree foliage and foreground textures. With a little help from my diluted bleach solution I created the winding pathway, taking the viewer on a journey past the sheep, through the autumn landscape and beyond.

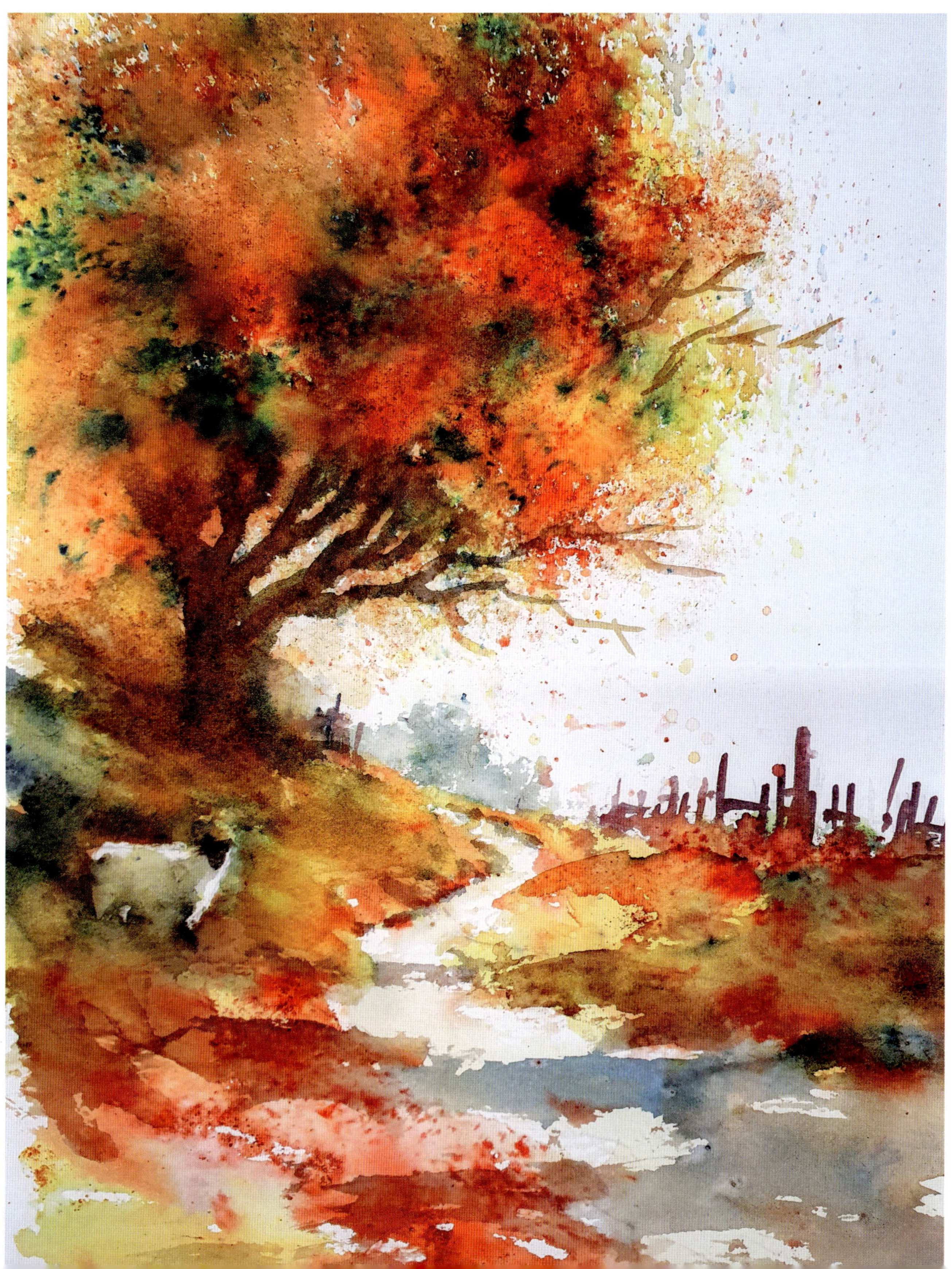

Stencils

I discovered that I could create an added dimension to my paintings by combining stencilled patterns with the unique properties of Brusho. You can see examples of how I've used this experimental technique on the following pages. Although the process looks complicated, it is in fact very achievable.

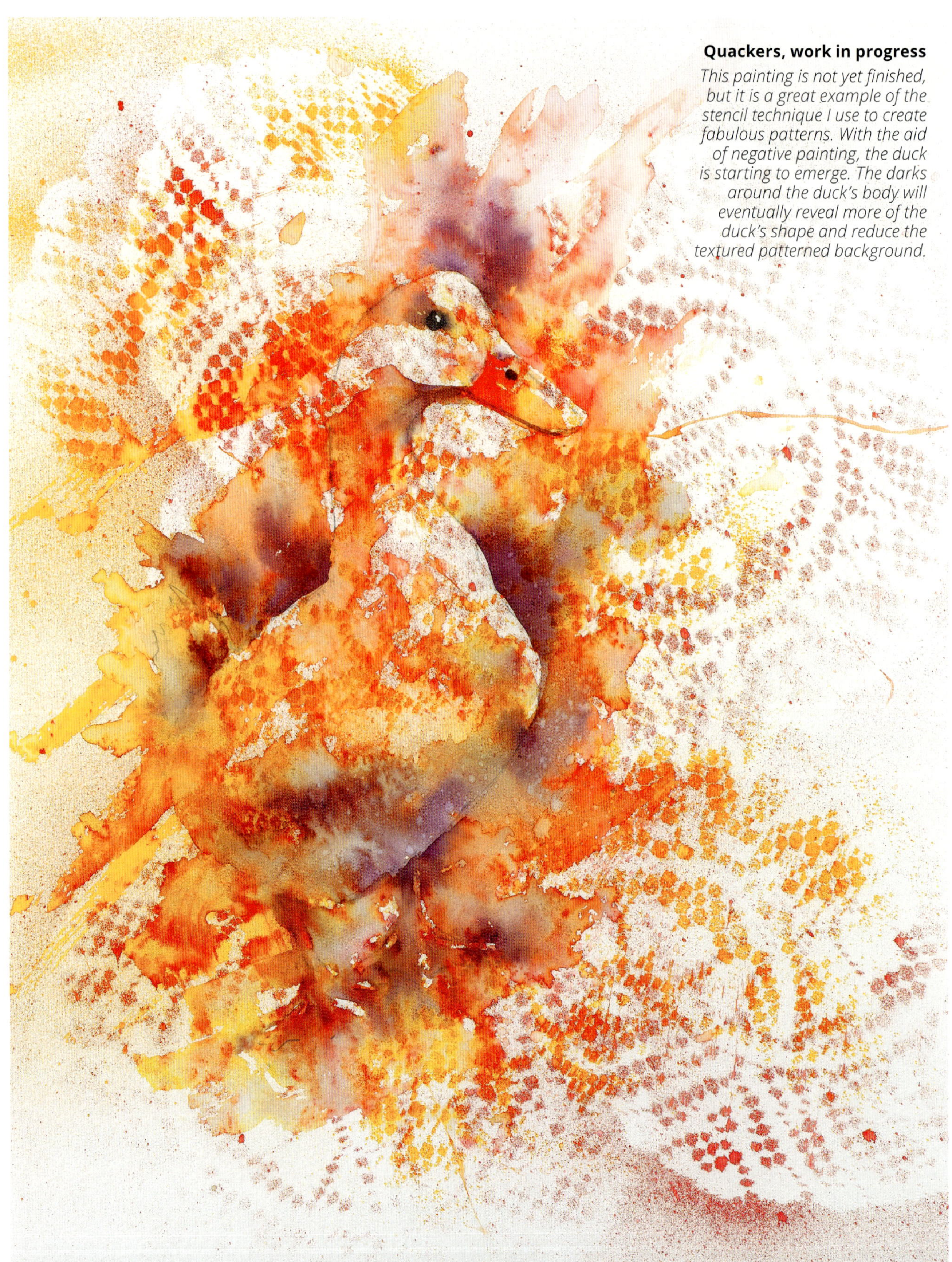

Quackers, work in progress
This painting is not yet finished, but it is a great example of the stencil technique I use to create fabulous patterns. With the aid of negative painting, the duck is starting to emerge. The darks around the duck's body will eventually reveal more of the duck's shape and reduce the textured patterned background.

Red Rooster
This stunning rooster appears from the stencil background with the aid of some negative painting. Here I have used a little wax resist and a small amount of bleach on his beak for the finishing touches.

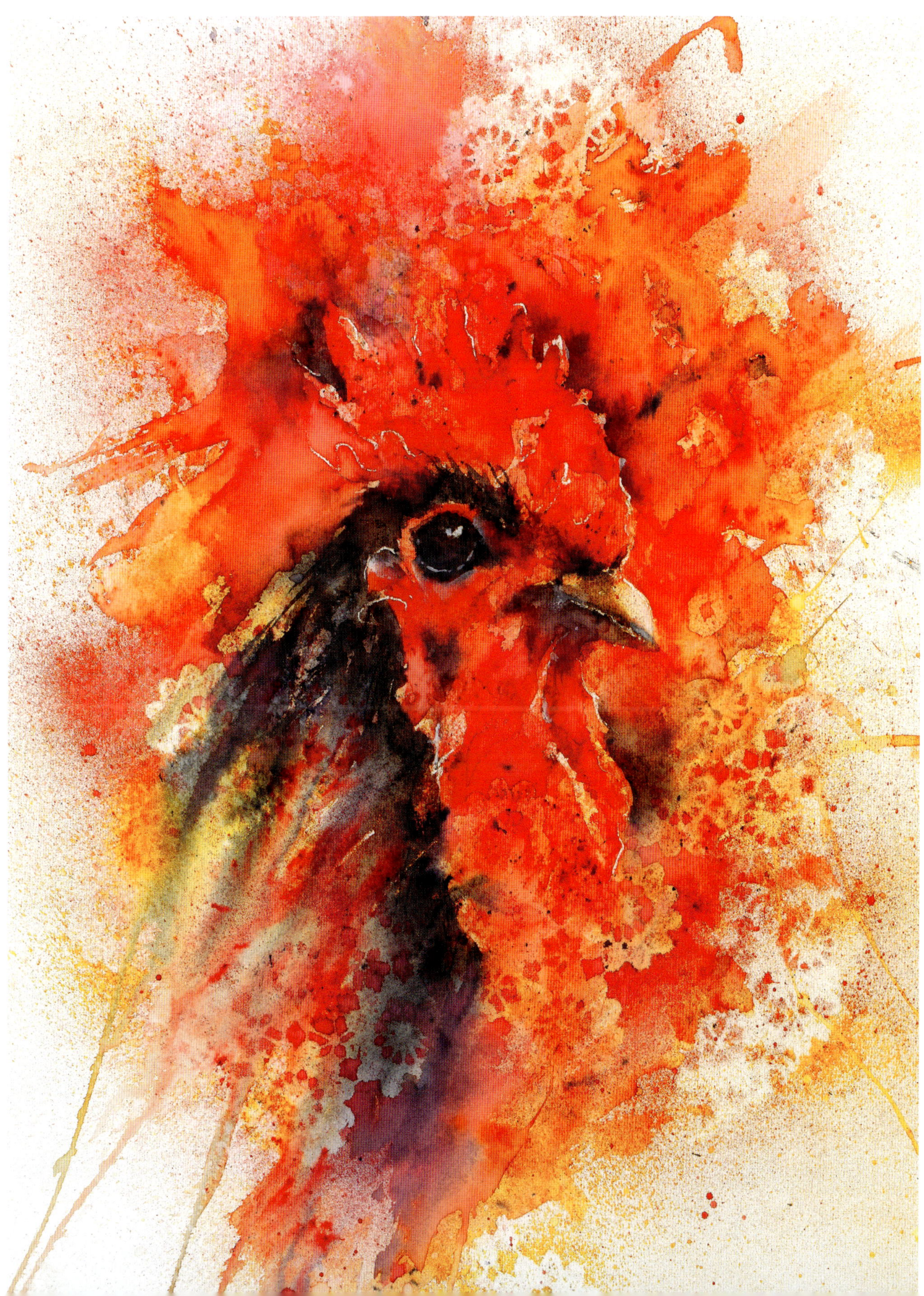

Floral Emerging

This is one of my favourite Brusho florals. It took a long time to complete this piece as I have incorporated many different techniques such as sprinkle and spray, application of bleach, stencilling and lots of negative painting to bring the main flower forward and link the colours and stencil patterns together so that they work in harmony.

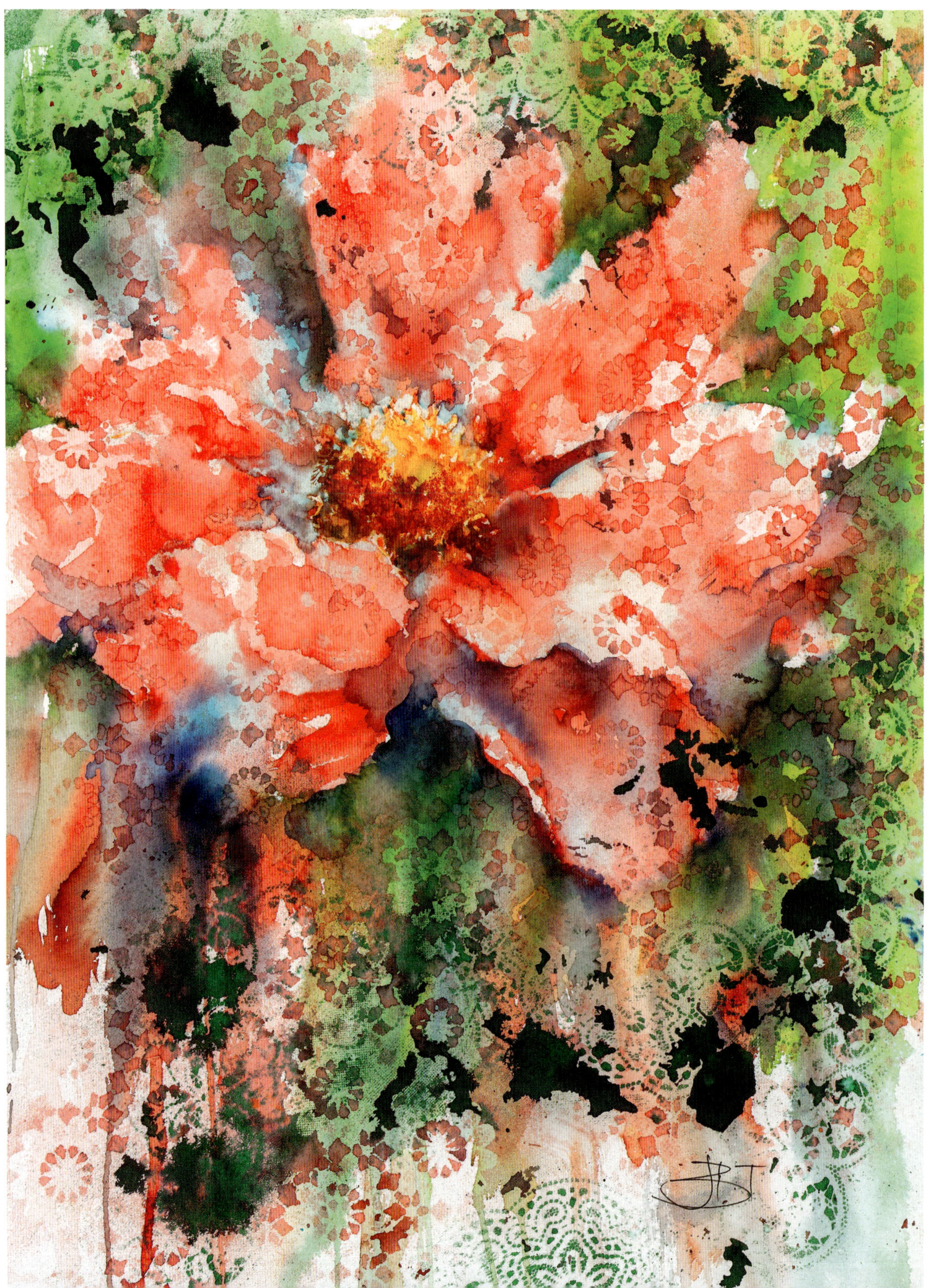

Outlines

The outlines are all reproduced at half actual size. Please either use them scaled up 200 per cent, or use them as a guide. They are also available to download free from Bookmarked: www.bookmarkedhub.com. Search for this book by title or ISBN: the files can be found under 'Book Extras'. Membership of the Bookmarked online community is free.

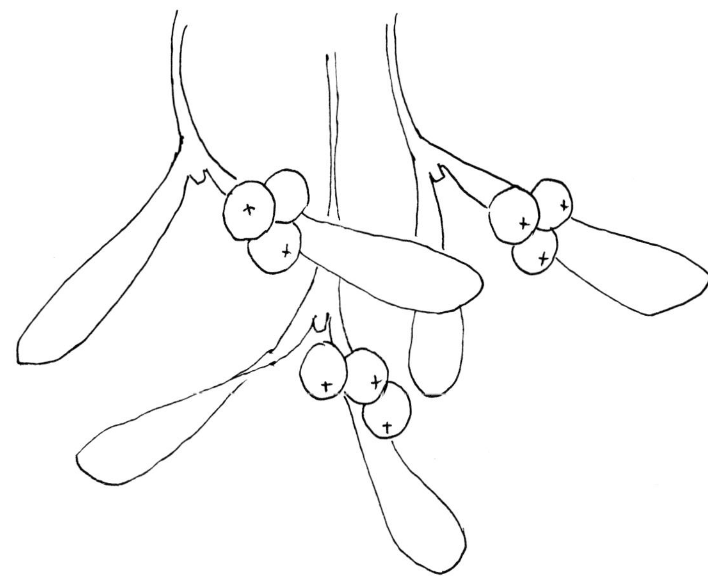

Mistletoe outline, Demo 5, pages 42–45

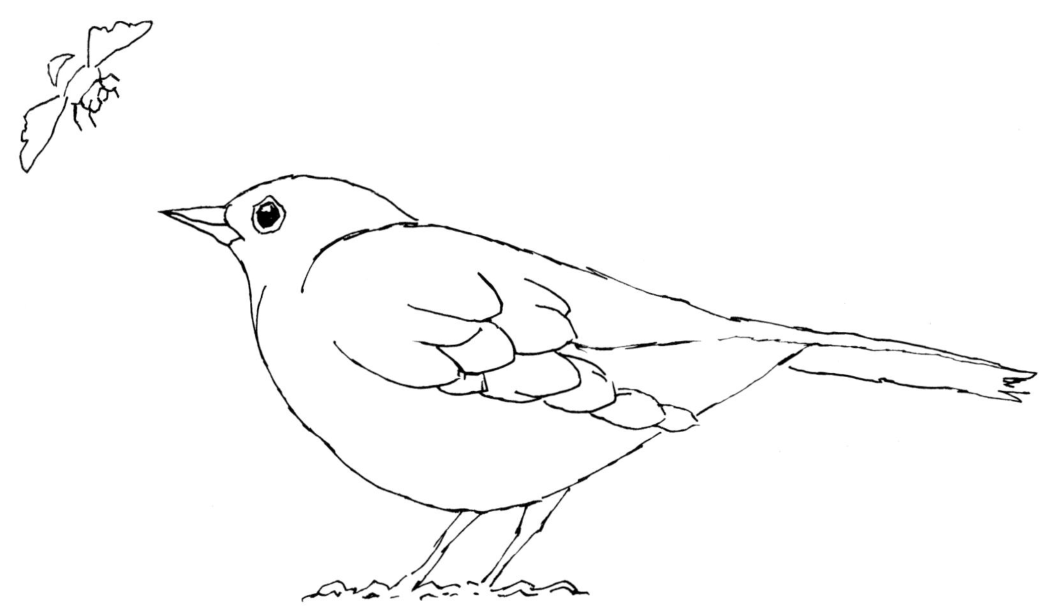

Blackbird outline, Demo 6, pages 47–49

White Duck outline, Project 1, pages 52–57

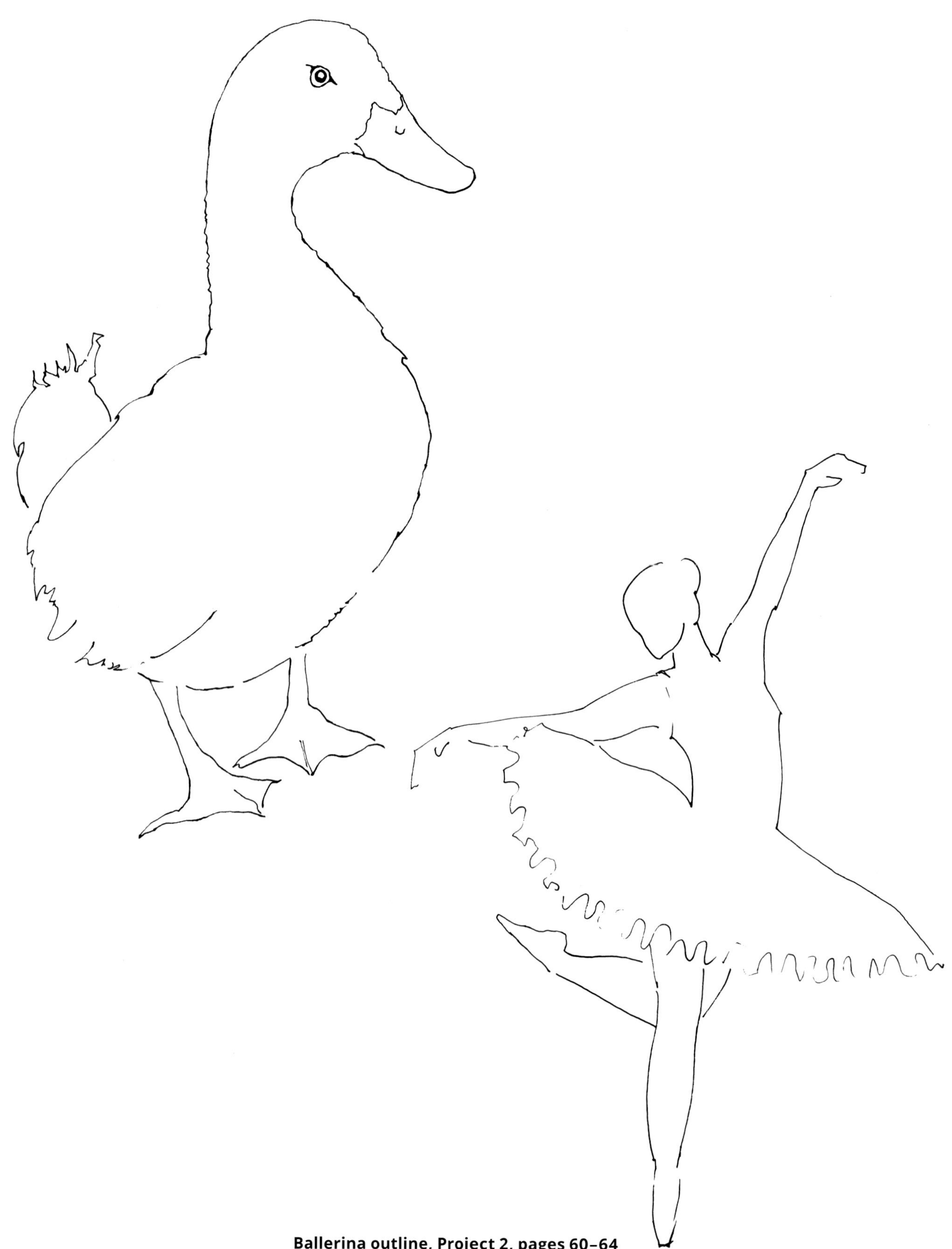

Ballerina outline, Project 2, pages 60–64

Echinacea outline, Project 3, pages 66–71

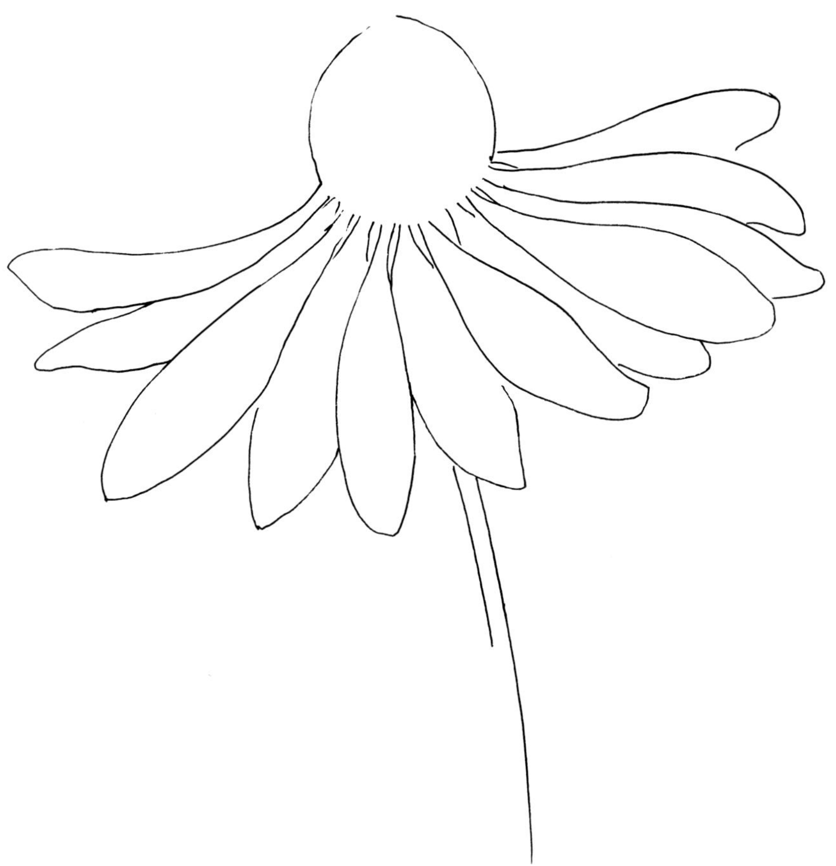

Bumblebee outline, Project 4, pages 74–80

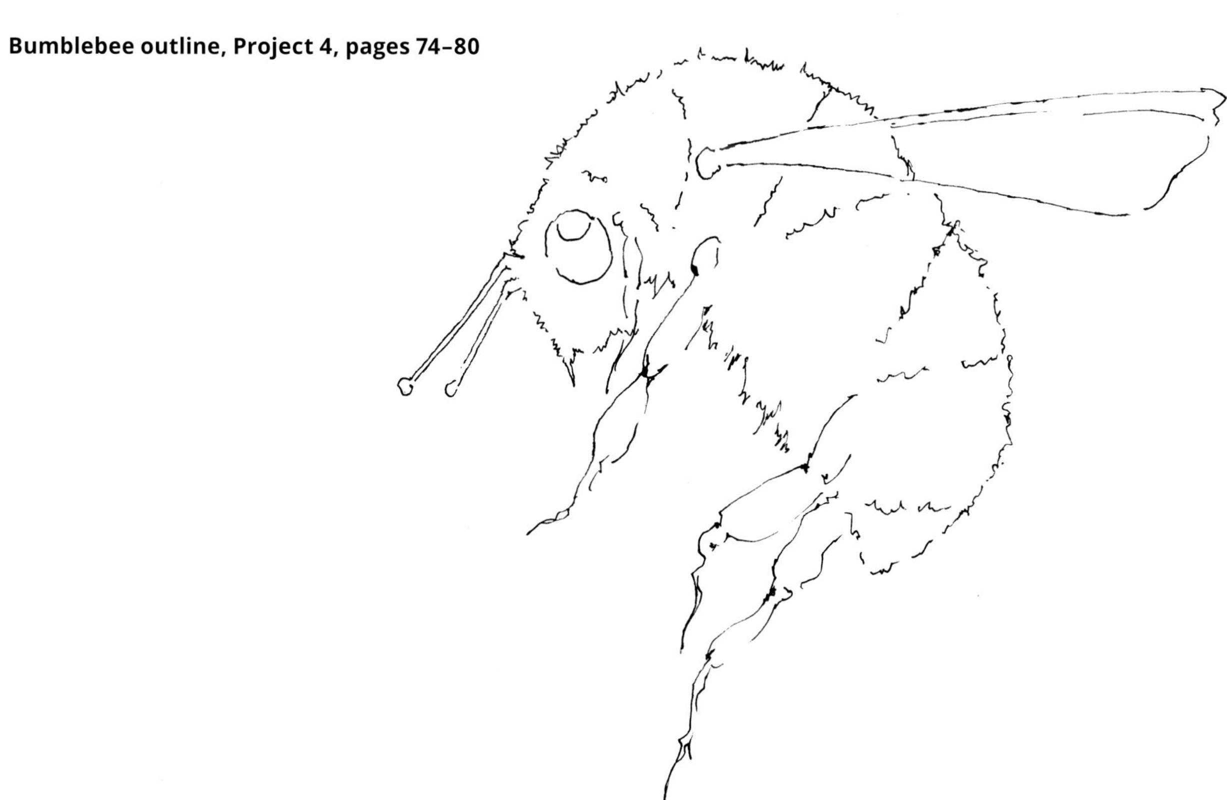

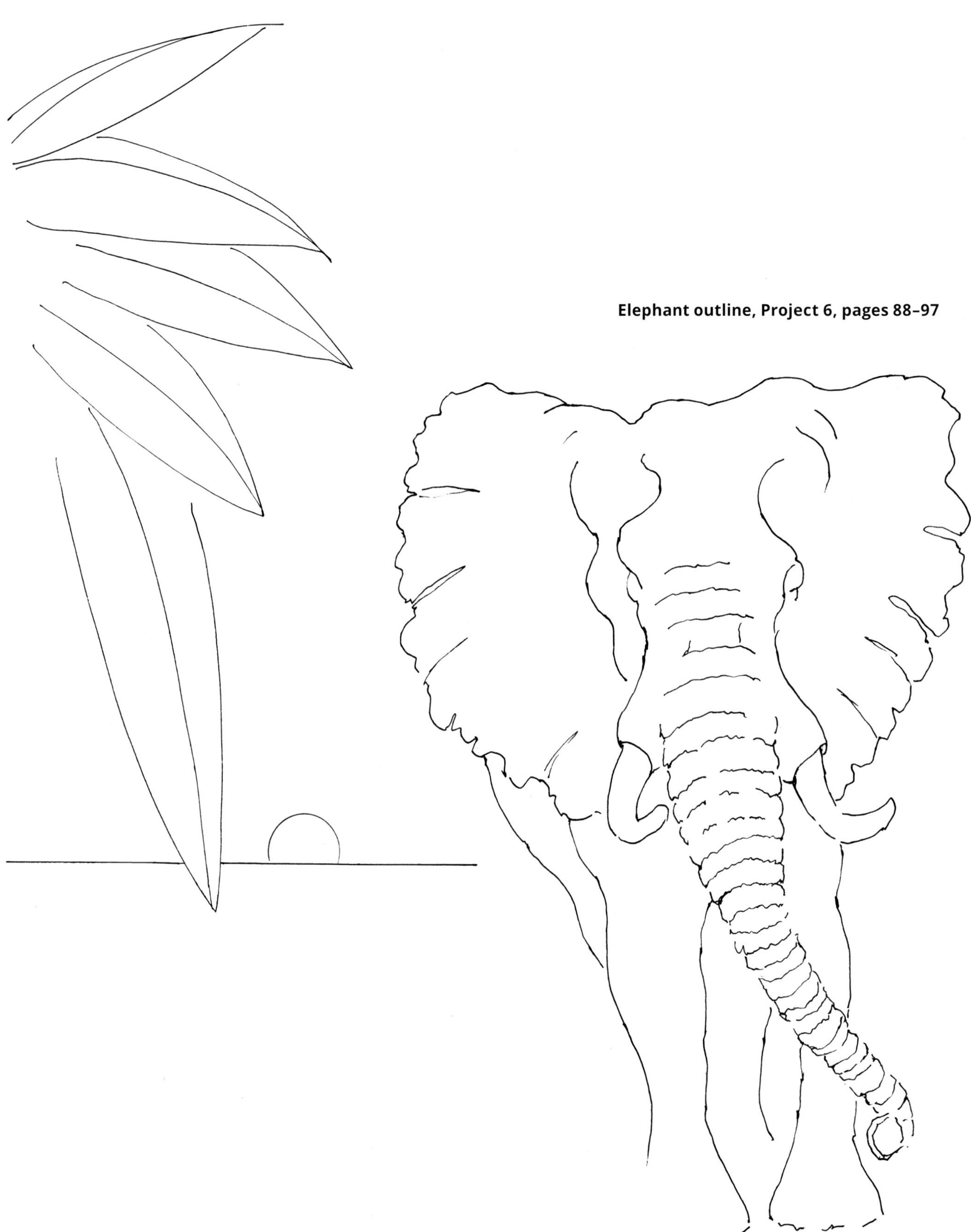

Palm Trees outline, Project 5, pages 82–86

Elephant outline, Project 6, pages 88–97

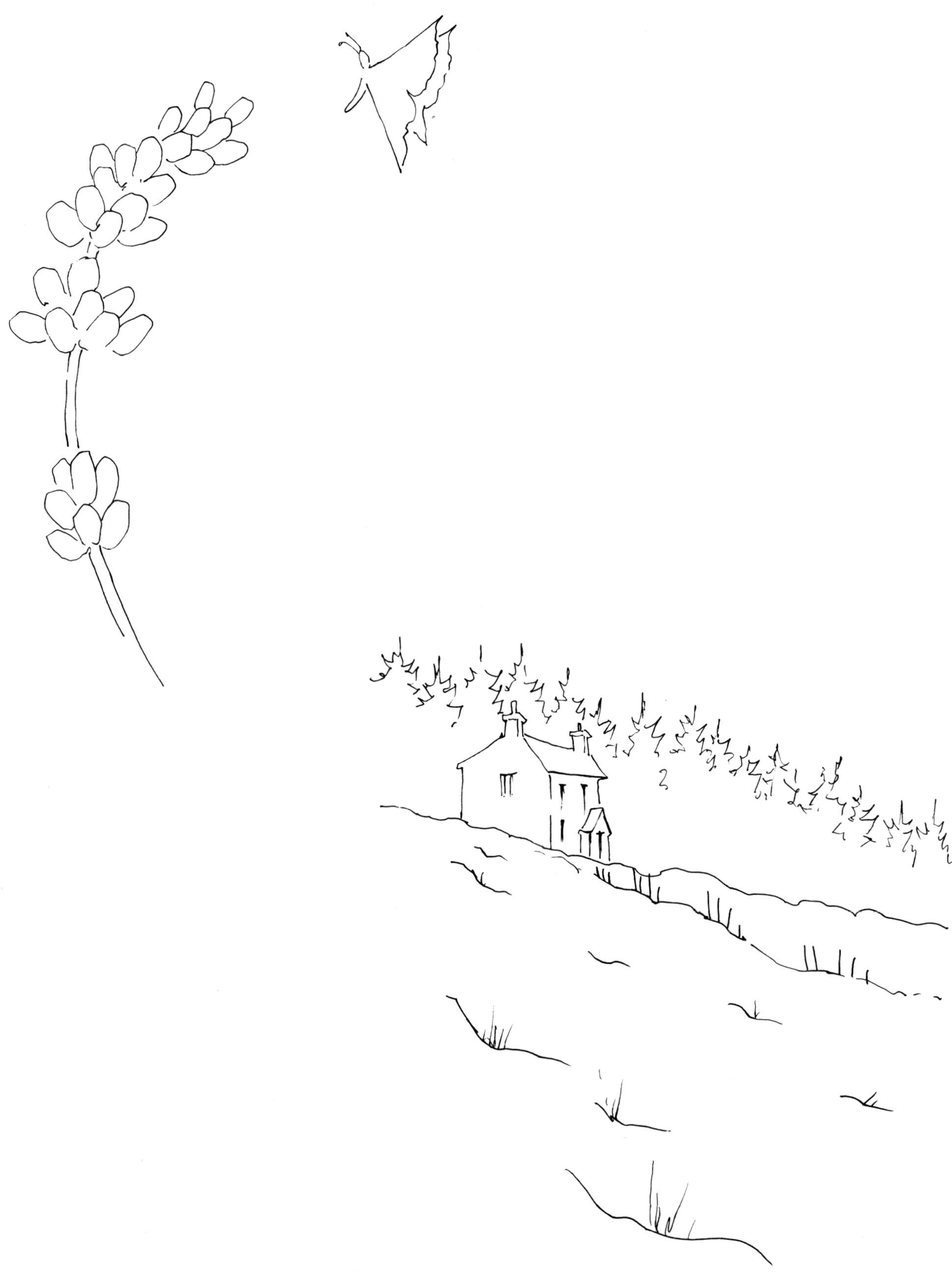

Cottage in the Snow outline, Project 8, pages 108–113

Allium outline, Project 9, pages 116–122

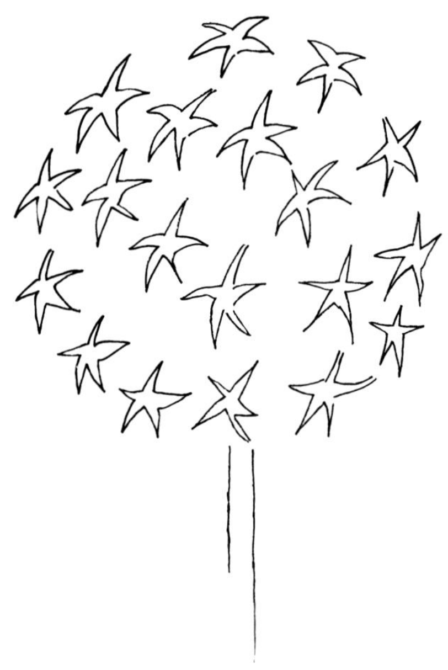

Crashing Waves outline, Project 10, pages 124–131

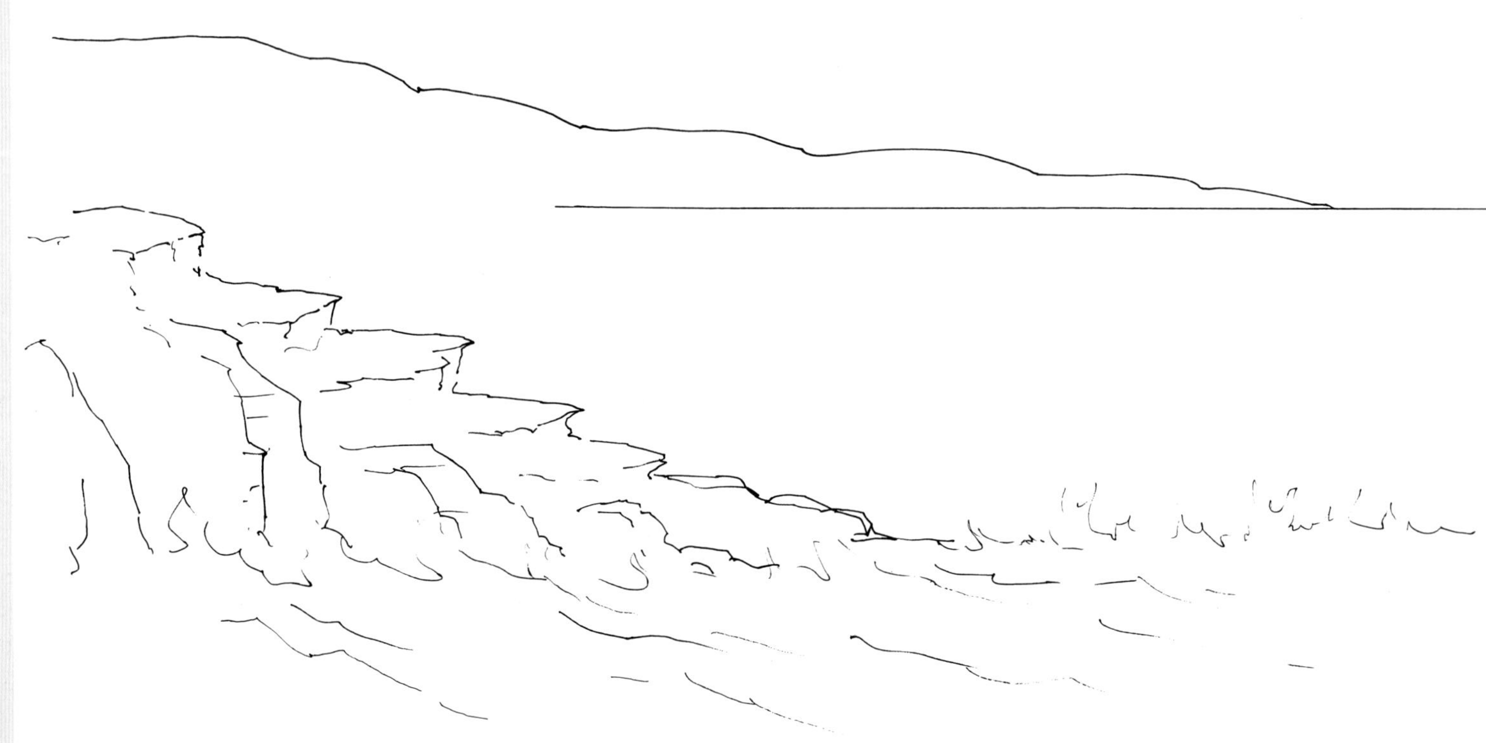